Bad Movie Beware

100 Movies that No Human Being Should Ever Watch

by

Jason Gilbert

To Joe:
A tome of Hollywood's intestinal rejects! Enjoy!
- Jason Gilbert

Bad Movie Beware!

Copyright © 2015 Jason Gilbert

Except as permitted under the U.S. Copyright Act of 1976, no part of this publication may be reproduced, distributed or transmitted in any form or by any means, or stored in a database or retrieval system without the prior written permission of the publisher.

ISBN-10: 1511783052
ISBN-13: 978-1511783057

How Did This Happen!?

Back in 2009, when I was on MySpace, I did a few movie reviews as a joke, starting with *Mutant Chronicles*. I'd been looking forward to that movie for a while, since the previews looked amazing.

What I got was an hour and a half that could've been better spent sitting on the toilet with the screaming s**ts.

I did a rant with torrents of profanity because, let's face it, no post on MySpace was complete without a monsoon of f-bombs. Shortly after that, my mom suggested *Basic Instinct*, claiming it to be one of the best Michael Douglas movies ever. I found the movie hilarious because his character was so hopelessly stupid when it came to the prospect of getting laid.

It was also great material for my next rant on MySpace.

I got on board with the cool kids on Facebook in 2010, and Facebook had this nifty little feature called "Notes." The purpose of writing a note was what people just use their status update for these days: rant, rave, and post something either intellectually stimulating or so utterly ignorant and misinformed that one would have to wonder how the hell this person manages to tie their shoes in the mornings without killing themselves. I began posting regularly in the notes, starting with such gems as *Asylum*, *Garfield's Pet Force*, and the infamous *Alice's Adventures in Wonderland*. That last one was a real piece of work and got me a fair amount of attention from my friends as their favorite one I'd done yet. A few of them had even had to read it twice out loud to their friends and family because they enjoyed the humor.

As I kept posting, my wife decided to toss me the idea of starting a blog. At the time I wasn't really aware of what the hell a "blog" was. My only understanding was that it was an online journal where people could post about their lives day-to-day, making people whose lives were similarly lonely and depressing feel better about the fact that they still lived in their mother's basements and kept stringently to the "Cheetos and Mountain Dew" diet to maintain a healthy virginity. She explained that my assumption was far from accurate and showed me a few blogs. As it turned out, people posted blogs for all kinds of things! Not that there weren't Mother's Basement Dwellers posting about their latest anime porn purchases, but most of the blogs she showed me were actually quite educational. One was a weekly lesson on how to be a more effective fisherman, another was different ways to prepare quality meals with minimal ingredients, and there was even one suggesting a simpler lifestyle by getting rid of excess stuff (that one would become big to me in later years).

I decided to follow the same kind of mindset of the Angry Nintendo Nerd (later known as the "Angry Video Game Nerd") and make my blog about bad movies that I would watch so that people wouldn't have to accidentally stumble upon these nightmares without due warning. The theme would be an unwritten idea. "Don't watch these movies. Let me take the bullet and spare you the misery."

Before I could set it up, we decided to move. That's the thing about renting: you don't like where you are, you move. Unfortunately, it's much simpler to say than it is to do. We ended up finding a place, but time and energy got refocused into that, and my blog and Facebook Notes were put on hold. It irked me because I was actually enjoying watching these movies. It gave me an outlet for my tendency to roast the hell out of anything or anyone in the room.

That, and some of them were just plain fun to watch even though they were agonizingly awful.

Once we got settled in and turned over the old house, things went back to normal. But, I wasn't writing or watching movies because I was still running around getting details done. Change of address, transfer of bills, call DirecTV, get the internet turned on, stock the kitchen, all the fun joys of moving into a new place.

One day I came home from work ready to just sit down and work on the book that I was writing at the time (it actually turned out to be one of those ideas that was great until I actually wrote it down) when Melissa showed me what she'd been up to that day. She typed in the address www.fail-flix.blogspot.com, and brought up my new blog.

Fail-Flix was born.

Since then, I've reviewed over a hundred movies and developed a loyal fan base. It's still going strong and has grown far bigger and faster than I'd imagined. I hope you enjoy reading these reviews as much as I enjoyed writing them. Read them, get a good laugh, and don't say I didn't warn you if you decide to watch one of these nightmares!

Cheesy Slasher Flix

Ah, the slasher flick! Their real heyday was in the 1980's, but it actually all really took off with the original *Halloween* in 1978 and spiraled into major industry movement after that. Credit *The Texas Chainsaw Massacre* and the early Video Nasties all you want, but *Halloween* uncorked the stopper on cut 'em up fun for the whole family. The two biggest? You guessed it: *Friday the 13th* and *A Nightmare on Elm St.*

These dingle berries, on the other hand, were the fodder.

A Bothered Conscience: Indecisive Disorder

My darling wife was gracious enough to curse me with a $5 four-pack of movies entitled *Backwoods Butchers*. I should have known that I was screwed like the new guy on the cellblock when I opened the case and saw that they had managed to cram all four movies like Mexicans in a Pinto onto one poor DVD.

But, I digress.

Onward to waste of time and brain cells number one: *A Bothered Conscience*.

Kenny McGavin is a hermit that lives with his son in a trailer out in the middle of nowhere. He has posted signs warning people to stay away and kills anyone who comes onto his property.

The movie opens in 1974 with a lady dressed in Tommy Hilfiger clothes and toting a $600 Nikon Digital SLR camera.

Yeah. Second giveaway that I am in for pain.

Kenny brutally murders her, then kills a group of hunters while muttering "Cain't you read my signs?" in what must be the most forced redneck accent since *Cold Mountain*. Twenty years (and almost 45 minutes later), Kenny is murdered by a vengeful U.S. soldier and discovered by his now grown son.

Lucas now takes up his father's hunt, but not without beginning to lose it completely. The spirits of the people that he and his father have killed over the years soon drive him to madness. Then he is attacked by zombies.

Yes. Zombies. And one guy pretending to be the *Grudge* girl. Badly.

During all of this, the movie cuts to random sequences starring random characters that have ABSOLUTELY no bearing on the story whatsoever other than the fact that they will get killed by Lucas at some point. The soundtrack is made up almost entirely of a single banjo, a fiddle, and a harmonica. The characters are obviously either in it because they are buddies with the director/writer/producer or they are under the sadly mistaken impression that they will get paid in something besides pizza and soda.

After this movie drags out for what feels like three or four hours of ungodly boredom, Kenny shows back up and informs a wounded Lucas that his death was faked in order to "test" the boy. Lucas, according to Kenny, failed. Kenny kills him and walks off.

Then end. No, really.

VERDICT: Toss it to the hogs, Ma!

The rest of the country has such a skewed idea of Southern living, and to see them try to act like us is often funny.

Not in this case.

This movie had to have been written on the wall of a bathroom stall in a public restroom. The random fodder for Kenny and Lucas to hunt is so painfully obviously "Hey, dude! Lemme be in your movie! PLEASEPLEASEPLEASEPLEASE!!!!!"

Also, would it kill the director/writer/producer to make up his f**king mind on what kind of movie he wants to make!? First, it's a slasher flick. Then, it's a psycho-thriller. Then it's a ghost movie. After that, a zombie flick. Back to ghost movie. Back to thriller. Ghost movie. Thriller.

It may have actually helped this broken and forgettable dog turd if he had settled on "Suckfest" and called it a day.

A Brush with Death: Like, totally lame. Totally.

Going on week three with no day off, and I'm wiped. Nevertheless, I said I would get this week's review done, and I do what I say I'm going to do.

Unfortunately, the writer/director of this pile of monkey poop does not.

Cheerleaders are awesome, right guys? Let's just get that out into the open right now. But movie cheerleaders? Yeah, about the only thing they have going for them is looks. Brains? Hell no.

God forbid they start talking. Makes you actually WANT Jason Voorhees to show up.

Five high school cheerleaders (read: twenty year-olds. Yeah, Hollywood actually frowns on hacking up real teens. Go fig.) decide to take a trip to a mansion out in the country for the weekend. Along the way, they run out of gas and are assisted by Caleb and his creepy pervert boss. Caleb is slow and stutters, often being called "retard" throughout the train wre...movie.

We cut to a scene where Caleb picks up two hitchhikers, a hipster couple traveling the road. He takes them to the gas station where Creep-O waits. The hipster boyfriend gets a bullet to the brainpan, and ol' girl gets tied up and stars in her own porno photo shoot courtesy of the Creep.

We flash back to the road. It was one of Caleb's memories.

Settle in, this kind of nonsense happens a lot.

The girls are back on the road, fun times in the summer heat on the way. They pass by an old decrepit mansion on the way but keep going since it isn't their summer hideaway.

Once they get to the mansion, Rankin, a local boy looking for some fun, greets them. They invite him along for a swim and a game of truth or dare. While the other girls are changing, Rankin moves in on Samantha and they begin to make out. Suddenly, he begins to throttle her.

Nope. Just a fantasy. Moving on.

In fact, by now we are 40 minutes into an 88-minute long movie. No s**t. Literally NOTHING happens in this movie until the last twenty minutes. We get a few "oh, that character got gotten" moments, but they're gore-less in a movie about a schmuck who paints with people's blood.

Oh, for f**k's sake, where's the damn remote!?

Anyway, Candice ends up missing, and the others go on to bed after Amber pulls a practical joke. Yes, their friend is missing and they stay clueless.

Like totally.

They all finally realize that they are at the Rue house where a boy killed his brother and family and painted their portraits with their blood. He's all grown up now and is more than happy to have Samantha, Creep-O, Candice, Megan, and Hilary over for dinner. Of course, after he's drained them all dry.

Caleb, who is Old Man Rue's son, brings in Amber. Caleb turns on his father, professing love for Amber (wtf did this come from!?) She escapes and is picked up by Rankin, who promises to take her to safety...after getting off the phone with Old Man Rue.

The end.

VERDICT: Duh!

"Mommy, I'm bored. Can I go play in traffic?"

This movie had more plot directions than *War and Peace*. I'm slightly ADHD, and watching this pile of steaming dog turds was almost as confusing at times as a variety show. One minute the plot's here, then it runs down a secret tunnel and launches into outer space only to land back on Earth right over there.

It's a thriller! It's a slasher flick! It's a teen scream!

It's gorilla stool on a stick.

The acting was horrendous, the lines being delivered with less emotion than Russell Crowe in ANY role. The cheerleaders are beyond ignorant and often say their lines while standing in one place like statues in a museum.

The pacing of the film is slower than Christmas. I don't care how creative you think you're being, there is NO excuse for having absolutely NOTHING happen during the first half of your movie. Even *Lord of the Rings* had stuff going on the whole time!

It was like watching *Seinfeld* with stupid girls as the entire cast.

Bikini Girls on Ice: Stupidity by the numbers

I stumbled upon this turd biscuit while perusing my Netflix queue and had to see why one customer said it was so bad that he actually cancelled his account and went to Blockbuster.

It was five minutes in and I fully understood this poor soul's reasoning.

A gas station in the middle of nowhere is the set, abandoned and run down. A group of bikini-clad college girls on their way to a car wash decide to set up there and end up fodder for the resident serial killer.

Note: it is a slasher flick but with no real gore. How the hell does this work!? I can tell you.

It doesn't.

Every element of a pointless kill-fest is there. You have the group leader doubling as the resident bitch, the girl-on-girl kissing, the group slut, one gratuitous breast shot during the obligatory sex scene, the innocent lead and her best friend, the hot guy who ends up dying, and the serial killer.

You know, we have killers with iconic names. Jason Voorhees, Freddy Krueger, and Michael Meyers to name a few. What's the name of the guy we get?

Moe.

No, really. F**king Moe.

And all he does is whine and breath heavy like a 12-year-old-boy playing monkey-spank with his hands wrapped in duct tape.

Plus, the whole thing takes place at a gas station. Where the hell is he gonna hide!? It's not like there is a lot of space here.

There is one scene where Moe has locked the girls inside a shed. But the latch is on the inside.

They can't get the door open, and they can't look down and see that the door is still latched.

Christ.

Granted, these girls are not ugly, but the characters aren't smart, either. I've seen better plotlines and acting in eighties throwback internet porn. The camera work was shoddy, looking like the filmographer was shooting with an HD Sony Handi-Cam. When the shot was supposed to follow the girls, it shook like *Blair Witch* but if Heather Donahue had Parkinson's.

VERDICT: On a scale of one to ten, I give this movie the finger.

While it's not as bad as *Troll 2*, it's up there with *Battlefield Earth* or *Mama Mia*. The acting is horrendous, and the kiss between the heroic leads is as awkward as a shut-in being walked in on by his parents while he is discovering his real identity in his sister's clothes.

The ending is predictable and quick, but not quick enough as the movie is a grueling 81 minutes long when it could have been covered in thirty minutes or during one of those infomercials that comes on at 3am.

Butchered: Yes, a pound of bad acting, please.

There are some things you have to remember and consider when watching independent movies, a.k.a. Indie Flicks.

A) They have virtually no budget. Any money that they have managed to put toward production has been gained either by fundraiser or donation.

B) The movie was written, directed, produced, and (usually) stars the same one guy who has painted his name all over the ending credits along with the three other people he got to help him out with camera and sound.

C) The actors are, nine times out of ten, people who have never done this before and are only doing it because they are buddies with the director/writer/producer. Don't expect a good performance from them.

That being said, I can easily say that while *Butchered* wasn't awful, it definitely has its problems.

Onwards and upwards!

Our story begins with the escape of our killer. He butchers (see what I did there?) the two guards that chase him, and he even manages to take out the dogs. He then takes a girl hostage, thus beginning our opening credits where they feature a news story about Terence Skinner, a maniac Gulf War vet who went nuts in his uncle's butcher shop and killed a bunch of people.

The news bit is broken up by a montage of scenes showing Skinner literally taking apart the girl from the last scene while the whole thing is backed by a pretty decent sound beat.

Skip ahead to a group of kids celebrating their escape from high school and transition to college. Each character is introduced in order of stereotype. We have the Horny Party Animal, the two hot chicks who are always together (they are not sluts; they just have friendly vaginas), the über-loyal black best friend, his "I take nothin' from nobody" girlfriend, the aspiring Stanford College Boy, his Girl-Next-Door girlfriend (you will NEVER see her naked), and College Boy's older brother who thinks he needs to stay home and work on the farm.

They all decide to go camping on a secluded island that they have been romping on since they were kids. It is to be their last night of partying and random sex before college, the military, or wherever the hell else they plan on going (only three of the seven actually specify where they are going).

It all goes to hell quickly when Skinner shows up and starts killing them off one by one, usually with an ax to the chest. The movie is slow going at first, filled with inspirational pep talks between all of the characters.

In fact, I've not heard this much crap from the heart since *Steel Magnolias*. It's like a chick flick with gore. The writing is just bad, and the acting is worse. In fact, I've seen better performances from nervous middle-school kids than I saw from these "actors."

The movie actually got better once Skinner showed up and started his massacre. Ever had one of those where you're actually cheering for the killer?

Yeah, this would be it.

Sixty-six minutes later, it's over. Yup. One hour, give or take. So, what happens? Well, once the heroic Stanford boy and girl-next-door off Skinner, they motor off on a boat, kissing as the sun sets on the words "6 Months Later..."

The epilogue is tacked on at the end like Eeyore's tail. Girl and boy are at Stanford together, trying to move past the horrors of running from the Butcher on the island. As they fall asleep, a figure emerges from the bathroom. Of course, being shot with a harpoon and beaten over the head with a club did not kill him.

He is Jas...I mean Mich...I mean Terence Skinner!

VERDICT: Meh.

I could sit through it again, but only for a laugh. It's not terrible, but it ain't great. The writer/director/producer obviously loves *Friday the 13th* and *Halloween*, so he made one and slapped a different sticker on the box.

If flattery is the greatest compliment, then this is straight up butt kissing.

To say that the acting is wooden is a compliment. To say that the acting and dialogue are bad to the point of hilarity is about right. In fact, it probably would have been better if Kevin Costner had actually shown up to train these people. Then at least they could perfect saying every line in the same tone with the same facial expression. Some of them were trying so hard that they looked like they were seizing.

If you are looking for boobies, blood and ignorance, have at it. If you are looking for a good addition to your slasher flick collection, look elsewhere.

Cheerleader Massacre 2: Pom-poms, boobies, and killer toys. WTF.

A buddy said something to me the other day that rang fairly true. "People go to horror movies to see two things: boobs and people get hacked up."

Granted, not all horror movies are the same, but Slasher-Flicks tend to follow that trend. A group of girls gets naked, at least one guy screws one of them, and then a maniac kills most everyone except one girl who DOESN'T get naked and has the balls to stand up and fight.

Cheerleader Massacre 2 follows that formula. Stringently.

The *Cheerleader Massacre* movies are actually part of a 6-pack, starting with *Slumber Party Massacre* circa 1982, followed by *Slumber Party Massacre 2* (1987). After those two we had *Sorority House Massacre* (1986) and *Sorority House Massacre 2* (1990). Do I have any desire to watch these movies? Negative.

Will you all probably put them into the suggestions for me to archive because you get a sadistic thrill out of watching me suffer through this relentless pile of cinematic fecal debris? Way more than likely.

A group of cheerleaders is on a bus heading to a weekend camp and competition. They blow a flat along the way and stop. The driver gets out and is attacked by an unseen killer. The girls go outside and find him dead, then scatter when a flying machine with three saw blades whips through and decapitates one of them, then comes back around and slices another in half.

Yes. Flying machine. No, I'm not lying. Nor am I drunk.

After the unit turns the troop into a pile of meat and parts, it chases the squad leader into the hills. She falls down into a crevice and is killed when the toy follows her and begins to fling CGI blood everywhere.

After the title card rolls, we are greeted by a blonde girl with oversized boobs in a bathtub. We get a 1-minute montage of her bathing the puppies. She gets a phone call and talks about camp. We never see her again after this.

Yes. Her only purpose was nudity.

We then meet Anna, our protagonist for the film (obvious) and her best friend, Janice. Anna is the innocent "girl-next-door" member of the local cheer squad on her way to camp for the weekend, and Janice is her ride. Before they leave, Janice's father gets a distressed phone call from work and runs off to the secret lab in the house.

Meanwhile, the rest of the squad arrives at camp. We have the typical bitchy squad leader and the two girls who act as her minions. The head counselor is a balding old pervert who surrounds himself with ditzy blondes, and his co-leader is a hot blonde with about a fraction more sense than he has.

Don't worry. It doesn't impede this masterpiece.

Notice also that I don't really know half of their names. Like the first movie, it's not really important. In fact, this movie makes it abundantly clear who are the important characters and who are the meat bags sent for certain death at the hands of Hasbro.

Yes, I went there.

Meanwhile a hot top-heavy redhead and her girlfriend wake up from a night of topless sleeping. They, also, have nothing to do with the storyline. In fact, I might just refer to these characters from now on as throw pillows.

They are decorative and nice to have but serve no other real purpose than to sit on the couch and usually get tossed in the floor when one sits down for an evening of beer and *The Walking Dead*.

In another scene, a group of boys are having car trouble during their drive to meet up with the cheerleaders at camp for a weekend of sex.

Back at camp, the squad, Red Team, is wondering where the Blue Team is as they were due at camp the day before. In 24 hours they will be disqualified, but the team decides to practice anyway.

During practice one of the counselors decides to sneak away to drink and take a shower. She is electrocuted when she touches the showerhead and is then dragged away by an unknown figure.

Practice ends when Minion B is almost electrocuted by a power line that snaps loose and swings down to the field.

Back at home, Janice's dad is killed by an insect-like robot while trying to figure out who stole the source code for his mechanical weapons.

By the way, we are now halfway through the one-hour movie. No, really. HALF of the movie was really not much more than bad acting, boobies, and horny teenagers.

Kinda like college.

One of the boys shows up at the apartment where the busty redheaded throw pillow lives, and they proceed with the obligatory Gratuitous Sex Scene. During their soft-core romp, a mechanical bug shows up and slits their throats. Lots of CGI blood and poof! More dead bimbos!

The other two boys show up at camp, and the minions dope the squad leader and sneak out against Anna's insistence that they obey the curfew. Janice is laid up on the bunk with a sprained ankle.

Minion A meets her boyfriend at the docks, and they start to undress for Obligatory Gratuitous Sex Scene 2 when he hears a noise in the woods.

By the way, these movies are actually only supposed to have one obligatory sex scene in order to follow the formula. Any others on top of that are optional. Just saying.

Anywho, Minion A follows him and discovers his body. She screams as he falls away in two pieces. She suddenly has her head crushed by a giant mechanical saucer-looking thing.

I didn't see how Minion B bought it because I actually fell asleep during that scene. Yes, this movie, despite the HUGE amounts of nudity and gore, is so boring I actually passed out. Let me sum up her death for you (found an online summary): Boobies. Screaming. Blood.

In fact, I was pretty much in and out during the rest of the film because it just dragged on like Renee Zellweger's speech at the Academy Awards. I saw enough snippets to know that everyone runs, screams a lot, and dies. The three-sawed flying gadget from the beginning is back in full force, and Anna was running through the woods evading it by the time I was able to slap myself back to the world of the lucid.

The figure in black shows up and unmasks to reveal that it was Janice controlling the robots all along. She stole them from her father and planned to use them to wipe out cheerleaders everywhere and cause a feminist revolt. She urges Anna to join her. Anna refuses, and they struggle until she manages to hold Janice in the path of the flying saw machine.

It rips into Janice, and the scene fades as Anna cries over her body. A few weeks later Anna receives an email. It's Janice, in a video made before camp, urging her followers to begin the revolt.

The End.

VERDICT: Lick the windows!

This movie, while superior to the first movie in all technical aspects, was mind numbing. I actually watched in horror as my IQ points plummeted for an hour, when I wasn't sleeping because of the boredom.

The last movie I watched that was this retarded was *Sand Sharks*. Yes, you read it right. *Robo Croc* was a f**king intellectual MASTERPIECE compared to this skid mark in the underwear of Netflix.

The acting, once again, was awful. I could chalk it up to bad writing, but if Bob Hoskins can pull off Mario and be remembered as the only good thing about the *Super Mario Bros.* movie, then these troglodytes should be able to do SOMETHING with this disaster of a script.

Okay, I've danced around it enough. The gadgets. WHAT. THE. HELL.

Who, on a pile of camel s**t, thought that cheerleaders getting slaughtered by top-secret government weapons would actually make for an exciting and interesting movie!? I mean, really!?

The tried and true formula of a mysterious figure killing off brain-dead naked cheerleaders would've probably saved this movie, but noooo. "Let's shake it up a bit and add robots!"

Robots. Jeez.

And not only robots but CGI effects that make anything SyFy puts out look like *The Lord of the Rings*. It looks like the same PlayStation 1 they used to animate *Primal* was stolen for the purpose of piling this crap up in the middle of the pen for the pigs to roll around in.

Daddy's Girl: Innocence has lame writing

Daddy's Girl could have been great. Even though the story has been done to death, it's still interesting to watch how creepy kids can be. You have *The Good Son* and *Orphan* among the good ones.

But *Daddy's Girl*, for as much potential as it had, ended up being not much more than a failed attempt to rehash the same story elements. Frankly, McCauley and Esther did it better.

Gabrielle Boni stars as Jody, an angelically beautiful, red-headed eight-year-old who is adopted by William Kat and Michelle Greene.

Jody has an obsessive attachment to her foster father, and throughout the movie we see her go deeper and deeper into psychosis as she begins to off anyone she thinks is trying to take her away from Kat.

The writing is hokey at best with Jody prattling off cheesy one-liners every time she works someone over.

The adults are just plain stupid. I mean, really.

It's almost as if they knowingly set themselves up just to see if she really will take them down. "Oh, let me stand in this spinning chair and reach up high while this creepy little girl holds it for me."

She does have a rather Jason Voorhees-ish workhorse method of killing off people, but I doubt Kane Hodder would have been as endearing.

I want to say that this movie was made for television, but I can't find any websites that will own up to having that much information on it.

Predictability is the name of the game here, but the ending trashes what could have been great. She cries as daddy finds out what she's been up to, and the camera pans out as she screams that everyone leaves her.

Sweetie, you kill people.

I'm pretty sure I read this crap in a Fear Street book at some point when I was a teenager. Her foster cousin, Karen, is responsible for bringing things to light. Boni does do a great job in one scene where we see Jody go about as nutty as a Peter Pan Peanut Butter distribution center, but the rest of the movie, she has a hard time putting away the cute in favor of sinister.

In short, she looks more like a little girl denied her ice cream than a serial-killing elementary school kid.

Just saying.
VERDICT: Eh.

For a non-violent violent movie, it gets tedious. The acting is good for as bad as the writing is, but I can't expect much from an 8-year-old who was given weapons and told to start taking people down like Michael Myers after a sex change.

If you want to see it, go for it, but don't have the expectations of twisted scenes and whatnot that you got in *Orphan*. I'm not saying kill Jody off, but the ending could have been better. It's not a bad movie, but it's not really good, either.

Disturbed: Beer goggles won't save this one.

What in the hell did I just watch?

In my time as a reviewer of all things cinematically s**ty, I've found a few gems that just stand out like boils on the anus of the industry. Most of them have been indie flicks. Not that I have a particular problem with indies, I don't. But indies tend to really show it when there is a particular lack of effort on the part of the people involved.

I'm not going to lie, I do advocate for independent film and theater. Independent film is what the industry thrives on for new ideas because, Lord knows, Hollywood sure as hell hasn't come up with anything truly original in years.

Then we get s**t stains like *Disturbed,* and my faith in the independent industry gets shaken like the bowels of a customer at Taco Bell.

The film opens with a copout…I mean "prologue"…featuring a politician who is recording the events of trial. Turns out the guilty guy, Mason, is being sent up death row for killing a lot of people, particularly women, due to his hatred of women stemming from an incestuous relationship with his mother.

Ew. Cliché, but ew.

Cut to Ashley and her sister and brother, Peyton and Alex. Peyton is supposed to be in middle school, judging by her behavior, yet the actress is obviously old enough to vote. Ashley is the older sister and a real estate agent, yet she's maybe the same age as Peyton if not a year older. Alex is the slacker in the family and is also the brother of writer/director/producer/every-other-job-on-the-film guy, who also happens to play Mason.

Yeah. One of those. I'm surprised the credits weren't on poster board.

Oh dear God. The acting. OH GOD, THE ACTING IS HORRIFIC! What the…is there no script!? What the hell!? It's all improv!?

(Beats head on desk. A lot.)

I can make it. I sat through *The Gay Bed and Breakfast of Terror,* damn it!

From this point on, the plot meanders in about four hundred different directions. Okay, I'm exaggerating. Three hundred and seventy-two. Really, it's just a nightmare trying to cypher out what's pertinent and what's fluff. I can save some time, though. About every scene up to the end of the film is filler. There are events that happen that are never discussed or referred to again.

I'll just skip the fluff and get straight to it. Mason ends up getting into the house during a party that Ashley and her siblings are hosting. One of the goers notices him and points him out to the group. Ashley looks up, right at Mason as he is backing away into the shadows, then back to the guest.

"There's nobody there."

WHAT!? Are you friggin' BLIND!? YOU JUST LOOKED RIGHT AT THE GUY! What the hell is up with these people!? It reminded me of *Thankskilling*, really. You know, the scene where the turkey disguises himself as a six-foot redneck by simply putting on glasses and a mustache and everyone is cool with it.

Anywho, shortly after the events of the party, Alex leaves to get more beer for himself and his girlfriend. Mason shows up and kills off Alex's girl, then waits for Alex to return home and stabs him in the stomach with a knife.

Ashley encounters Mason upstairs and a struggle ensues. Mason beats down Ashley, strips her, and rapes her on her bed while Peyton watches. Afterwards, he takes Ashley to the shower and starts to assaulter her again when Alex shows up and tackles him. They struggle, and Alex uses his karate to send Mason over the bannister and twenty feet down to the floor.

Alex and Ashley go downstairs, but Mason is gone. Alex heads outside and discovers Mason by the pool. He jump kicks Mason into the pool, killing him.

Because swimming pools are deadly and s**t.

The EMTs show up and take care of Ashley and her siblings while the coroners haul off Mason. The ambulance pulls over on a dirt road, and one of them opens the body bag and greets Mason with "Hello…brother."

The End. Thank God.

VERDICT: Somebody flush this turd!

There are no words that can describe how bad this movie is, but I can think of a few really creative and colorful ones, most of them involving monkeys, footballs, and cotton candy.

I said I was creative.

The acting and the writing went hand-in-hand like a marriage made in hell. Why? The lack of a script wasn't the only thing that hurt this heap of s**t, but it was the one major issue that stood out like pervert at a Putt-Putt birthday party.

It probably would've worked if the actors were actually able to act. I mean, hell, ACT like you know what you're doing. I haven't seen dialogue this awkward and meandering since *Love, Actually*. They talked over each other constantly, and there were far too many times that they were obviously struggling to keep the scene going.

The girls in the movie came off far too whiney. Ashley was the overbearing older sister in charge, and was obviously no older than the girl playing Peyton. Oh wait: Peyton was her real name too! Same with Alex. That's not breaking the fourth wall for effect, that's called L.A.W.

"Lazy-Assed Writing."

The movie ends with a sequel obvious, but one can hope that it'll never happen. Sequels tend to be worse, and there isn't enough heroin in the world that could make me able to sit through something worse than *Disturbed*.

What disturbs me is the fact that someone kept telling Randy Aldridge that this was good stuff, and that the action and scenes were fabulous. It's the only thing I can think of that would've made this shot-by-camera phone film possible. Otherwise, it's just another case of time that would've been better spent watching a toilet flush.

Dreamaniac: Nightmare of stupid proportions

Finally got to one that has been in my Netflix queue for a while. This one looked like it would suck just from the cover, but I figured I'd endure it anyway since that's what I do.

Maybe I'm just a glutton for punishment.

I think they call that masochism, or something.

Anyway, I got about thirty seconds into this movie before I realized that when it comes to cinematic intestinal dysfunction, *Dreamaniac* is a shart.

Ready? Here we go.

Alan has a dream one night about a beautiful woman, so he decides to bring her to the real world using black magic. That evening, his girlfriend Pat is throwing a party at the house that he is housesitting. The guests show up, including the mysterious Lily, who happens to be Alan's dream girl.

The party is as wild as it gets with drinking, drugs, bridge, charades, and sex that is about as awkward as the moment you realize you just shot a nugget into your shorts while standing in the middle of Best Buy on the day after Thanksgiving.

After about twenty minutes of this montage of eye-clawing boredom, Lily begins to kill people using tricks she must have learned from Wyle E. Coyote. One guy, for example, is tied to a pole with wire and electrocuted while wearing only his whitey-tighties.

I mention this because the homosexual overtones in this movie are blatant and not as "Oh, NOW I get it!" as the second *Nightmare on Elm Street* movie.

But, I digress.

Lily possesses Alan, and they both carve and hack their way through the party guests one by one until only Pat and her sister remain. Pat decapitates Alan with a portable power drill, and Lily is just about to hack Pat and her sister to pieces when the men in white show up and chastise Lily for escaping the mental institution. They leave with her, apologizing to Pat and hoping that she did not cause too many problems.

Cut to an office where a "sleazy" Hollywood writer is reading the rest of the script to someone on the phone. Yes. The whole movie was just an indie film. While he is stewing over what to call his newest *tour de sewage*, Lily appears and butchers him, splattering blood on the script and covering up most of the word "succubus."

Only "suc" is visible, which about sums up the whole movie.

VERDICT: Annihilate!

It would be nice if movie studios would flush after using a public restroom.

This movie was bad, even for an indie flick. If the campy overly dramatic acting wasn't bad enough, the plot just got weaker and weaker as the torture dragged on.

This movie was so bad that they actually (pointlessly) put a couple in bed post- (or pre) coitus on the cover because they knew that the only thing that would sell it was sex. And yet, they couldn't even do THAT right in the movie!

How do you screw up fake screwing!?

All of the girls in the movie were dressed in over-the-top 80's glam, and all of the guys were dressed like pretty-boys ready for a night at the Birdcage.

From the time the credits hit the screen with the sound of a keyboard being played by the Phantom of the Opera's mentally disabled stepbrother to the moment the end credits rolled, I felt like I had done something horrible to deserve an early trip to hell.

Evil Remains: Oblivious

This looked somewhat promising. Hot girls on the cover, a haunted house with a gory and tragic past, and a plotline that is fleshed enough to get the idiots...I mean, coeds...to the house, but thin enough to kill them off in horrifically violent and senseless ways.

God, I love horror flicks!

But what did I get? *Tresspassing.* Okay, so the title of the movie in the opening credits is different from the title on the cover.

(Double-checks).

Yep. I'm in for another monkey turd. ONWARD!

Mark wraps up a rather interesting interview with Dr. Rosen (Kurtwood Smith) and meets up with his friends Eric, Kristy, and Kristy's girlfriend Sharon. His brother Tyler is also along for the ride as they take a trip out to the old Bryce house to film and try to document ghosts and other supernatural phenomena for Mark's final thesis.

Okay, so it's a haunted house movie. Just like I thought.

Soon strange things begin to happen. By soon, I mean a good half-hour into the movie. Otherwise, this awkward stain just DRAAAAAAAAGS on about Mark's angst over his thesis, Eric's obnoxious behavior, and Kristy and Sharon being lesbians.

Oh, and Carl Bryce killed his parents in the house.

Soon we get to Tyler in the basement setting up his camera. We hear Eric get into a struggle in the kitchen above, and Tyler goes to check it out, accusing Mark of beating the crap out of Eric when they can't find him

The walls in the house begin to bleed profusely, and Mark and Tyler go to the attic to investigate and discover Eric's body bleeding out into the wall joints.

Meanwhile Sharon and Kristy have been on a nature walk talking about their feelings when they discover that the woods are loaded with bear and rabbit traps. Sharon snags her heel in one and has trouble walking. The make their way back to the house and spring a trap in the front yard.

In the attic, Tyler walks right into a giant bear trap that crushes him to death, and he bleeds out as Mark panics. A masked maniac emerges from the shadows and chases Mark into the house. He runs out the front door to see Sharon and Kristy approaching but is yanked back inside and butchered.

Kristy and Sharon run away but fall into a pit and end up in a dirty sanctum of sorts in the basement of the house. Carl Bryce enters wearing his dog mask, and Kristy ambushes him. She and Sharon flee, but Carl finds them in the woods and kills Sharon.

Kristy runs into a shack where a mechanic is working, but Carl shows up and offs the mechanic. Kristy is able to escape and run across the road. Carl is after her, but he is crushed by an eighteen-wheeler.

In the next scene a pretty blonde grad student is interviewing Dr. Rosen about the Bryce house and Kristy. He claims that the house is not haunted and that Kristy did not kill her friends, but the student disagrees.

VERDICT: Confusticated.

Okay, so the whole movie is centered around the house being haunted, but there is a serial killer? You had one job, Mr. Writer/Director.

ONE.

So let me make sure I've got this right: You wanted to shoot a scary haunted house movie, but then you decided mid-shoot that you wanted it to be a slasher flick? Who told you this was a good idea? Your mom?

The acting is good, I'll give it that much. And the suspense is very *Texas Chainsaw Massacre*. The problem is, I was so geared up for a haunted house flick. Not complaining, but you're killing me here.

The dog mask was cool, though.

Really and truly, it wasn't horrible. The plot was a little random, and it dragged out like bad case of the turds after a night of drinking.

That being said, it was still a chore to watch. The pacing, as I said, makes this movie about as appealing as the idea of licking a sweaty fat man under his moobs. Once the action picks up, it gets interesting, but the rest of it is about as nail-biting as *Sense and Sensibility*.

Frozen in Fear: Like eating yellow snow...

I thought I ordered this tea without ice.

Argh.

Back in the saddle with movie number two from the Serial Killers collection I got from a buddy at work. He did warn me that none of the movies in the collection were good, and I didn't doubt him. Typically, there's usually one good one on the disc.

I'm terrified that *Frozen in Fear* may be the one.

The original title of the film is *The Flying Dutchman,* which was weird because it had nothing to do with the famed ghost ship captained by Davy Jones. But, if you go to IMDB.com and search for *Frozen in Fear,* you'll get a smorgasbord of s**t that has nothing to do with this movie.

Because, you know, everyone totally tries to look up this pile of feces.

The film opens with Sean, a young boy who walks in on his mom banging another guy. He runs out of the house, and his father goes in and catches Mom in the act. He exacts revenge by dragging both her and Sean out onto the ocean in his boat and drops Mom overboard. She grabs him along the way, and Sean loses both parents to the sea.

Flash-forward to present day (if present day took place in the 80s). An art dealer purchases a painting from an old woman and brings it back to New York. Lacy sees it and drags her assistant, Polly, with her back to the town where the painting was purchased.

Moira, the old woman who sold the painting, explains that a local man named Sean did it. Lacy and Polly also meet the sheriff, Ethan, and hear about the town mayor, Ben, who also happens to be Sean and Ethan's father.

These are the only four residents in this hellhole.

I mean this *quaint* little hellhole.

Polly heads back to New York, and Lacy meets Sean, who is a kind and quiet man. In fact, he never speaks, and she soon discovers that he was rendered mute after watching both of his parents die in a boating accident.

BUT WE KNOW WHAT REALLY HAPPENED.

Lacy trips and is injured in the woods. Sean finds her and takes her back to his place. We discover that Sean is more than a little creepy, copping feels and kissing Lacy in naughty spots while she sleeps.

Oh yeah. During all of this, a couple of girls are grabbed and hauled off with a bag over their heads by an unseen assailant. Big whoop-di-doo.

No, really. These events take a back seat to a montage of Lacy tracking Sean and boning him over and over again in his house. Polly gets worried and drives out to the town, and Lacy meets Ben, who has a complicated relationship with his sons and a slightly awkward relationship with his sister, Moira.

Ew.

Sean, as it turns out, is a serial killer that Ethan, Ben, and Moira have kept hidden away for years in his secluded cabin. Sean nabs Polly and is about to kill her when Lacy shows up with Ethan. Sean bests Ethan, who is drunk. Lacy rescues Polly, and Ben steps in to fight his son. Sean kills Ben, then is killed by Lacy.

Lacy and Polly go to help Ethan and discover that Sean has escaped and run off towards the lake. They follow him and find that he's fallen beneath the ice.

Back in New York, Lacy is at an art expo when she receives a phone call. It's Sean, doing his best Hannibal Lecter impersonation.

VERDICT: Umm...nah.

This was a made for TV movie with a decent amount of nudity in it, so I'm guessing maybe HBO or something. Who knows? Even better: who cares?

Let's start at my favorite go-to: the acting. This movie doesn't set any new standards with the acting prowess (or lack thereof) of the actors, but it isn't good. A lot of time it seems wooden and a little forced. Ah, f**k it. I felt like I was watching the *Carousel of Progress* at Disney World.

The writing, really, was probably the biggest issue with this pile of dog crap...I mean, movie. I'm trying to be nicer these days. Better myself as human being and such.

It's not working.

Must...maintain...a**hole behavior...

The plot and dialogue seemed like they were just half-thrown together with no real direction for the movie to go. It meanders along like a lost toddler in a toy store and moves at a pace that would make the building of Rome look like a rush-job.

We get lots of scenery, Lacy asking about Sean, lots more scenery, shady characters, Lacy asking about Sean, Polly whining, Lacy asking about Sean, more Polly whining, Ben making out with Moira, Sean and Lacy playing Legos: Perv Edition, more Polly whining, Ethan getting drunk, and credits. Masterful writing, let me tell you. I'm sure even Stephen King could learn a thing or two.

Sadly, as I said earlier, this might be the good film on the collection. I still have two more movies to go, and it really can only go downhill from here. If you're into TV movies, give it a look. If you're into keeping your sanity by not being so bored you'd actually consider using a hot steam iron on your face just to see what happens, avoid.

Rob Zombie's Halloween 2: Uh...No, Rob

The first remake of the original *Halloween* story was one of the most epic and staggering cinematic experiences ever. The original *Halloween* was cutting edge and pushed boundaries never before touched, spawning off the *Friday the 13th* series as a copycat as well as a few other failed franchises.

In fact, I think *Friday the 13th* may have been the only successful one. I mean REALLY successful.

Rob Zombie took this old, hardcore movie and made it depraved and deep, exploring more of Michael Meyer's past and how he lost his humanity. It was disturbing and very real.

Part two was not.

With the second film, Rob tries to invoke more psychological aspects to Michael, but ends up dragging out a very simple storyline.

After allegedly shooting Meyers in the face, Laurie Strode ends up living with Annie and her father, Sheriff Brackett.

Michael, we learn at the beginning of the movie, is far from dead as the round merely grazed his skull. He wakes up miles outside of Haddonfield, kills the two drivers in the Coroner's van, and begins a two-year-long journey back to Haddonfield to find Laurie.

Laurie is mental, having been traumatized by the encounter with Michael and having to see the scars on Annie's face as a constant reminder.

What killed me the most was that Loomis, the good side of one of the three epic slasher vs. good-guy story points, was reduced to a sniveling, greedy diva who used the events in Haddonfield to gain profit. Gone is the intelligent, passionate Loomis from Donald Pleasance and Malcolm McDowell's masterful interpretation in the first movie. The character is unlikeable, plain and simple.

The movie, otherwise, begins on a very frightening note, but as it progresses, it gets worse and worse, ending in a climax meant to be epic but ending up being depressing.

I can't give the ending away because the statute of limitations is about ten years, but I can say that the intelligent, striking subject matter of the first movie is reduced to a brutal slash-fest with pointless characters that are nothing more than fodder for a more violent, grunting and talking (YES, HE HAS A LINE!) Michael Meyers.

This flick wasn't poo, but it wasn't good, either. It's a classic case of the original being far better. Zombie should have stuck to the original storyline and added his splash of utterly painful realism rather than trying to see how artsy he could be.

The dream sequences stunk after the first one, which was the most frightening sequence in the movie.

Guess what?

IT WAS IN THE HOSPITAL AND A REMAKE OF THE ORIGINAL SECOND MOVIE!!!

If he had stretched that out to an hour and a half, this movie would have sent chills up my spine. Instead, I am resigned to say that Rob Zombie's *Halloween* began and ended with the first one.

The second one is just a rambling, frightless waste of two hours.

VERDICT: Meh.

Give it a one timer if you're curious and have seen the first one, but don't expect the same level of terror you got from the first movie. If you are a fan of the original *Halloween*, watch the first remake and leave it at that.

In the Dead of Winter: Banjos, keyboards, and buffoonary

Redneck serial killers on the run, killing everyone they come across. *The Dead of Winter* is promising. We have blood, we have violence, and we have hick morons reunited to make the snow red. What can possibly go wrong?

A LOT.

Tucker is released from prison after a stint he served for killing a guard dog. His buddies Luke, Roy, and Dean pick him up. The first place they stop is the home of Sheriff Steve, and Tucker guns him down.

From this, we're to assume that Sheriff Steve is the reason Tucker was locked up. Tuck and his friends leave, and we get a montage of the snowy wilderness of Whereverthef**k in the great state of Whogivesadamn, USA.

They next meet a vacationing middle-aged couple hauling snowmobiles on a flatbed truck. Tuck and the gang tie up the couple and steal the snowmobiles.

Next up is a couple on their honeymoon. The girl is trying to seduce her new husband by pelting him with snowballs and shaking her hips like a bad silent film.

The Copenhagen Rejects descend on the couple like a bad case of anal warts and take the girl hostage to use for sex. They bury the man up to his neck in the yard after he stabs Roy in the foot with a knife.

The girl manages to steal Tuck's gun and holds the group back. Roy pulls his snowmobile up to the guy's head and waits for the word to run him over. The girl shoots Roy, but he isn't killed and runs over the honeymooner's head. The girl screams, there's a struggle, and Dean stabs her to death.

Yes. This, so far, is the entire movie. Montage. New characters. The four morons kill them. Redneck Skullduggery. Wash, rinse, repeat.

After another montage, a mysterious figure in the woods takes potshots at the foursome. The group scrambles and splits up. Luke agrees to try and get Roy help for his foot, which is frostbitten. Roy is dying of blood poisoning. Dean and Tuck push on, trying to find the person hunting them.

Bad Movie Beware!

They split up when Tuck sees the figure duck behind a tree. Dean scouts ahead, and Tuck shoots him by mistake. At this point, the movie flips back and forth between Roy and Luke, and Tuck forging ahead on his own.

Luke parks Roy under a tree and pushes on, following a dark figure out onto a frozen lake. Luke falls through the ice and drowns. Roy dies from exposure.

Tuck runs into the figure, who turns out to be Sheriff Steve. As luck would have it, Tuck shot Sheriff Steve on his birthday—the day he got a bulletproof vest from his wife. They fight, and Tuck manages to get Steve's gun. Tuck tries to shoot, but the gun is empty.

Sheriff Steve recovers and traps Tuck in a cluster of bear traps. He walks away, deciding not to kill Tuck directly. He leaves Tuck on the side of the river, trapped and exposed to the weather.

The End. No, really. That's it.

VERDICT: Naked, falling backwards into a hog pen.

This movie...what the hell, where do I start!? It's a camcorder movie, so expect the same cinematography you get with internet porn. While I don't have anything against these indie flicks, it's still easy to tell when they are trying, when they aren't trying, and when they have no idea what they're doing. What the f**k did they use to film this s**t!? An iPhone 6!?

No wonder it's a little bent.

The acting is abysmal. Even with a poorly written script, the line delivery was on par with an elementary school production of *Scarface* with a heavy dose of *Deliverance*. The redneck characters were way overdone, and the victims were so helpless that I wondered how they managed to survive even up to this point.

The music was probably the worst part of this movie as far as production goes. It's as if the writer/director had a friend who knew a friend who knew a buddy who had a kissing cousin who knew how to play keyboard, and he paired them up with Uncle Sister-Auntie to play banjo for every scene in the film. No, really. This SLASHER flick had the most upbeat techno music EVER.

You'll notice that they synopsis is kind of short because I didn't take the time to describe every montage in the movie. Probably a third of the movie is the techno-savvy Trailer Park Jug Band playing the redneck dance club inbreeding mix while the characters either walked, drove, or laid there contemplating whatever. God forbid we have characters that actually have SOME sort of development outside of craving beer, chaw, and gentle touch of a close relative at Christmas.

Do yourself the favor of avoiding this movie like it's a monkey covered in Liquid Ass.

Mother's Day Massacre: Throw Momma under the damn bus

Movie number three in the epic $5 four-pack is, so far, the worst in the bunch.

When I watched *Halloween*, I got what I expected: Michael Myers killed a bunch of people on Halloween, which is the anniversary of the night he went nutbags and butchered his sister. *The Amityville Horror* took place in Amityville, of all places (imagine that)! Yet, I watch a movie called *Mother's Day Massacre*, and I get a dose of randomness not seen since *The Sweetest Thing*.

It was as if the writer/director opened up Word on his computer, and then proceeded to bash his head against the keyboard until he was almost unconscious. He then saved the file and sent it to some third world illiterate country where the population is primarily mentally disturbed chimpanzees with a note that said: "Edit this and have it ready in three days. Thanks!"

A woman finds out she has chlamydia and knows that her husband, Tex, has visited his whore, Delores, again. She storms into Delores' house and comes upon a woman with two small children and the worst Scarface impersonation EVER. Cue the bad stage combat, and ol' soccer mom gets her hair redone with a cast iron skillet.

Skip ahead an unknown number of years to the world's oldest third grader about to graduate high school and trying to have a romantic bath with his girlfriend. But they aren't allowed to see each other naked.

I can't make this up.

This awkward couple is Jim and Doreen. Jim's father, Tex, shows up as a surly (read: overacted) redneck that gets his kicks abusing his son.

Skip ahead six months, and we find Doreen post miscarriage with blood pouring out of her hoo-ha and puking up the last bit of fake vomit that Spencer's Gifts had. We can only assume that these two somehow had sex in the past six months.

They break it off, and Jim ends up discovering a lost dog and a reel of footage in his dad's shed. The next-door neighbor, Jen (read: Suzy Rottencrotch) seems like she is going to start dating Jim.

Am I the only one who is wondering why this movie has been on for thirty minutes now and we have seen no massacre!?

They gather at the movies with Jen's boyfriend Bobby, his buddy Petey (shoot me now), and Jen's friend Steph. Doreen is also there and has gone from naive little girl to smoking bad girl (Suzy's sister, Sally Rottencrotch). They are having a good time and then decide to go to a random abandoned town and look around.

They happen to end up in the same house that is occupied by Delores and her two now grown mentally retarded sons. Petey decides to take advantage of a hole in the wall.

What idiot goes into an abandoned house and sees a hole in the wall as a glory hole!?

He gets trapped and hacked up by a giant fat dude in shades who squeals like a pig. Steph is next, getting dragged off by a cross-eyed dude with mommy issues. Bobby gets worked over with a knife and dropped out a window. At this point, Doreen, Jen, and Jim decide to leave.

Gee!

One Week Later...yes this screen actually pops up. No, it's not over.

No, we can't burn the disc, there's one more movie on it.

Jim, Jen, and Doreen are trying to cope with the events in the town. Cut to Incest Hollow where we find Delores snarling that Jim took the whole crop...

Of what!?

Anyway...she visits Tex and demands compensation only to get slapped around. She leaves and returns after Tex goes off to sell some drugs or something. Not really clear on that because the writer forgot to put that one in.

Delores and her artards storm the house, killing Jim's idiot brother and injuring Jim as he and Doreen take cover. Tex shows back up, and we find out that he is in cahoots with Delores. He shoots Doreen in the eye (not that she really added much to the train wreck) and is ready to kill Jim when Jen arrives and shoots him in the face.

The bullet grazes his cheek and he goes down. Delores screams and Jen blows her head off. The police arrive and Tex cries that Jen is the murderer. Before she can explain, she is gunned down.

Cut to a truck stop where Tex and the big pig dude in glasses are sitting in the car. Tex goes and kills off a trucker, then hands the keys to Pig

Man. Cut to a hospital where Jim has gone bat guano and is being taken care of a very familiar male nurse with crossed eyes.

The End. Thank God.

VERDICT: Throw it into a yard fire!

This movie was so random it was unreal. The review is not random on purpose, and I have not gotten things out of sequence. It jumped around THAT MUCH. I left out a few tidbits, like Tex being in league with a doctor who molests his patients while they are under hypnosis, simply because there are large scenes like this that add nothing at all to an already broken story.

Also notice that there is no mention of Mother's Day. NONE. So why the hell call it Mother's Day Massacre!? Maybe because "So Random" was already taken by Disney Channel? Who knows!?

I'm still trying to figure out how Jim and Doreen managed to have sex if they couldn't see each other naked. Turkey baster?

This movie was up there with *Troll 2*, which has already set the standard of how bad movies can get. If ever a film was shat, this one would be the one. I have used some rough toilet paper in my day, but film takes the cake.

Rabid Love: Musical montage from hell

Ah, the 80s. Hands-down, the 1980s was the greatest decade to be a kid. You had your timeless classics, such as *The Goonies* and *Ghostbusters* as well as dozens of others because your dad knew how to do that trick with two VCRs. *Full House* and *Alf* were in their prime, and everyone watched *Muppet Babies, GI Joe, He-Man,* and anything else to do with toys or was on the *USA Cartoon Express*.

And slasher flicks. The BEST slasher flicks.

And no hyperlinks.

Jesus.

So as I peruse my collection of movies I find that a fan has given me yet ANOTHER great 80s slasher flick! *Rabid Love* calls to me in its great glam and blood-soaked sultry voice, saying "Come to me, my eighties-loving child. Come to a world of girls wearing legwarmers and flashing their boobies. Come to the era people getting killed in the most ridiculous ways possible because it's funny."

What? "Copyright 2013?" What the hell is this s**t!?

Rabid Love stars Hayley Derryberry, who also happens to be the writer and producer of the film. In fact, the director, Paul J. Porter, also has a large role in the film. He's also the producer. And the Associate Producer (he gets himself coffee and takes notes for himself when he's about to present to investors). And the Editor.

Anyway, onwards!!

Heather and her friends, Summer and Julie, go on a weekend getaway that is to be their last before they all separate and go off to college. Along for the ride are Heather's boyfriend, John, and his obnoxious best friend, Adam.

While they are enjoying their stay at the cabin, John meets up with a local photographer, David, who is trying to get pictures of the bear that has been rumored to be attacking hikers in the area. David helps John reset a bear trap and pricks him on the back with a needle or something during the process.

John writes it off as a bug-bite and invites David over for dinner. That night John begins to complain of fatigue and rubs his shoulder where David pricked him. He retires early, and the others go on with their evening.

I might as well bring it up now. That way, should you decide to watch this movie, you can't say I allowed you to be blindsided, thus failing in my venture to unearth the crap that makes you curious whilst perusing the shelves at the video store (they'll come back, dammit!!!).

Remember when 80s flicks would begin or end scenes with a snippet of whatever music was popular at the time? The trend carried over into the nineties as well, then stepped back towards the turn of the century and became a radio snippet. This movie not only has 80s music, it has songs no one has ever heard of.

Plus, about a half an hour of the movie is comprised of montages. That's right! They don't play a snippet! They play the whole f**king song!!

Aaaanyway, the next night, David shows up to dinner, and we get another musical montage of everyone eating. David is quiet and shy, and Julie is obviously interested in him. John retires early again, Adam goes into the next room to continue to get wasted, and Heather and Summer go outside so that Julie and David can be alone. David promptly leaves, assuring Julie that she will see him again.

That night, during yet another musical montage, John has sex with Heather then rolls over and goes to sleep.

Yeah, it's significant. I know, right?

John sneaks out for a run, and Summer follows him. They meet up in the woods, hook up, and the scene fades as the song ends.

The next morning, Heather and Julie go out looking for them. Heather stumbles across Summer's body, David appears and tells them to call the police.

I can probably sum up the next bit with: "Some stuff happens." Believe it or not, I've skipped A LOT in the summary. The bulk of the movie is character development. Considering that this is a slasher movie, it comes off as boring and uneventful. By the time things started rolling, I was rooting for the killer.

By the end of things, David has killed off a wandering hippie chick from a group he killed earlier (yes, you read that right), has caught Julie in a bear trap, and has Heather on the run. It is revealed that he is a mad scientist who has a created a "Super-Rabies" strain and is conducting human trials.

Heather finds his lab and, in a fit of synthesized 80s music, destroys it. David hears the montage start…I mean, his lab explode, and goes after it. Heather returns and is cornered by John as the montage comes to a close.

David appears and is attacked by John, who kills him with a bite to the neck. John attacks Heather, and she is able to escape. She grabs David's gun and shoots John.

As Heather, Julie, and Heather's cop friend, who had nothing to do with the plotline other than transition into the chauffer at the end, begin another montage while driving off into the distance, Heather comes under the control of the rabies strain (remember the sex scene?) and kills the cop and Julie. The montage transitions into credits as she runs away.

The End

VERDICT: Needs a vaccine.

Let me start by saying that, like *Slaughtered,* this movie has its pros and cons. It's not a "terrible" movie, but it does kind of deserve its place in the "Bad Movie" genre. It has its good points, but it also has its problems.

I have to give it to Hayley Derryberry: the concept is good for a slasher flick and potential Bad Movie. A mad scientist wants to create a rabies strain that can be used in biological warfare and is testing it on people. But a lot of the writing has its hiccups. The opening scene where Heather is jogging and runs up on two girls slaughtered by a bear (according to IMDB these girls are her sister and her sister's friend) has no bearing on the story whatsoever.

Supposedly there is a short film also done by Derryberry that spawned this movie, and it might shed some light on a few characters and plot points, but I was unable to find it anywhere. But I shouldn't have to watch it to get what's going on.

The 80s look was pretty spot-on. In most indie-flicks that take place in the 80s, you see mistakes such as characters with digital cameras (as in $2000 DSLRs) and cell phones that they try to write off as "gadgets of the future" IF they say anything at all about it. The props and clothing styles were refreshingly accurate, and Porter managed to steer clear of dropping media references from the era. Many indie films tend to focus on these in order to go "Lookitme! lookitme! I take place in the 80s!!!"

The makeup and gore effects, though done on the cheap, were surprisingly well done. The cuts and slashes weren't obviously gelatin and corn syrup, and the bite on David's neck wasn't obviously one of Miley's pasties hosed in ketchup and adhered to Brandon Stacy's skin as he pretended to die from his mortal wound.

Though the acting was well done and the camera work was above average, the musical montages were WAAAAAAAAAAAAY overdone. Almost half the movie was musical montages while we watched the characters look determined or lost in thought while walking. If I want to watch a movie about people walking, I'll hit up *The Lord of the Rings*. While my favorite movies of all time, there is quite a bit of walking.

All in all, not a terrible movie. I can say I'd recommend it if you want to watch a good indie-flick for a change of pace, but be patient because you can't skip the montages. Some of the critical plot points take place during them, and you'll end up lost if you hit the fast forward button.

Return to Sleepaway Camp: Camp Crappymovie

I had never seen the *Sleepaway Camp* series before this for two reasons: A) It was billed as a *Friday the 13th* wannabe. B) Good luck trying to find it, as it is rare.

After receiving a text from Steve, I sat down to watch *Return to Sleepaway Camp* since it had two of the original cast in it.

I should have known that I was in for some utter poop when the theme song started (Sleepaway Camp, performed by the greasy step-siblings of the Red Hot Chili Peppers).

Enter Alan, that token fat kid we all went to school with who was totally devoid of social skills and smelled like hot garbage due to his refusal to change his clothes or bathe regularly in a manner that involved actually using soap.

Naturally, everyone picks on Alan. We're supposed to feel sorry for the kid, but he's loud and obnoxious. Generally, he instigates his confrontations.

In other words, our hero brings on a lot of his own bulls**t.

He also has a thing for the hottest girl at Camp Manabe.

Yeah, you can imagine how that goes.

She's nice and all, but her friends easily pressure her into luring Alan into traps so that they can torture him. A police officer is in and out but has to use a vocal vibrator to speak due to throat cancer.

Ronnie, played by the original actor Paul DeAngelo, returns as head counselor. Of course, things begin to happen around Camp Manabe, people start dying, and he suspects that Angela has returned.

Angela was the original killer from the first movie. The death sequences are creative and over the top, but they are overshadowed by the rest of this ass-fest. Paul DeAngelo is legendary in the B-horror genre, but that does not mean his porn-style acting is entertaining to watch.

In fact, the storyline and acting is more reminiscent of a Disney Channel Original Movie gone horribly wrong and filled to the brim with over-the-top blood and gore. At least some nudity would have offset the fact that the original director thought he could bring the series back to life with what he learned from the two God-awful sequels.

The story, also written by the director, goes in so many directions it's less like a movie and more like random webisodes strung together into a haphazard Nickelodeon's *Salute Your Shorts Halloween Special* starring a sadistic maniac who likes to deep fry people's heads, blow them up with gasoline, castrate them with a Jeep (don't ask) and set up elaborate traps that would make Wyle E. Coyote scratch his noggin.

I have to wonder how the killer managed to construct a bunk bed with spikes in such a short time frame, or knew exactly when and in what direction a victim would drive off and into a razor-wire trap strung across the road.

If Porky Pig had come out during the ending sequence where Felissa Rose was trying to recreate her horrific face from the first movie and said "B-de,b-de,b-de-That's All, Folks!" I would not have been surprised in the slightest.

VERDICT: Outhouse fire!

This movie was actually less of a chore to watch than *Evita*, but more entertaining to watch than drying paint. But not by much.

I've seen bad slasher flicks, but this one took the cake and laid a massive Cleveland Steamer right on top of it.

I was told that the original was fairly good, and I was expecting more from this one since it had the same guy behind the helm.

What I ended up watching was the equivalent of going to the porta-john at a community event and finding out the hard way that it is full, you just added to the problem, and you have no toilet paper.

Some movies are fun to watch, even when they're bad.

Watching this movie was like staring at a motion photo of skin tags on a ferret.

Secrets of the Clown: As if I really wanted to know...

After probably two of the most eventful weeks of the entire year, I'm back! Normally I have a line-up of holiday flicks ready for slaughter, but things got crazy. Anywho, what better way to bring in the holidays than a good ol' scary flick?

It would've been something had I actually found one.

For those of you who have a fear of clowns, this movie is harmless. *IT* was crazy; I'll give you that. Tim Curry brought horrifying life to Pennywise the Dancing Clown, and let's not forget the iconic *Killer Klowns from Outer Space.*

Actually, let's forget about that one. Yeesh.

Secrets of the Clown is another camcorder independent movie, which is fine. I really don't take issue with the genre as a whole. I've seen a few good ones, such as *Off Season.* But what kills me is when the people behind the camcorder are clueless and, more or less, sharting a movie for cheap thrills and a chance to see a lot of boobies.

The movie opens on two people in bed who are awakened in the middle of the night. The girl, of course, is topless and the guy is a complete tool. I specify this toplessness because, despite what you might hear in some reviews, this is the ONLY time you see nudity in this movie.

Not as bad as *Thankskilling*, at least. Yet.

They are killed by a figure that seems to be a clown, judging from the hand that carries the knife. The next day, enter Boobie...I mean Bobbie. Ah hell, the first one might be a little more accurate. This dude is the hero of the film, and he's a total nimrod. Just wait and see.

Bobbie and Val seem to be having relationship issues stemming from Val's obsession with a porcelain clown doll she keeps handy. She leaves, and Bobbie's best friend Jim comes over to help him drink his sorrows away. Jim breaks the clown doll to get back at Val and goes outside to smoke. He is killed, and Bobbie finds the body with the clown doll next to it.

Val returns to Bobbie in the hospital and they rekindle the relationship. Bobbie later tells her that he can sense Jim's spirit in the house. Bobbie's friends Ken, Mike, Louie, Kelly, and Jon agree to meet at the cemetery to pay their respects to Jim.

Jon is acting like a jerk to everyone, constantly telling Louie and stupid he is and insulting anyone who speaks. He goes especially nuts when Bobbie wants to hold a séance to talk to Jim and find the killer.

Mike ends up punching Jon in the face, and he storms off before Bobbie can stop him. Jon goes back to the car and is killed by the clown hand.

Now what kills me.

In the next scene, Bobbie is writing a speech for Jon's funeral. He begins it with, "Jon was the best friend anyone could ask for." Dude, he was an uproarious a**hole. Let's be real. I've got friends who can be a little much too, but at least I can admit it.

Anywho, at Jon's funeral the friends get together and decide to hire a psychic to contact Jim and identify the killer. Val is upset by this and goes out the night of the séance. The psychic (they never say his name, I looked twice) arrives and begins to talk to each of the group about the recent events.

During this, Val has a revelation and tries to call Bobbie. He doesn't answer, and she turns around and heads back. The car breaks down, and she is forced to go it on foot. A strange old man picks her up, and he reveals that he is part of a coven searching for her. She escapes after killing him and is picked up by another driver.

Relax, he's just a pervert. No biggie.

Ken has been attacked by the clown demon, and Louie has been killed. The psychic recognizes her, and he reveals that he is a warlock and has been alive for centuries. He promised Val, his prize student, eternal life if she simply killed someone she loved. She was supposed to kill Bobbie, but it backfired and the psychic came for payment.

Ken comes back as a zombie and attacks Val and Mike. Bobbie struggles with him and kills him by stomping his throat in.

Mike: "You killed Kenny!"

Bobbie: "I'm a bastard."

No. Really. I can't make this up.

Val arrives, and chaos ensues. The clown demon appears and kills Kelly and Mike. He works for the psychic, and Val rebels and says that she chooses Bobbie over immortality. She battles the psychic, and Bobbie is caught in the crossfire when the clown attacks him. Val uses the clown doll to vanquish the clown demon, and the psychic disappears in a puff of smoke.

Bobbie awakens in the hospital to find Val by his side and the doctor running tests. Val offers to take him for a walk, and the doc, who turns out to be the psychic, stops them. Bobbie blacks out and awakens to find the aftermath of a fight and the psychic dead on the floor.

Val tell him that she couldn't kill him because she loves him and that the psychic knew that he could die even though she can't. As they leave, the psychic opens one eye.

Please, God, don't make a sequel.

VERDICT: Keep that s**t to yourself!!!

Even for what it is, this movie is a gargantuan donkey turn floating on the top layer of film in the water stagnating in the film industry's toilet. The acting is absolutely horrendous. It's as if they learned from none other than the master himself: William Shatner. They all recite the lines as if they're reading them, and everything is overdone to the hundredth degree.

Actor 1: "Where are you going?"

Actor 2: (With intense urgency as if the fate of all Cybertron hangs in the balance) "The bathroom to take a whiz!"

Not kidding. Every. Freakin'. Line.

The plot is weak at best, with crater-sized holes for added fun. Who is the coven after Val? What is their story? Was she born into it? Was she found? It ends up being a storyline made up of plot points that go nowhere and ride the tails of the main plot as weakly as possible.

Though it's cheap and Halloween store special, I'll have to give kudos to the gore. The blood and wounds are theater department quality, but from a good student and not the Mass Comm major looking to fill in elective hours.

On the whole, if you're into horror movies about clowns, look away from this one. If you're into the camcorder indie genre...look away from this one. No, really. It sucks. It sucks on every level. It sucks about like an asthmatic prostitute with an iron lung. Just because you have a friend who will take off her shirt and a buddy in a heavy metal garage band does not mean you can make a movie.

Hell, I think EVERYONE has that one friend who will go all out just to be on camera.

Slaughter High: School spirit is in the crapper

Ah, 1986!

1986 was a good year for film, noted for landmark releases like *Crocodile Dundee, Ferris Bueller's Day Off, Top Gun,* and *Aliens* (my personal favorite) just to name a scant few. I could go on and on, but the list of fantastic movies that came out that year is just too long.

Of course, 1986 wasn't exactly s**t proof.

Slaughter High isn't so much a slasher flick as it is a nod to the eighties slasher movies, particularly the well-known and beloved *Friday the 13th* series. In fact, *Friday the 13th Part VI: Jason Lives* is one of the most loved in the series and the movie that initially brought him back from the dead.

Unfortunately, the B-movie industry took this idea as an invitation to really hammer out some copycat-style crap onto the market like this dung pile of a movie. I remember seeing the cover on the video store shelf as a kid, and I'm glad I never gave it much thought because I might never have had the mental capacity as a child to move past the horrible acting, let alone the bad plot.

Speaking of a bad plot…stop me if you've heard this one before.

Marty is the school nerd who is the constant butt of the jokes of a group of friends who just refer to themselves as "The Group," led by Skip and Carol. On April Fool's Day, they play a prank on Marty that causes an explosion in the chemistry lab and leaves Marty permanently disfigured. Carol tricks him into stripping in a shower stall in the girls' locker room, and they jab him in the junk with a javelin. They also shock him with a car battery rigged up to a towel rack, dunk his head in a toilet, and then ultimately almost kill him.

All in one scene.

Ten years later, "The Group" reconvenes for a high school reunion only to find that the school has been closed since graduation. They decide to stay and drink anyway and find one room in the building that has been decorated for the reunion. They also discover that their old lockers, along with their old belongings, have been moved into the room.

Marty's old locker is also in the room, and they wonder what ever happened to him after the prank that landed him in the hospital. Skip tells them that the last he heard Marty was institutionalized, and they figure that he has moved on.

Wait a sec.

Excuse me if I have to take a moment to wonder HOW being institutionalized because a group of scumbags disfigured him would go hand-in-hand with him "moving on." I would think that being locked away for years on a steady diet of lithium and Pop Tarts would be a constant reminder that the group leader, Douchebag McF**k-Nugget, caused the explosion that burned his face off.

Anywho, the group runs into the caretaker and informs him that they are just touring around reliving old memories. He warns them to be careful and is then killed as soon as they are out of sight. A figure lifts him off his feet and impales his head on a coat hook.

This is the first kill of the movie, and it's pretty gruesome, so at least we're off to a good start. It's also pretty much hitting the "GO" switch on the Murder Machine. Marty is obviously back, and he's picking off the group one-by-one with an assortment of javelins, beer cans filled with poison, tubs of acid, and metal framework wired up to the school's main electrical system.

By the time the third member of the group is killed, they figure out what the viewer already knows: Marty is back and he won't stop until all of them are deader than Stephanie Meyer's writing career.

The movie moves quickly, and the characters make the token dumbass decisions that end up doing nothing more than make it easier for Marty to pick them off. Because, you know, I totally want to take a bath inside an abandoned building. And what's the best thing to do when we're trapped inside a building with a deranged serial killer on the prowl?

Screw our brains out, of course! Duh!

By the time Marty is done, only Carol remains. He traps her in the same shower stall that she got him trapped in during the opening scene of the film and impales her with (presumably) the same javelin that the group tortured him with all those years ago.

And then he wakes up.

Wait, what!?

That's right! Why just end it there? Why not add a few more measly minutes to this derp-fest by making the ENTIRE MOVIE a dream sequence? Marty kills two nurses as he flees the mental hospital and heads for his old school to make the hour and a half dream we just watched a reality.

The End. Cue credits and bad theme song.

VERDICT: Stuff your alma mater up your a**, *Slaughter High*.

Watching this movie is equivalent to looking up the wrong cheerleader's skirt during a pep rally. Just when you think you're about to see Suzie Rottencrotch's goods, she kicks up her leg in a standing split and you get full view of where she keeps her tobacco chew.

This movie appeals to young little boys who run over to the horror section and look at covers that have skulls and s**t. It's that movie mom would never let us rent.

But *Hellraiser* was perfectly okay.

Little did I know, at the time, that mom ACTUALLY had taste in movies and could spot a pile of s**t stinking up the shelf from a mile off.

First things first.

The acting is absolutely horrendous. Most of the cast is British and trying to use fake American accents. What ends up happening is an ear-piercing mix of the two that ends up making them sound largely like rednecks trying to talk like them thar Europeans.

The theme music is laughable, even by 80s standards. The mood music in this movie sounds familiar because Harry Manfredini, the same guy who did the music for *Friday the 13th*, did it.

Frankly, the characters in the movie are complete s**theads. They take bullying Marty to the extreme in the beginning

But what are a few pranks, right?

Needless to say, you don't like any of the characters that Marty is killing off, which kind of sucks in a sense because you want someone to survive for a possible sequel. Then again, you also feel justified rooting for the killer, so maybe it's not so bad.

What I can say about this movie is that the pacing is outstanding. There is constantly something going on, and the kills are super-creative. Where it falls flat is the cheap cop-out of making the entire movie Marty's dream. That's the thing that seals the deal on this movie being the liquid goop inside the dried shell that forms around the cow patty.

Slaughterhouse Massacre: The meat tastes funny...

I started off the week with *Autumn*. It's a zombie flick, set in Britain, and chronicles the day-to-day goings-on of a group of survivors that are holed up in a school gym. Or store. Or something.

Bored. To. Tears.

Deciding that only heroin would make this movie interesting, I hit Netflix in search of something juicier. Oh, dear God, did I find it. *The Slaughterhouse Massacre* jumped out at me like a tranny-granny clown at a mom-n-pops trailer park haunted garage tour on Halloween night.

Slaughterhouse, like so many others, is a camcorder movie done with some clever (read: inept) editing and classic-style special effects (more like "Hey, we went to Wal-Mart!"). But, the film boasts "intense" nudity and sexual situations and massive amounts of blood and gore, so I gave it a look.

The movie opens with a couple making out in a car parked in front of the local slaughterhouse. The girl insists that she wants to have sex in the room on the table where they kill the animals. The boy is hesitant, so she begins to masturbate graphically in the seat.

Okay, so far the film is delivering on its promise of intense sex.

The boy gives in since he's missing the action, and they enter. Cut to Mickey Sickle, the lone worker in the place. He is hacking up a cow and leaves the room. The couple sneaks in and strips as soon as the coast is clear. The scene is almost hardcore.

Somewhere, this chick's parents are crying.

They flip over to missionary and the girl screams. Cut to present day, ten years later. We meet Mandy, her boyfriend Justin, his best friend Bobby, and Bobby's girlfriend Tina. Justin is a tad unfaithful and likes to try and get into the pants of the school slut. Bobby hangs out with a guy named Stoner (yeah, he likes weed). Bobby also likes to party.

Speaking of parties, the group attends a house party later that is fully stocked with alcohol, drugs, food, lesbians, and sex. Mandy walks in on a guy using the bathroom...twice.

Okay, it was funny once, Herr Director. Let the gag die.

Bobby and Justin have made an arrangement with Stoner to go to the slaughterhouse and pull a prank to scare the girls. They all leave, and

Mandy and Justin spend the evening fighting because Justin was all over the school slut again.

And this is the last we see of the slut.

Yes, each character is a stereotype. Mandy is the "Girl-Next-Door" type who never does anything wrong, Tina is the partying best friend, Justin is the horny school jock, and Bobby is the hopeless party animal. Stoner is…self-explanatory.

The group breaks into the slaughterhouse, and we get a montage of the areas we're likely to see again. The one of particular interest is the guillotine area where cows are beheaded.

We are now about halfway through the movie. Nothing has really happened yet. Jeez.

The group arrives at the area where Sickle was killed and recites the rhyme that is supposed to bring him back. It doesn't seem to work, and they try to leave but inexplicably get mixed up. Bobby runs across a figure he thinks is Stoner, and it actually turns out to be Sickle.

"Gotta split," Sickle says, grinning. He takes one good slash, and Bobby falls away in two vertical halves. This is the tone of the rest of the movie. Sickle is a wisecracking slasher fiend who takes joy in tossing around jokes as he toys with his victims before killing them.

Someone a Freddy Kruger fan, much?

Tina finds Bobby and flips out. Justin and Mandy hear her and find her in the room in shock. Justin searches around and goes to her. "Where's Bobby!?"

What the hell? Did you not see him, ya twat!?

Holy bad editing, Batman.

Sickle attacks leaving Tina wounded. The three escape into a storage room and lock the door. Justin breaks out a window that is small enough for the girls to get through. Mandy and Tina leave to get help, and Sickle kills Justin.

Meanwhile, Stoner meets up with a good ol' boy cop with a highly overdone redneck accent. "Lemme see some eye-dee, boy." "Whatchew been doin' boy?" "Yew comin' with me, boy."

Have another Copenhagen-flavored donut, boy.

Sickle finds Tina and Mandy in a storage building and decapitates Tina. He chases Mandy, but she fights him off and escapes back into the slaughterhouse. She finds Justin and remembers that Sickle has to be decapitated in order to return to his eternal rest. She lures him into the cow guillotine room and into the guillotine.

Oh, and let it be noted that even though the hole is a good 3ft tall by 5ft wide, she still cannot get through without stripping off her skirt, which matches with her inexplicably open blouse. So she is now running around in her underoos.

Sickle follows her through the hole, and she throws the lever holding up the blade and ends his reign of ridiculousness...I mean terror. Stoner shows up, sees the scene, and helps her out of the slaughterhouse. The movie ends with what has to be the most epic finishing line in cinematic history.

"We need to go to the police."

Shoot me.

VERDICT: Mad cow disease.

This movie follows formula of your basic slasher-porn flick. Lots of blood and gore, boobies, and a gratuitous sex scene that borders on something you'd find on the internet. But following formula doesn't mean that a slasher-flick is going to be worth the film it's shat on.

The writing is, to say the least, awful. The characters have no real reason for anything, and even the plot twist where Mandy admits she's pregnant is anticlimactic. Having stereotypical characters in these movies is par for the course, but part of the fun is figuring out who is what during the first act. Pretty much giving them a sign and having them overact to it with dialogue written by your kid sister is a little lame.

Sickle is a joke. The guy has very few lines, and they tried so hard to make his voice sound like Freddy Kruger that it's laughable. What few lines he has are quips and jokes that fall flat and add no shock value to anything he does. What made Freddy great was how dark his humor was. If they had made Sickle less chatty, he would've been more effective.

And edit, for the love of God! Scenes where characters walk through a door and out of the shot change camera angles to that same character still standing in the doorway doing the same activity they were doing before the camera had a conniption. In Bobby's death scene, it was blatantly obvious that they either didn't have the funding or the time to properly edit and rewrite the scene. Both halves of Bobby are in plain view, and they still spend time looking for him without noticing that he's half the man he used to be.

Yeah, I'm singing the song too.

All in all, this movie leaves scary behind in favor of T&A and campiness that isn't even endearing. If you want scary, watch something more visceral and psychologically warping. *Yo, Gabba-Gabba* is just terrifying.

Train: More like "Train Wreck"

What looked like a promising roller coaster of thrills and chills turned out to be a case of the squirts on the monorail.

Thora Birch heads up a no name cast in this film, which one would think would help. But, the boring story, bad acting, and pointless plot twists kill what could have been a cool flick.

Then again, how many other movies have the whole "Euro-Crazies steal people and hack them up for parts" thing?

Let me answer that one for you: A LOT!!!

Thora plays Alex, a female college wrestler who goes to Europe with her team and her boyfriend's team for a competition.

When she, her friend Claire, Todd (Alex's boyfriend), Sheldon (Idiot Best Friend) and the assistant coach Willy (Stone Face...must be related to Ron Pearlman) stay out too late at a party and miss their train, they are invited with their coach to take a small train to their next match.

As it turns out (surprise, surprise), the train is a body-transport for an insane doctor who kidnaps American tourists and harvests their organs and parts for the underground black market.

I'm all about slasher flicks, don't get me wrong. But *Halloween, Friday the 13th,* and *Texas Chainsaw Massacre* weren't BORING!

"Yeah, he got killed. No, wait. He's still breathing. They cut off his penis. Yawn. Next?"

The dialogue was simple and not much more than "What was that?" and "Where the hell are we?" followed by one or two "What the hell is going on here!?" After about thirty minutes, the script consists of mostly grunting, screaming, breathing and crying.

And more grunting.

I was waiting for something interesting to happen. ANYTHING. What if Thora went to the bathroom and the train derailed, her bathroom floor coming apart and leaving a trail of toilet water and used feminine hygiene products strewn all over Prago-wherever-the-hell? That would have been more entertaining than this movie.

It was like watching a documentary on naval fungus.

VERDICT: Take the bus.

This movie defines bad slasher flicks. I don't know why modern-day directors think this crap is scary, but the only time I cared whether one of these cardboard cutout characters bought it was when Claire was fed to wild dogs and that's because she was cute. I mean, yeah, they cut off her leg, but that's what prosthetics or wooden peg legs are for.

Bottom line, I'm going to pretend that this movie never happened.

Monster Fails

Monster movies have always been a staple of the horror industry. *Dracula*, *Frankenstein's Monster*, *Godzilla*, all of them have been featured or mentioned in countless movies and television shows. But monsters don't always get it right.

In fact, this group just gets it WAY wrong.

Almost Human: Well, not really even remotely close, but okay

Almost Human was another from my guy up in Mt. Holly, NC. He's actually found a video store up there that is alive and well! It's a B-Movie Lover's Dream Come True! Family Video houses some newer movies and a vast sea of cinematic drivel that would make Uwe Boll sweat like a whore in church.

So, as you can imagine, this place has pretty much become my acquisitions warehouse. When he pitched *Almost Human* to me, I knew I was in for a little over an hour of headache and alcoholism-inducing moments of stupidity at the Fox News level. The reviews for the movie hadn't been that favorable, and I'd read a few on IMDB before watching it.

So, of course, I gave it a spin.

Seth is running from a mysterious blue light and ends up at Mark's place. Mark's girlfriend, Jen, comes in as Seth is screaming to Mark that they've already taken Rob. Mark takes the rifle and begins to search the house after the trio hears a noise from the back.

Keep in mind that "searching the house" is actually "walk up and down the same hallway over and over until something happens."

A horrible shrieking noise fires through the house, and the three humans hit the floor screaming in pain. Mark suddenly gets up, walks outside into the light, and is taken.

Okay, so far the opening is decent.

Fast-forward two years. Seth is plagued by nightmares about the abduction, and Jen works at a diner and is engaged to a new guy. Cut to two hunters in the woods who discover Mark lying naked behind a tree (really didn't need that s**t seared into my brain, but whatever). They try to help him, but he suddenly unleashes the same shriek we heard before and kills them both with his bare hands.

Cut to Seth, who is concerned about the latest news reports about strange blue lights in the area along with mysterious power outages.

Cut back to Mark. He kills someone else. This time at a local gas station. Cut back to Seth. He's worried. Cut to Jen. She wants to go home because she doesn't feel well. Cut back to—

Oh, for Christ's sake.

A fair amount of the movie goes on like this. We get a minute or two of Seth, a minute or two of Jen, and a minute or two of Mark killing people. It's as if the writer/producer/director wanted to make sure that everyone got a symmetrically equal amount of camera time.

Aaaaaanywho, Jen finally gets back home to find that Mark has killed her new fiancé. Mark wants Jen to join him and is about to take her when Seth shows up and rescues her. They run to the shed and discover three slime-covered sacs next to the body of Jen's fiancé.

And cue the sex jokes.

Mark ambushes them and knocks Seth out. He drags Jen off to the house. Seth wakes up as one of the sacs begins to hatch. One of the hunters from earlier on in the film emerges and tries to kill Seth. Seth kills him off with an axe and kills a second sac-man before he can fully hatch.

In the house, Mark rips Jen's pants and underwear off, clearly about to rape her. He suddenly spits out a long tentacle that latches onto her crotch. A lump starts moving down the tentacle.

I think I saw this in a cartoon once…

Seth comes in and saves Jen by blowing Mark's head off with a rifle he found on the way up. He leaves the room to investigate another noise, and Mark's headless corpse comes after Jen. She fights, but a giant slug launches from the stump where Mark's head used to be and shoots down her throat.

Seth reenters just as the slug vanishes, and he carries Jen out to his car to take her to the doctor. She wakes up and tries to kill him. He wrecks the car and escapes, flagging down a driver. Jen attacks, kills the driver, and Seth kills her by smashing her head in with a large rock that he gets from the side of the road. Just as he is about to hit her again, the police shoot him.

Credits. Instantly.

WTF just happened?

VERDICT: Meh.

Okay, this movie wasn't actually awful. It had its moments, no doubt. It didn't look like an indie film, but it didn't look pro, either. In truth, it would've tanked in theaters.

For starters, the acting is sub-par. Many of the emotions conveyed are not a far stretch for a trained actor. Panic and terror are fairly easy. The actors struggled more with acting normal than they did screaming their heads off while running from an alien that looked like Paul Bunyan. To call the non-action scenes wooden isn't far off.

The effects aren't exactly mind-blowing, but they're great for an indie flick. Nothing CGI here, it's all real effects. Fake blood, puppets, make-up, nothing is cheaped-out using fake computer effects. Kudos to Joe Begos (writer/producer/director) on making sure that the effects were good.

My biggest issue with the film is the unoriginality. It's more or less a straight rip of *Invasion of the Body Snatchers* with some *The Thing* and *Evil Dead* tossed in like the mint one uses to keep the toilet bowl fresh and blue.

The plot also seems to meander and make little to no sense at times. Like Rob. What the hell happened to Rob? We heard about him at the beginning of the movie, and then he was never mentioned again. And how did Mark know where to find Jen's new house? And why is Seth not in the loony bin or under some kind of counseling?

All in all, not a bad flick. Not a great one, either. It could use some work, but fans of the genre will probably enjoy it. The ending, or lack thereof, killed it for me.

Altered: People panicking for 90 minutes

I've been looking at this flick for a while now, though I never have really had the urge to watch it until recently. It's been sitting in my Netflix queue simmering like a bad bowel movement for a year or two now.

Now most of you know I'm a sci-fi fan (as in Science Fiction, not SyFy, the Crappy Movie Network), so it seems logical that I would pick this movie next since it's been a while on the sci-fi side of things. Alas, this was more of a monster movie…with events happening for no reason whatsoever.

Three friends capture a raging alien monster in the woods, and they tie the thing down and haul it to a buddy's house. Wyatt lives in constant fear, having stemmed from the abduction that he and his friends experienced fifteen years prior.

Hope is Wyatt's very patient live-in girlfriend. She doesn't have much of a sense of humor about Wyatt's buddies showing up in the middle of the night.

In fact, Kristen Stewart has more personality than this chick.

Hope is warned not to look into the alien's eyes, but she does and is under its control. She attempts to free it, and then tries to kill herself before Wyatt tackles her and ties her up in another room.

As it turns out, Otis, Duke, Cody, and Wyatt were all abducted along with Otis's brother back when they were fifteen. Otis's brother was killed during the experiments, and he has been seeking revenge along with Duke and Cody while Wyatt chose to hide.

So far, the story isn't bad and neither is the acting. The alien effects are also snazzy, but the transitions make the movie about as hyperactive as a kindergarten class on a cotton candy rush. Most, if not all, of the scenes are people freaking out and screaming.

So it's kinda like you're average episode of *Yo, Gabba-Gabba*.

Aaaaaanyway, Otis is bitten and begins to rot, and the sheriff shows up to answer a distress call from a neighbor. He sees the alien but is shot in the struggle and dies. Hope is still tied up in the other room, but Wyatt lets her loose once the alien is packed up into a cage and put in the back of the van to be hauled off.

Hope and Wyatt leave with a terminally injured Cody while Duke stays behind with Otis. Wyatt and Hope discover that Duke swapped the alien out with the sheriff and plans to torture it. Duke is killed and Cody dies before Hope and Wyatt can return.

Wyatt gets into a battle of minds with the alien but is saved by Otis. Otis turns on Wyatt and is killed. The alien tries to battle Wyatt again but is shot in the face by Hope. They escape into a bunker just as the alien ship destroys the farm.

Oooooookay.

VERDICT: Excitingly uneventful.

One of the things that stuck out like an infected boil on this movie's a** was the fact that every action was carried out first and then explained later. I mean, come on. Once or twice is one thing, but when every move and every decision is made on the fly and then explained away later it seems random and the point is missed.

The acting isn't bad at all, and the effects are great. I get why they can't just shoot the alien, but Hope does it anyway and they manage to come out alive. It would've saved about ninety minutes of shouting and drama if they had done it earlier.

And putting duct tape over your girl's mouth is usually a bad thing.

All in all, this movie is fairly underestimated, but I got a little numb to the action and drama about halfway through. Okay, I get it.

You got molested by E.T. years ago and you want revenge.

Kill it in a porta-jon somewhere and get away before getting blasted. Problem solved.

This movie wasn't terrible, but it could've been better in places. Great effort, but a little less random action followed by lectures would've been nice. Give it a look if you're feeling up to it, but staying with it takes some effort.

Assault of the Sasquatch: Oh, my poor brain...

This week was a week of mystery. I wrapped up *Prescribed Danger,* a medical mystery by the fabulous Gwen Hunter. I've been on a major *Warehouse 13* kick, and then I decided to look into the mystery of Bigfoot.

Or at least a lousy, slack-a**ed attempt at what would happen if he got set loose in the big city.

Cue opening sequence! A group of bear poachers led by the nefarious Drake (Kevin Shea) have bagged a bear and begin dismembering it when they hear a roar from the woods. The two younger poachers set out to find the source of the noise only to be met by the Sasquatch (read: a dude in a gorilla suit with a Rob Zombie mask).

Dragula...I mean, Bigfoot...tears apart one of the young poachers and chases the other back to camp. Drake shoots Bigfoot with a sleeping dart, but he wakes up just as they are dragging him onto the truck. The beast tears apart the other poacher just as Drake slams the door shut.

The state park police show up and arrest Drake for poaching. Krystal, one of the cops, takes Drake in the car while her partner, Ryan, drives Drake's truck back to the station.

Back at the station, Drake is locked up and another prisoner, Talan, is escorted in. He recognizes Ryan and attacks but is held back by the arresting officer. Turns out that Talan is the same guy who killed Ryan's wife years ago. He eyes Ryan's teenage daughter, Jessica, just before being locked away.

Then Bigfoot escapes.

Two losers who videotape everything (and apparently whack it to Sasquatch footage and lore) happen to be outside a house when Bigfoot appears and breaks in. He kills the girl inside and escapes, and we get these two Mother's-Basement-Dwellers screaming into the camera during random scenes for the rest of the movie.

Thankfully, Bigfoot kills the fat one first. His voice was grating.

The rest of the movie is more dialogue than action, with the occasional scene of Bigfoot killing someone until he manages to trap the remaining cast inside the station. Talan manages to escape.

Make it stop.

Krystal decides to release Drake after Drake explains that he knows how to stop Bigfoot. The secretary, Amy, also happens to be a butterfly knife-wielding ex-stripper. We find this out when Jessica is cornered by Bigfoot and Amy shows up to kick his a**.

Oh God, more monotony.

After all kinds of feelings and heartfelt emotions are talked about, Bigfoot breaks into the station and besets on our cast. He kills the desk cop, George, and rips Amy's legs off. Krystal is able to escape after Bigfoot separates her from Jessica in the tunnels, but Talan stabs her.

Bigfoot emerges and kills him.

Oh, the suspense.

Ryan distracts Bigfoot while Drake, Jessica, and Krystal escape into the warehouse. Drake stays behind and scuffles with Bigfoot, which ends with a large container box being dropped on Drake. Goodbye, Drake.

And goodbye to the only character in the movie worth watching

Ryan and the girls manage to make it to the tunnel where Bigfoot emerges. He passes them by, running off into the night as Ryan explains that Bigfoot now has a new home...in the city. DUHN-DUHN-DUUUUUHN!!!

VERDICT: You're kidding, right?

Of all the f**king things you can cheap out on, you go all Jew on the actual Bigfoot costume!? Seriously! It's a f**king gorilla suit with Rob Zombie's face and Bob Marley's hair! And the guy can't be much taller than 5'6". Bigfoot is supposed to be eight feet tall, isn't he!?

The acting is atrocious, the lines forced with all of the grace of a condom on a cactus. Kevin Shea is the only noteworthy actor in the movie, but with writing like that, he had to work with what he had. The Creepy Sasquatch-baters didn't help, their bit being way over-acted and old after the first two times they appear.

The script isn't much more than "What was that!?" and "How do we get out of here!?" It was interlaced with some feel-good mush and scenes that are supposed to pull at the heartstrings. All those managed to do was give me gas.

All in all, walk away from this one. It will wreak havoc on your eyeballs, your common sense, and your bowels. Anyone got a bottle of Beano?

The Beast of Yucca Flats: Shh...Don't interrupt the narrator!

Of all the garbage I've seen, nothing prepared me for this hot mess of a film. The 1960's must've been an era for whatever crap might actually fit into a week or less of shooting. This movie was forced upon a poor, defenseless reel of film in 1961 and stars a Swedish former wrestler who, I guess, was in dire need of a cheeseburger.

The film opens with a woman who has just gotten out of the shower and is drying her hair in the mirror. Sorry guys, but the boobies were cut in the version I saw. She is strangled by a strange figure and left dead on her bed. The murder is never mentioned or acknowledged in the film again.

Ever.

The narrator begins by telling us about renowned scientist Joseph Javorsky of Russia, who defects to the United States and brings a briefcase full of Russian secrets with him. During his run from the Russians, two assassins attack him. He manages to escape deep into Yucca Flats but finds out quickly that the place is an atomic bomb testing ground.

The narrator then introduces us to a new couple who are beset upon by Javorsky, now a rampaging mutant. He kills the male driver in the vehicle, then takes off with the woman. A motorist discovers the man dead in the road, and the narrator then introduces us to Joe, the local sheriff.

In fact, get used to hearing the f**king narrator... a lot. The movie was filmed with no soundtrack. No, really. In order to avoid syncing lips and effects, they added in voiceovers later on and characters only speak when you can't see their faces. Guns only fire when their muzzles are off screen.

And the narrator. Heavens to Murgatroyd, the narrator! The entire movie is narrated except for snippets of badly voiced dialogue tossed in like dirty underwear into a laundry basket. And, what's worse, this a**hole repeats himself constantly. I get it, jerk-off! "Jim and Joe, two men responsible for the safety of the desert community of Yucca Flats. Jim and Joe, two law men caught in the wheels of change."

Gag me with a pitchfork.

Aaaaaanywho, Joe wakes Jim up from a night of boozing and women to help him find whoever is killing people in the desert. Meanwhile, a family pulls off to the side of the road in Yucca Flats to take a break on their long drive. The two boys run off into the desert while Mom and Dad stretch. They return, but somehow events lead back to them getting lost in the desert after Dad is shot at a few times by Jim from an airplane.

I began to lose track, frankly, because this movie gets really random, really quickly. Hell, it's only 54 minutes, so it all has to go quick.

Thank God.

The Beast discovers the boys (after the montage of the narrator summing up the events thus far...twice...Jesus) and they escape into a cave to avoid him. He finds them and chases them into a clearing where Jim and Joe ambush and shoot him. He feigns death, then grabs Jim and begins to strangle him. Joe grabs the rifle and fires several shots into Javorsky, finally killing him. Maybe.

The actor wouldn't hold still.

The end. Thank God I drink.

VERDICT: Bring in the nukes!

At least *Track of the Moon Beast* had a plot. Sort of. They most certainly had f**king dialogue!!! But then who am I!? I'm just a sad little man who reviews bad movies and stuff. What the hell do I know? Dialogue!? Pssh!! Dialogue is for pansies!

Then again, I have total respect for the silent film era, and this movie might have been able to pull it off. But no! They had to go halvsies on it because the director/writer/producer didn't wanna fork over the cash to at least put a f**king soundtrack in his already useless movie!

The voice work is absolutely horrible. It's almost apparent that the actors weren't even in the same room. It's like the crew showed up to each person's house on different days and said, "Read these lines, and we'll record it. Direction? Nah! Just go where it takes you!"

The storyline was weak only because of the lack of everything else. It could've been a decent science fiction government conspiracy flick, but it just wound up being about as useful as a bag of gluten-free marshmallows and a brick of compressed cow dung.

S'mores, anyone?

Breeders: I hope that alien has been tested...

I decided to take advantage of the box of movies my aunt gave me a year ago and took a look at one that has had me curious for a while. I was expecting crap, of course, but it didn't even meet my expectations on that level.

Breeders originally had a subtitle with it: *The Sexual Invasion*. However, people took one look at it and saw it for the large Cleveland steamer that it really is, so they dropped the extra title and stuck with *Breeders*.

In New York City (surprise) five women, all virgins, are assaulted by a mystery rapist. They cannot remember much of anything. Dale, a detective with no acting experience, is tasked with finding the criminal and bringing him to justice. He is aided by Dr. Gamble Chase (I'm not kidding), the sultry doc with a sordid past (that we never hear about it) and a distaste for men (maybe lesbo, but she's too stoic to tell for sure).

The five ladies are, according to the back cover, smokin' hot. I'm here to tell you that once they are disrobed (every woman in this movie except the doc gets naked), they look more like gender-confused teenage boys who won't stop taking their mom's hormone treatment behind her back.

The tan-lines are HUGE! I mean, the girls have color, then BAM! So white you can see through them!

The acting is about as good as chicken liver boiled in vomit. All the characters simply stand there and observe the scene while they deliver their monotone lines. I mean, c'mon! At least they were trying in *Troll 2*!

The alien is the biggest laugh as he looked more like a cosmonaut in a rubber suit with HAZMAT gloves and shag carpet for skin. The musical score is plain awful. I'm guessing they hired a drunken circus midget to play the keyboard for them, then fired him at the last second and hired on some third grader who agreed to work for M&M's.

Throw in some inconsistencies and you have an hour and half of what must have been the most ignorant coaster that I have ever spun in my DVD drive. I'm not kidding when I say that it jumps from plot point to plot point with the same random M.O. as an episode of *Spongebob Squarepants*.

VERDICT: Positive for a life-sucking disease that will shorten your life by an hour and a half.

This movie is an itchy crotch fungus that won't go away and smells right through the clothing. I had to laugh at the fact that every cliché was met, right down to the all-knowing computer that knew what the parasite was, where in Manhattan one could find a specific brick dust, what the alien location was, and how to get there.

My question: WTF DIDN'T YOU USE THE COMPUTER FIRST!?

Oh well. One more for the vault, I guess.

Die-ner (Get it?): Hey, waitress! This food tastes like it was marinated in stupid!

"Pulp Fiction meets Zombieland?"

Um…no.

What killed me about this movie from the word "go" was the title. The "Get it?" part of *Die-ner (Get it?)* isn't me, folks. That's the title of this window-licker. It's like that one fat kid we all knew in middle school who smelled like too much cologne, fancied himself the "Class Clown," and laughed like hell at all of his own jokes.

The movie opens with Ken talking to Rose inside a nondescript roadside diner in a small town located in Godknowswhere, United States. She tells him her life story and then realizes that he is a hitchhiking serial killer and tries to run away. Ken kills both her and Fred, the cook, then locks them in the cooler.

A young couple having obvious marriage issues wanders in and sits. Ken throws on an apron and plays himself off as a late-night waiter at the diner. He is about to kill the couple, Kathy and Rob, when Sheriff Duke wanders in for a coffee. Duke sees zombie Fred walking around in the kitchen and tries to talk to him.

Ken goes into the kitchen and tries to rally Fred back into the cooler when Duke comes back and tries to talk to Fred again. Fred lunges at Duke and bites him in the neck. Kathy and Rob rush back to help and discover that Ken is not who he says he is.

Actually, Ken straight up tells them he is a serial killer.

What follows is a constant cat and mouse game between Ken and his hostages while dealing with a zombie outbreak. As far as the story goes, the entire things takes place inside the diner, so there really isn't much to tell. It's much like my love life as a teenager.

Lonely and rather sad.

Things escalate quickly when Rob and Kathy knock Ken out in the bathroom, tie him up, and try to hotwire their car. Kathy is distracted by a zombie and manages to take him out. When she gets back, she discovers that Fred has gotten loose and is eating Rob.

Inside, Ken comes to and realizes that he's been tied up. Duke turns into a zombie and attacks Ken. Kathy comes back in and kills Duke, then cuts Ken loose and demands that he help her escape.

They are about to leave when Duke's partner, Jessie, comes in and holds them at gunpoint. Ken fools him into thinking Kathy is the killer, and Jessie shoots her in the shoulder. The diner door opens, and a swarm of zombies shuffles in and overtakes Jessie.

Ken tries to make a run for it but goes out the back door and right into a horde of zombies. He screams that he has no regrets as the zombies proceed with the obligatory disembowelment scene. Inside the diner, Kathy screams as Rob comes in and approaches her.

The movie ends with the big rig outside the diner starting up. The camera shifts up to the windshield, and we see that the driver is a zombie.

VERDICT: Food poisoning.

What killed me the most about this movie was how hard it tried to be a Kevin Smith or Quentin Tarantino film. All of the dialogue was nothing but casual conversation, casually delivered. Even when things were supposed to be intense, the calm and cool line delivery just made the characters seem cardboard and monotone.

It was like watching a zombie movie starring Ben Stein as the protagonist. His weapon of choice? A rifle that looks like Ferris Bueller and shoots Ben Stein's money out of his a**.

The acting is just plain bad, even for an independent film. The camerawork in this movie was just as slack as the acting, with bad shots, shaky cam in the worst spots, and shadows that shouldn't be constantly distracting me from the non-action of the movie.

Let's get it straight: I can totally appreciate old-school makeup styles. But, the reality is that those styles are done. They're part of a past generation, and trying to use them in a modern setting even as a nod just doesn't work. The current zombie is expected to look like the zombies in *The Walking Dead* or at least the *Dead Rising* video game series.

But the writing. Dear God, the writing.

Most of the lines in the movie were pointless, and it was far too evident that they were trying (and failing) to be funny. I couldn't laugh because I was so dumbfounded in the decisions the writer/director made for the characters in the script. How did he even concept this movie? Will I wander into a random diner and find the outline written on the stall in the men's room?

"For a good time, DON'T WATCH THIS MOVIE."

What could've been at least an entertaining indie flick is utterly drowned in bad dialogue that is poorly delivered and sub-par effects that make most indie flicks look high-tech. Not saying that a diner isn't an ideal location for a zombie-survivor lock-down movie, but I certainly would want more personality from my fellow survivors than these people had.

Dracula 3000: I am...Suckula.

I remember being a kid and watching Bela Lugosi portray Dracula in glorious black and white. The opening theme was Tchaikovsky's *Swan Lake,* and Lugosi was deep and brooding. Dracula always carried a certain mystery about him that made him both fearsome and seductive at the same time.

Much unlike the a**-gasket they got to play Dracula (oh, my bad, "Count Orlock") in this piece of dog poo.

Like the other movies y'all typically read about on this site, *Dracula 3000* straight up sucks a** on toast. Casper Van Dien heads up a cast of no-names along with Tiny Lister and Coolio.

Yes. Coolio.

Most of the characters are named after the classics. Van Dien plays Captain Van Helsing, his first mate is Aurora Ash (hot blonde), Coolio is 187 (you wish, buddy), Lister is Humvee, Mina Murry is an intern, and the Professor Holmwood is our wheel-chaired genius who rounds out this lackluster cast of heroes.

And then there's Count Orlock, who I was half-expecting to sparkle.

The Captain of the *Demeter* space ship is videoing his final moments, saying that his crew is dead and that they are all doomed. He is clutching a cross when the video goes blank.

Enter our group of heroes aboard the *Mother III* (aaaand our *Alien* nod). Van Helsing claims salvage rights to the *Demeter,* which has been floating derelict in space for the past 50 years after communications were lost.

Ash warns against it, but Van Helsing ignores her and proceeds. Mina suits up and goes aboard, followed by Humvee and 187. Shortly after boarding, 187 and Humvee find a room full of coffins.

187 is attacked by Count Orlock and turned into a vamp. Humvee fills the crew in, but they are attacked by 187. Van Helsing shoots him multiple times, but it takes a little research and ten minutes of people running through corridors and looking at video diaries to realize that the only thing that can kill a vamp is a broken pool cue stick.

What. The. F**k.

After offing 187, we find out that Mina has been turned during all the hubbub and that Ash is a droid programmed for law enforcement. Ash and Van Helsing take her out, but Orlock intervenes. As it turns out, Van Helsing comes from a long line of vampire hunters. Ash runs off to get help and returns to find that generations of old farts killing the undead does not make one a vamp hunter overnight.

Van Helsing is turned, and Ash kills him off.

Dumba**, corner pocket.

Count Orlock spends the rest of the movie running through the corridors of the ship a-la *Evil Dead* while Humvee and Ash discover that the good doctor is now a vamp. Orlock chases them into the main control room, and they shut the door on his arm and sever his hand.

They set a course for the sun, and then Ash reveals that she was originally programmed for sexual entertainment and pleasure. Humvee leaps at the opportunity, the original Demeter Captain appears in a video blog and accepts that the needs of the many outweigh the needs of the few, and the ship explodes.

For no reason. Period.

VERDICT: Stake it through the eyeball!!

As if the story wasn't bad enough, it seems that the entire budget went right into Casper "All I've ever done is *Starship Troopers*" Van Dien's pocket. The set is obviously a battleship memorial or something along those lines, and the slow-motion camera work is just depressing.

On the bright side...never mind. There isn't one.

The writing is atrocious, with most of Coolio's lines being ad-lib because, well, it's Coolio. Mina is annoying, and the Doc freaks out and becomes a sniveling little girl before he finally stops whining and vamps out. Ash is a blonde bombshell, but she also got her technique from Kristen Stewart.

The only actor with any talent is Tiny Lister, and he even suffers since all he has to bounce off of is cardboard cutouts of human beings.

The story is simple to the point of madness, yet this battleship-sized turd log is 86 minutes long. Granted, most of it is the characters running aimlessly though endless corridors while the scenes are broken up at random by the video diaries from the original ship captain before his demise.

In the end, I've seen golf with more hard-hitting thrills and chills.

Eegah!: Movie leave bad smell in air

Another face-first plunge into the *Best of the Worst* collection I got for Christmas turned up this awkward piece of corn Hollywood ate back in the sixties and forgot about. *Eegah! The Name Written in Blood* is the last of the first disc in this cornucopia of crap, so at least it has that going for it.

That and a glimpse at an early Richard Kiel.

Yeah, him. You know, the guy from *Happy Gilmore* with the nail stuck in his head?

Now you remember? Awesome. Apparently, he was something of a lady-killer back in the day (yeah, I kind of did a double take at that one, too).

The movie opens with Roxy stopping off at the gas station where her boyfriend Tommy works. Tommy is a classic fifties carhop, complete with the over-done boyish acting and surfer-style greasy hair. "Gee, I'm sorry, sir!" he gushes as he wipes the spilled gasoline off of a customer's car. "Guess I was just thinkin' about my girl!"

Roxy continues on after Tommy agrees to meet her and her father for dinner. Eegah appears in the road, and Roxy almost hits him. She passes out in a faint, and Eegah admires her from the road. He's 7'1", so it looks more like a creeper standing over an inflatable woman, but whatever.

Yes, I went there. With bells on.

She comes to as Eegah flees from the approaching headlights. She sees Tommy, crying out, "Oh Carl!" as she hugs him and tells him what happened.

Carl? Who the hell is Carl?

Roxy relays her story to her father, who laughs it off and sends her on her way to a party where Tommy is playing guitar. He sings a classic fifties tune that no one has ever heard of from beginning to end, then is convinced by Roxy to go searching the desert for signs of the giant she encountered.

Her father also agrees to come, and they soon discover one of Eegah's massive footprints. Mr. Miller agrees to go on an expedition to find Roxy's giant. The next morning he is dropped off via chopper and searches, but is attacked by Eegah.

Roxy and Tommy get the memo that the chopper pilot was stood up by Mr. Miller and go searching for him in Tommy's dune buggy. What we get next is a five-minute montage of him driving like a maniac in the sand...

Sand? But they're in the...oh, nevermind.

They call off the search for the evening and make camp. Out of the blue, Tommy pulls his guitar out and sings a song. Another. F**king. Song.

Yes, kids. It's a bit of a musical.

Eegah comes by, and in some turn of events (I may have missed it because I was the midst of massaging away the migraine), Roxy ends up over Eegah's shoulder and is hauled back to his cave up in Shadow Mountain. She finds her father there, and they are in the presence of Eegah's dead relatives, who he still speaks to as if they were alive.

By speaks, I mean he grunts, groans, mumbles, and gestures. Kind of like Kevin Costner in most of his roles, but taller.

The next half hour of the movie is a montage of Tommy searching the desert for Roxy as she and her father develop a tense friendship with Eegah while plotting their escape. At one point, she even gives him a shave, stating that he's actually kind of cute.

Yes. That makes perfect sense. Get captured by a gigantic cave man who wants to bang you before he eats you and give him a makeover. I'll make sure to update my survival journal.

Eegah takes Roxy outside and tries to get frisky with her, allowing Mr. Miller to escape. Tommy ambushes Eegah, and Roxy and her father escape. Eegah comes around just as Tommy picks them up in the dune buggy. They take off, and he is left howling and raising his arms in the air.

The movie doesn't really say how long it's been since Eegah's cave, but we next find Roxy at a party at her house where Tommy is singing with his band. Eegah is on a rampage and has followed them to the city. Well, more like an inconvenience than a rampage. He scares a few pets and a few people, damages some property, and tosses a guy into a swimming pool.

Be still my beating heart.

Meanwhile, Roxy has been preoccupied with Eegah ever since they got back from the desert. She decides to take her mind off things by dancing, and Tommy soon joins her. Another of his band mates tries to move in and punches Tommy in the face. Tommy retaliates shouting that Roxy is HIS girl.

This is funny to watch since we JUST saw this dude say, "Wow-wee, wow-wow!" in the previous scene. They scuffle, and Eegah invades the party. Tommy rushes him but is decked by Eegah. The cave man picks up his club and rushes the police that show up on the scene, but they shoot him.

Roxy, Tommy, and Mr. Miller stand over Eegah's body as it floats in the pool, and the credits roll after a highly forgettable profound line from Mr. Miller.

The End.

VERDICT: Ugh...blurr...blah-blah...Eegah...Blah...Mmmorgop...

I've now watched four movies in this collection, and this one takes it home on the camp factor. Yeah, I caught it too: IT'S KING FRIGGIN' KONG.

Okay, now that the obvious is out of the way, the breakdown. The acting is laughable. The only person who didn't over-act was Richard Kiel, and grunting like a constipated wookie isn't really a stretch. Tommy's character is a complete tool, and the shoo-wop fifties jive he's putting forth is about what you expect when visiting a theme park or watching a campy fifties musical that was shot in the sixties.

Oh, wait...

Three songs were played in this movie at random times, and none of them had anything to do with anything. They were the typical 50's sap songs, and I found it funny that Tommy was obsessed with Roxy but sang three songs about three different girls. So either he's a musician writing songs about what was popular back then, or he's a complete douche-canoe and can't keep his microphone in his pants.

I vote douche-canoe, sans the cheating.

The plotline is weak and pretty much a blatant rip of *King Kong*. Only Eegah didn't climb a skyscraper and swat at planes. Why? Because at least that would've added some awesomeness to the film. No. We get *Beauty and the Beast*, but Beauty is a dingbat and the Beast is Richard Kiel with no nail in his head.

Yeah, I didn't recognize him at first either. Needs the nail.

Feeding Grounds: This one gave me food poisoning

Yet another from the endless collection of utter nonsense that Netflix likes to call their award-winning instant content for those who prefer streaming to discs in the mail. Yeah, it's another indie flick. Yeah, it's bad.

The director tried going more for the characters rather than the scares, much like the movie *YellowBrickRoad*. Unlike *YellowBrickRoad*, which was masterful and shocking, *Feeding Grounds* is boring at best. It was more like watching what not to do/say when on a road trip with a hot girl and you actually want to get laid.

The movie opens with a hobo waiting by a black SUV at a gas station. A gorgeous young girl walks up, and he asks her for a ride. Her girlfriend shows up with a knife and shoos him away.

Yeah, *that* kind of girlfriend.

Already off to a great start!

These two drive off into the desert, have some fun in the sand (Yup, I'm digging this movie so far), and then drive off to their planned destination.

They both soon become agitated and violently ill. In a brief moment, they pull over, one takes off into the desert, and the other is taken inside the car by...the hobo...how the!?

Anywho, scene change to the driveway of a hippie and his three former band buddies. Four girls show up in a red car, and they all take off for a weekend of fun in a remote cabin in the desert.

On the way, we see aggression between two of the guys in the car, and we don't find out until half way through the friggin' movie that the band caved in on themselves and split because of artistic/personality differences and money.

For the next half an hour, we get a montage of these people hanging out in random parts of the desert as they continuously stop on their way to the cabin to view the scenery.

On one of their stops, they find the bloody remains of the two girls from the opening and flip out. Soon the group begins to deteriorate into madness and sickness, each disappearing one at a time as they accuse each other of murder, dishonesty, and thievery.

Who the hell wrote this? Disney!? Only one of them stays normal, and she explains that the creature on the loose has not taken her because it knows that she is one of them.

Like the hobo, this plot point goes nowhere.

Finally, in the final two minutes of the movie, we see the hand of the monster as it prepares to face off with über-chick.

Flash to daytime.

A police officer radios in on two abandoned vehicles in the desert. He finds über-girl in a giant pile of poo asking him if he has anything to drink. The end. Really. That's it, that's the whole movie. Nope, not shorting you. It. Done. Fini.

VERDICT: Delete.

This movie is solid evidence that your mom does not always have the most objective opinion when it comes to your art.

Let's face facts, kids. If you finger-paint a rainbow in dog diarrhea and highlight it with toe fungus, Mommy is going to tell you it is beautiful and hang it up on the fridge (then toss it while you are at school).

That is, essentially, what this movie is. It's an hour and twenty-one minutes of poo art spattered onto film for all to see.

As if *The House that Screamed* wasn't bad enough! Do these people actually WATCH indie flicks? It would help! That way they'd know what NOT to do.

Do NOT make a horror flick a character study without using characters with substance.

Stephano the Stoner is not a deep character.

Find people who know how to act. Even better, find a writer who knows how to write a cohesive plot that makes sense to people older than 13! Got an original idea here. It's a whopper. If you're gonna make an indie horror flick, MAKE IT SCARY.

I'd rather watch two straight hours of Honey-Boo-Boo footage than watch this movie again.

Mega Shark vs. Crocosaurus: The waters went foul QUICK.

Believe it or not, I was a HUGE Godzilla fan when I was a kid. I had (still have) a Godzilla action figure, and I saw ALL of the movies.

Of course, I also saw the disastrous remake with Matthew Broderick where Godzilla was a mutated iguana.

Real original, guys.

Watching these movies is like dating the school slut: you know what you're in for. The feeling I got when watching *Mega Shark vs. Crocosaurus* was the same feeling one would get if all Susie Rottencrotch wanted to do was hold hands. And, to top it all off, this steaming pile of doo-doo stars none other than Jaleel White: aka **STEVE FRIGGIN URKEL!!**

The movie begins with the most boring opening next to *Battlefield Earth* with the opening credits looking more like they were done in Microsoft Word. An illegal diamond mine is torn apart by a 1500 ft. crocodile. Meanwhile, Dr. Terry (Urkel) is perfecting a device that can draw or repel sharks aboard the battleship he is stationed on.

No really. They have a tank full of great whites on the ship.

A giant shark, the Megalodon, leaps from the water and ambushes the ship. Let's begin by saying that the CGI was not as bad as *Primal*, but definitely done on a Sega CD gaming console. Here's where it gets interesting. The first time we see Megalodon, he's twice the size of the ship. He flips like Jackie Chan and smacks the boat with his dorsal fin. We then see the crew firing at a dorsal fin as big as a skyscraper (yeah, real effective). He leaps from the water again, only this time he's about the size of an 18-wheeler.

Wait a sec…he can change size?

Nope. It's a screw up.

Basically, the director and editors were too lazy to notice that there are scenes in the movie where Megalodon and Crocosaurus are smaller (or bigger) in some scenes than they are in others.

Flash-forward and we are introduced to Nigel: a complete rip of Crocodile Dundee sans the accent. Joining them as their recruiter is Agent Hutchinson, a sexy but stern secret agent who is part of an elite military group whose soul purpose is to hunt down and destroy Megalodon.

They embark on an adventure that takes them to Florida, where Mega Shark and Crocosaurus clash as they realize that Mega Shark is after Croc's eggs.

The croc has laid hundreds of them, and they begin to hatch and terrorize Miami and Orlando.

Mega Shark swallows a nuclear sub, but the plot point is dropped when the idea of activating a volcano off the coast of Hawaii and sending them into it takes precedence.

The two beasts bumble through the Panama Canal and end up in place with the baby crocs in tow and continue to battle. Terry sends his device into the water, and the volcano erupts, deep-frying all of the monsters.

Yay, happy ending, everyone's happy. Except me. Is it too much to ask for, at least, a minimal plot?

After the credits, Nigel asks Terry to join him on an investigation that a giant lizard (Godzilla) is loose in Japan.

Please shoot me.

VERDICT: Duh.

This movie was so ignorant my IQ actually dropped three points just watching it.

Low budget CGI is one thing; half-a**ed CGI is unforgivable.

Monster movies had their heyday in the fifties, but serial killers, ghosts, and demons have since taken the reins. The Asylum works hard at making movies to cash in on cheap thrills, but they fail because they make minimal effort.

Not that making a movie about a giant shark fighting a giant crocodile has any chance of being even remotely intelligent, but it could be more entertaining. It was a Syfy Movie but more resembled a Hallmark Sci-Fi flick (Hallmark is still on my sh*t list for *The Last Sentinel*). And every time Jaleel White spoke, all I could hear and see was Urkel. Two gigantic monsters are about to devour us all, and our only hope is a squeaky-voiced teenage nerd with a crush on the girl next door and a cheese fetish.

I feel safer already.

I haven't seen a lamer monster battle since Shannon Doherty fought Paris Hilton at a party. When it comes to Hollywood crap, this one is a bad case of dysentery.

Osombie: Bin Laden is a zombie...and so are the actors

This tale of gut-wrenching stupidity came as a suggestion from one of the many fans (you guys are awesome!) on the Facebook page. She is one of many die-hard zombie fanatics, so if she is saying that this movie is bad, she might be on to something.

A GIGANTIC UNDERSTATEMENT.

I mean I get it: a lot of Americans aren't really over the 9/11 attacks and want a shot at Bin Laden, even though he's deader than Kristin Stewart's facial expression. This is very apparent with this movie. The plot is not a whole lot more than going after Bin Laden with a twist: he's a walker. He's Bin Laden with a taste for human flesh.

The movie opens with an attack on Bin Laden's hideout in Afghanistan. Soldiers infiltrate and shoot the place up. Bin Laden awakens from his sleep and injects himself with a serum just before being shot dead by the American troops. As they are shipping him out by chopper, he returns from the dead and kills them all, then washes ashore and begins his trek across the desert turning anyone he comes across into a zombie.

Deep, I know.

Scene-change to a small squad of American troops sent on a top-secret mission by the government to destroy the zombie plague in the Middle East. They are set upon instantly by a group of walkers and take to the best tactic that they can muster: the "stand-in-the-middle-and-shoot-in-all-directions" tactic.

God knows watching them shoot was better than watching them act. Jesus, it was like watching a bad soap opera in monotone starring *iRobot* and the *Stepford Wives*.

One of them takes off his shirt for the occasion. I guess he's Team Jacob because he almost refuses to put it back on for the rest of the movie. Another one, Tomboy, is a lollipop-popping pony-tailed blonde who also just so happens to be a samurai warrior. She gets tired of shooting and proceeds to slice-and-dice through the horde.

Joker, the comedy relief in the movie (and I use that term with all intended sarcasm), spouts of bad jokes the entire time. Besides his jokes, the dialogue is not much more than "Look out!" and "Let's move!"

No, seriously.

There is a video game called *Dead Rising* where the player can choose how they want to play the game: either following one of many story lines, or just trying to see how many zombies they can kill in a set amount of time. The writer and director of *Osombie* opted for the latter, and the bulk of the film is shootouts between the soldiers and zombies. One human dies in every encounter, and the fighting is broken up by relentless montages of the group trudging through the desert.

After about ten minutes of this, we meet Dusty, who is in Afghanistan looking for her crazy brother. Derek was a fire fighter during 9/11, and his entire troop was killed when the buildings went down. He lost his mind and vowed to kill Bin Laden himself. He flies to Afghanistan in search of the supposedly dead Al Qaeda leader.

Okay, now it's getting a plot. A bad one, but I'll take it.

Dusty joins our military friends to find her brother, and is now an extra character in the fights and montages. One scene after the death of Joker (no big loss) shows that the director was suddenly inspired by Kevin Smith. Two of the characters, Chapo and Chip, are caught up in very casual conversation while Tomboy goes to work on a group of zombies with her sword.

Fast forward because the movie drags like this up until the last ten minutes or so. We finally get inside the Al Qaeda base and discover that Bin Laden is alive-ish and sitting in chains with his men. They open fire on Derek, Dusty, and Chip. Dusty and Chip run for it to escape an air strike, but Derek stays behind and shoots Bin Laden in the face with a bazooka. The base blows up, the air strike calls off due to the apparent self-destruction of the place, and Dusty and the group are taking Derek for dead.

As the group is walking into the sunset, Derek reappears and starts chatting them up. They walk into the horizon in pleasant conversation as the credits begin to roll.

VERDICT: NO.

I understand the concept of using casual conversation as a comedic move to lighten the tone of a scene in a movie, but it only works when certain people do it in certain movies. This is not one of those movies.

I will say this: the CGI and make-up effects were excellent. The zombies were over-the-top gruesome, and the effect of their heads getting blown off (though torn right from the source code in *Resident Evil*) was highly entertaining.

That is about where the entertainment ended.

The acting was sub-par even for what it is. Tomboy telling a dying Joker, "I was gonna have your babies," was about as believable as the Carolina Panthers ever going back to Super Bowl and about as random as *The Sweetest Thing*.

WAIT! I know what happened here.

If Kristen Stewart and Keanu Reeves had babies, then these actors would all be brother and sister. And the girl that played Tomboy was AMAZING in that she NEVER messed up her perfect make-up no matter how many zombies she took out. Maybe it's her secret.

Maybe it's Maybelline.

If you want to completely turn off your brain and drool on your Mickey pajamas while the nice lady feeds you Jell-O, go for it.

Parasitic: Worst case of crabs EVER

This one was done by none other than Tim Martin, the man behind the creature effects of such films as *AvP* (*Aliens vs. Predator* for those of you who don't keep up with that kind of thing) and *X-Men Origins: Wolverine*. Of course, since ol' Timmy has insane Hollywood backing and a network of people in the industry to work with, I had rather high hopes for this movie.

Alas, my hopes were loaded into a spud canon and launched gloriously into the side of Old Lady Myrtle McCreeper's place with the grace of a bag of poo thrown into an exit sign on the interstate.

Parasitic opens with a shot of a meteor crashing to Earth while two rednecks are fishing. They get their catch, explore the crash site, and find nothing. The fish they catch is taken to a local eatery, cleaned (more or less), and made into sushi for a customer who brings the sushi back to a nightclub and delivers it to Val, the voluptuous owner. Val is disgusted by the gross-looking green sushi but wolfs it down anyways. Yes, let's eat sushi that looks like the Elephant Man blew his nose on it!

No, she is not that bright.

After closing, the crew is cleaning up and complaining about wanting to leave. Val falls ill and runs to the restroom. She begins to vomit a black, viscous liquid and rips off her shirt. Soon she begins to have chest pains that are so bad she has to take off her bra.

Yes, she is the very one you wanted to see topless. Tim Martin made sure this happened...right before her neck bursts and a tentacle comes out and begins to squeak and squirm. Val is now a monster. A topless flesh-eating creature with E-cups and a taste for human flesh.

Back in the main room of the club, the rest of the characters are whining because they are ready to go home and Val has the key. Steph goes to look for Val, searching the dark corners of the nightclub. Val finds her first and infects her with the parasite.

In the next scene, the others are whining that they want to leave. They notice that two of their party are missing, probably off screwing. Sure enough, the scene changes to a sex scene that is worse than the one in *Dreamaniac*. It's one thing to screw up real sex.

How do you screw up fake sex!?

The two lovebirds meet up with Val and Steph and are turned.

Back in the main room, the rest of the characters are whining about wanting to leave. What? I repeated myself? No, I didn't. See, if you actually ignore my warnings and watch this pile of sheep pellets (while keeping in mind that I am removed from all liability in the event that you dig your own eyeballs out because this movie sucks) then you will find that the entire movie plays out like this:

Monster!!

Val with a salamander between her boobs!!!

People whining.

Repeat.

In fact, it's not until about the last fifteen minutes of the movie that the other characters finally realize that they are vanishing one by one, and something is going on! YES. They spend ONE HOUR of a 77-minute movie whining about wanting to leave and ignorant about what is going on around them.

And ignorant in general because these characters are really f**kin' stupid.

Case in point: Grace, the handsome black dude, and the token fat guy nobody likes are barricading the doors against their friends now turned zombie minions to Val. The shove couches, tables, chairs, and shelves in front of the door. Grace decides that a guitar is all they need to finish it off.

A. Guitar.

As the creatures break in and close in around Grace, she grabs a stick and knocks the salamander off Val's chest (how she missed the girls is a complete mystery). Val and all of the zombies die. Grace stomps on the salamander until it shatters, and she and token black dude leave into the next room. A small parasite survives and takes over black dude.

Epilogue: it is now a monster holding Grace captive. The end.

VERDICT: Flush it in toilet paper.

This movie is chock-full of T&A. I've never seen a movie beyond *Sand Sharks* with this much T&A. There are so many Twits and A**holes in this flick that I actually cheered when any of them got killed off. Once again I've discovered a movie where not one, not two, but ALL of the characters are so stupid they drool on camera. The cast of *Jersey Shore* are friggin' Ph.D. holders compared to these numbskulls.

The effects are awesome, that I will admit fully and seriously. Tim Martin really went all out on the creature make-up and effects for his first film. It really would've helped if he had also gotten some actors to be in his movie. All of them spoke their lines as if reading them off of a teleprompter, and the screenplay played out as if it had been written by a horny eighth-grade little boy.

The sex scene killed me. I mean, really. It basically amounted to, "Oh baby-oh baby-oh baby," OH, PLEASE. As a follower of *True Blood*, I've seen my fair share of sex on the television screen.

This looked more like something out of a homemade Sex Education and AIDS Awareness Video.

Just sayin'.

Tim, go back to creature effects and leave this s**t to the pros. Obviously, he had no help writing this catastrophe and must have taken tips and advice under the supervision of Uwe Boll because this ended up being nothing more than a 77-minute-long dump into the toilet in the top desk drawer of Hollywood's office desk.

Pinocchio's Revenge: A REAL piece of...

The first thing that caught my eye was a fellow reviewer on Netflix touting this piece of garbage as a "movie that takes Disney's character and warps it." Really? Never mind that Pinocchio was a character from the book *The Adventures of Pinocchio* by Carlo Collodi.

Nope. Give credit to the Mouse.

Anyway, I was drawn to this skunk turd because I rather enjoyed the first *Child's Play*. The others sucked hard, getting progressively worse as time went on. How many times can an ugly doll kill people before we just move on to something more terrifying? Something such as *Teletubbies* making a comeback or Palin wanting to run for President?

(Shudders)

Anywho, since this movie looked like utter crap and about as appealing as flossing with Mama June's thong, I figured that I might as well give it a look so that I can at least say that I warned you.

The movie opens with the dramatic arrest of Vincent Gotto for the murders of several local children and his own son. He was found burying his son along with a strange wooden Pinocchio doll. Jennifer Garrick is his defense attorney, and she tries to talk him into appealing the death penalty. Vincent warns her about Pinocchio and tells her that he would rather die.

Enter Zoe, Jennifer's precious little girl. Zoe has a bully at school but manages to hold her own with harsh insults back at the girl.

After Gotto's execution, Jennifer drives home to help set up Zoe's birthday party. She sends her boyfriend, David, out to the car to retrieve Zoe's present. David returns with Pinocchio, much to Jennifer's confusion and horror since the doll is associated with a murder case. Zoe immediately clings to Pinocchio, and Jennifer decides that a few days wouldn't hurt.

What the hell am I watching, a character study!?

The next day (read: 30 minutes into the 96-minute movie) Zoe takes Pinocchio to school with her. That afternoon, her bully takes Pinocchio and tosses him over the fence. Zoe finds him and a rake handle is suddenly put between the bully-girl's bike wheels as she pedals by. The girl falls in front of a school bus and is hit, but she survives with bruises and a new fear of God.

At the 40-minute mark we see the sexy nanny of the house take a shower in a full-on nude scene. Sadly, she is not spectacular.

And the point of this scene is?

Ah, there it is. Pinocchio is watching her. I wonder if he gets wood? Ark-ark-ark.

That afternoon Zoe visits her shrink to discuss her issues and how she is dealing with her parents' divorce. He leaves the room to take a call, and Zoe and Pinocchio begin to talk to each other. Zoe trips out just as the doc is coming back into the room.

That evening David stays home to watch Zoe while Jennifer goes to work on a new case. Pinocchio tries to convince Zoe that getting rid of David would be a good thing. Before she can stop him, Pinocchio pushes David down the stairs into the cellar. David is rushed to the hospital with a cracked skull and in a coma.

Jennifer asks Zoe what happened, but Zoe tells her that it was Pinocchio. A medic informs Jen that Zoe was the one who called 9-1-1.

That night Pinocchio convinces Zoe to cut his strings, and he escapes to the hospital where he kills David by unplugging the life support machine. We assume it's Pinocchio, as the scene happens in first person.

Kind of like *Halo*, only stupid.

Jennifer gets wind of David's death and comes home to find that someone has bludgeoned the nanny to death. She sees Zoe and calls out to her, but Zoe tells her to run because Pinocchio is on the loose. Jennifer is struck with a fireplace poker and comes to as Zoe holds up the poker and tells Jen that she wrestled it from the doll.

Jen looks away to try and spot Pinocchio, but Zoe is gone when she looks back. Pinocchio charges her with a knife, and she slams him through the glass coffee table. When she looks, Zoe is in Pinocchio's place.

Twist ending. Totally didn't see that coming. And I am Miley Cyrus.

VERDICT: Chop the little b***d into firewood!!**

This movie doesn't really get interesting until the end, and even then the psychological aspect and twist seem thrown in at the last second to avoid becoming a *Chucky* rip-off. Even the nude scene didn't help. I don't mind a little nakedness, but when it comes out of nowhere and out of formula then it just gets silly.

Pinocchio looks creepy from the beginning, and while Zoe may have fallen in love with him as soon as she saw him, most little girls would probably run from him as if they were being chased by Freddy Kruger.

I actually thanked God when the credits rolled because this movie seemed like it lasted 3 hours instead of 96 minutes. It could've been trimmed down to about an hour and gotten the whole story across. No, really.

The only thing that would've saved this movie would have been the promise of a free meal at Waffle House for anyone bored or masochistic enough to subject themselves to 96 minutes of mindless dragged out drama and half-a**ed story-telling.

Piranha 3DD: Water contaminated with stupidity

As much as I love horror movies (what was your first freakin' clue?), I also enjoy a good comedy. Mesh the two, and I'm usually sold. *Evil Dead 2* was a classic in the genre, as well as the *Return of the Dead* movies and *Shawn of the Dead*.

This movie tries to follow in the footsteps of horror/comedies with slapstick humor and gore galore. Intense moments are interspersed with comedic moments that are meant to entertain and humor the audience. The writer and director only missed two KEY elements: the horror and the comedy.

Let me forewarn any of you that plan to watch this because you are masochists and watch these piles of skunk doo-doo despite my warnings to run like hell: this movie has a LOT of gratuitous nudity (which will probably entice most of you to watch it. Hey, don't say I didn't warn you). I say forewarn because it can catch you off guard at moments and leave you about as confused as an ADD kid watching a variety show (shaddup).

The first Piranha movie in this series, *Piranha 3D,* was a hit with the fans. It had plenty of blood, plenty of comedy, and lots of gratuitous nudity that one would expect from this kind of film. The ratings were extremely high considering what it was.

This movie is far different. The director actually managed to take everything from the first movie that was good and poop on it.

Maddy (Danielle Panabaker) returns home from college for the summer to work at the water park that was left to her by her mother to find out that Chet, her sleazy stepfather, has changed it and added an adult-themed section. He has also renamed the place "Big Wet" and is marketing with sex.

This is, of course, following our opening scene where a dead cow farts hundreds of baby piranhas into the water. The fish kill the two farmers, one of them being Gary Busey.

Guess he'll work for cheeseburgers, too.

Maddy is disgusted, and her friends go out for the evening with the goal of losing their virginity. Shelby goes skinny-dipping with her boyfriend but trips out and blames him for doing something wrong when a baby piranha swims up into her...

Oh, God. I see where this will end up.

Ashley and her boyfriend are about to have sex in his van when she accidentally kicks the parking brake and sends the van into the water. They become a quick meal for the fish.

Meanwhile, we find out that Officer Kyle is taking bribes from Chet to turn a blind eye to the fact that he's using a well and pumping in water illegally. Kyle is also trying to sleep with Maddy despite the pursuits of another boy in the park, Barry, who has had a crush on her since the seventh grade.

Maddy and Shelby sit on the dock and mourn the loss of Ashley when they are attacked by piranhas. They go to Mr. Goodman, a marine biologist who is an expert on the prehistoric piranha that attacked the neighboring Lake Victoria a year ago.

Mr. Goodman explains that the piranhas are probably using the drains to get where they want and that the park is in danger. They leave after a few more wild-eyed cryptic responses from him. What do you expect?

It's Christopher Lloyd for God's sake!!

Shelby is distraught by the attacks and tells her boyfriend to make love to her. She does not want to die a virgin.

Uh...k.

They have sex, but things go wrong when the piranha that made the Vagina Voyage comes back and latches on to Josh's penis. He pulls out and searches for a knife in the kitchen while the fish dangles from his member. He finds a knife and whacks off his pointer, then flees. Shelby awakens to find a fish on the floor next to the end of a penis and blood everywhere.

Just as Maddy and Kyle are about to leave to search the water park, Shelby shows up and delivers the line of the movie: "Josh just cut off his penis because something came out of my vagina!"

(Stands in kitchen in front of laptop in between bites of oatmeal and stares at screen speechless.)

Cut back to the water park. Chet has opened the place up, and the adult pool is full of nude partygoers with not a cup size under DD in sight. Maddy and arrives and tells Chet that piranhas may be entering through the drain system. He laughs her off as David Hasselhoff shows up as the celebrity guest for the grand opening.

Maddy soon discovers the well pump Chet is using to pump water from Lake Victoria into the park. She tries to turn it off but is stopped by Chet and Kyle. Soon piranhas begin to flood the park. People scramble and Chet tries to escape as the bloodbath ensues.

During his escape, he runs through a flag line and is decapitated. His head catapults through the air and lands in the pool where it is devoured by piranhas.

A little boy named David calls to Hoff to be rescued. Hoff ignores him until he suddenly has a *Baywatch* flashback and hurries to David's rescue, calling him a "little ginger moron."

Barry and Big Dave hurry to the pump room and turn on the drain in order to pump the water out of the pool. Maddy falls in and is sucked down to the bottom. Barry, despite being unable to swim, jumps in and rescues her. Big Dave dumps a barrel of chlorine into the main pump and lights a match. The explosion kills most of the piranhas.

Maddy soon receives a phone call from Mr. Goodman informing her that the fish can now move on dry land. She tells him she knows as one crawls out of the water and eats David's head. Hoff's final line of the movie is delivered. Yes, the line that brings the credits: "Little ginger moron."

VERDICT: Out of the pool!!

This wasn't the worst movie I've ever seen, though it certainly wasn't good, either. The entire movie builds up to the final scene where the piranhas launch their attack on the water park. No, really. ALL of the good comedy bits and suspense moments were saved for the end.

You just have to endure the rest of the movie.

The acting is abysmal, which is par for the course considering the movie. But even a parody needs to have a solid performance from the cast. The creature effects, however, were great. The piranhas look vicious and scary, and it was obvious that some serious work was put into their appearance and their animation.

The only real ding I have on this movie is that it hits one of my major taboo turn-offs: kids. Yeah, I know. It's pretty much understood that it's going to happen when an en masse public slaying happens, or a natural disaster hits, but I don't need to see it.

Chet runs over a little girl during his escape, and the little David kid gets graphically (though cartoonishly) decapitated in the final scene. Yeah, even I have my limits. Leave the kiddos out of it.

Other than that, this movie wasn't a complete disappointment in that it delivered as promised on its main feature: boobies. Boobies, boobies, and more boobies. There was enough T&A in this movie to make *True Blood* blush. So, in that regard, it lived up to its potential.

It just didn't do anything else. Period.

Honestly, the only thing that would keep me from watching it again is the fact that it exists. I wouldn't go so far to say that I would rather be mauled or permanently disfigured by some random woodland creature with some kind of abnormal psychological disorder than watch this movie again, but I can say that I'd take my chances being naked in a gorilla cage while looking for a contact lens before I press the play button on this aqua-fungus.

Robo Croc: Steve Irwin just rolled in his grave a little

Have you ever watched a hippopotamus take a crap?

They flick their tail around while farting explosively and send s**t EVERYWHERE. Now, imagine that each little lump of fantastic fecal fun flying from our flatulent friend is a plot point and the hippo is the movie.

Ladies and gents, I give you *Robo Croc*.

In typical SyFy fashion, this movie is one of those the looked great in concept but failed miserably in execution. I never did watch the bonus content (because there was no bonus content), but I can just see the producer now: "We were set to go, and everything looked great for the effects. We knew we were f**ked when Gary showed up with his Commodore 64 to work on the animation."

A rocket blasts off from an unknown launch pad somewhere between Whereisit and Whogivesadamn and explodes in the atmosphere. A capsule crashes in a zoo (once again, no location) and cracks open. Thousands of tiny nanomachines escape and fly up the right nostril of a large crocodile named Stella where they latch onto cells and begin to transform them.

A random zookeeper, Chef, is out feeding the animals. When he gets to Stella's area, she charges him, and he barely escapes with his life.

Enter Jim Duffy, the lead zookeeper and local hero known for bringing in the 20-foot croc Stella to the zoo. He is joined by Jane, an attractive new intern who has requested to work with him, and his boss. Don't even remember the guy's name.

Not like he's important anyway.

We find out that Stella has escaped her pen, and Duffy has been charged with getting her back. The military is involved, along with Dr. Riley. Riley is a stern, cold woman and refuses to give Duffy and his crew any answers as to why they are so interested in Stella.

Meanwhile, two losers in the water park next to the zoo join the summer party going on. One of them is Duffy's son, Rob. The other is Hud, who is filming the girls on his iPhone. Two of the guys in the park toss Rob and Hud in the pool when they catch them taping their girls, Julie and Sydney.

In the zoo, Duffy and Jane are tagging along with the military trying to get answers while Stella randomly attacks a nearby pond full of people fishing. She is beginning to lose skin and take on more mechanical attributes.

Rob and Hud end up getting locked in the men's room by Julie and Sydney's boyfriends. Meanwhile, a massacre has begun outside as Stella lays waste to the water park. She leaves after she kills everyone there except for the boys, Julie, and Sydney. They come outside and discover that everyone is lying around covered in strawberry syrup.

I mean blood. Yeah, totally blood.

Julie's boyfriend is eaten by Stella, and she and her friends go back and release Rob and Hud believing that Rob can get them out of there.

We are now halfway through the movie. Ugh.

Duffy and Jane find a piece of crocodile skin while they are saving Chef from the lion's area and realize that the scales are turning into metal. Montgomery reads them in. The payload on the crashed capsule was nanomachines that are capable of turning organic tissue into mechanical material that can be controlled. Stella's primary objective: Kill.

Gee. I didn't see that coming. Shoot me.

Duffy calls his friend Nigel in to try and capture Stella alive. The mission is a failure, and Duffy soon finds out that Rob is in the water park. He and Nigel take a chopper into the park and face off with Stella, who is now all robot.

Cool look. Crappy execution. Eh, it's SyFy.

Stella kills Nigel, but Duffy escapes with the teens. He instructs them to go to the pump house and stay there until he comes for them. Meanwhile, Duffy and Jane try to come up with a way to capture Stella. Montgomery gets called away to clean up an attack at the local fishing spot where Stella has killed numerous civilians. Despite Dr. Riley's threats, he makes the decision to destroy Stella.

A little late in the game, but okay. Can't get any worse.

Duffy and Montgomery nab an EMP (Electromagnetic Pulse) device and head to the sewers. Rob, Hud, and Julie decide to leave the pump house and try to escape in the sewers only to run into a very angry Duffy. Just as he's instructing them to stay put, Montgomery is attacked by Stella and Duffy leaves to go after the croc robot.

On the surface, Jane finds out that Riley has been helping Stella the entire time, sending the killer commands via her iPad. Riley punches Jane in the throat and takes off into the sewers to stop Duffy from neutralizing Stella.

Duffy runs into Riley and is relieved but finds out quickly that she's a turncoat when she fires her gun at him. Stella arrives, lured by the gunshot, and Duffy tosses the briefcase with the EMP inside into Stella's mouth. Riley tries to get it back, but Duffy sets it off. The blast shuts Stella down for good, throws everyone to the ground, and...what the f**k?

It disintegrates Riley. Really?

VERDICT: The hippo says it all.

In true SyFy fashion, a cool idea that would make a fun popcorn movie is taken and smeared in B-Movie dung by the infamous network that brought us *The Final Days of Planet Earth*, *Mutant Chronicles*, and *Supernova*. Lots of little plotlines get started but go nowhere.

First, we have Riley. She's a frigid b***h. She's also, quite obviously, I might add, the bad guy who is semi-controlling Stella. So the twist at the end where she turns is absolutely no surprise. In fact, I was beginning to wonder if they were ever going to flesh that one out because they sure as hell didn't do anything with Duffy's background with Nigel and his boss.

Also, what's the deal with Chef? He seems like an okay character with an interesting background who could move the story with some comic relief, but he gets hauled off instead and we're left with Hud. Hud is a loser with no sense of humor and an inability to act.

I could go on and on, but the Guinness is running low.

The biggest question I have is why, in the name of all that is Emily Wickersham's girl-next-door sexiness, is no one in the movie acknowledging that Stella looks like something from *The Terminator* by the time she reaches the water park? She's 100% man-eating beer can, and yet they still treat her like a living crocodile. They COMPLETELY ignore that fact that she is now, clearly, a Deceptacon.

She's an out of control can opener, people.

Of course, what would a SyFy movie be without a perfect ending that wraps up everything ultra-neat in less than thirty seconds? Stella gets fried, an EMP evaporates Dr. Riley (can't figure that one out, either, since they said earlier in the film that it doesn't affect living things), and Rob and Duffy each get their respective girl. The end, roll credits, cash and prizes.

Well, more like misery and a s**t stain in my memory.

Despite it's awfulness and failure, it really brings nothing new to the table. Truly, that's a common issue with all SyFy movies. It's litter box fodder, but not any different from the last turd nugget you scooped out and tossed into the toilet so you could blame it on your kid later.

Eating a large spoonful of coagulated sweat off a fat man's armpit, or watching this hippo dung again?

Hmm...

Sand Sharks: "Mommy, the beach smells BAD."

So the last time I had someone suggest a horror-comedy to me, I ended up with *Santa's Slay*. The movie was actually funny as hell in spots, so you can imagine what I expect when I see *Sand Sharks* billed as a horror-comedy.

The first five minutes of this movie had me drooling because my IQ dropped so low. Never in my life have I had a stronger urge to lick a window on a school bus.

There are bad movies, there are horrible movies, and then there are just stupid movies.

All of Me, for example (Lily Tomlin is a great lady, but her voice makes me want to kill small woodland creatures).

Sand Sharks is a moderate-budget B-movie with all of our well-known clichés firmly in place like a chastity belt on the Amish girl-next-door.

You have the money-crazed schemer, the good-guy courageous sheriff with a tragic past, the quirky sister/deputy, the über-sexy doctor who knows everything about all sharks except this one, and the token old guy who knows exactly what is going on and exactly how to stop it.

Jimmy (Schemer) returns to the island of White Sands to throw a huge beach party for the college kids on the mainland. His father, the mayor, agrees after Jimmy explains that he wants to use the money from the party to boost the town economy.

Meanwhile, Sheriff John Stone and his sister, Brenda, investigate a death on the beach that was perpetrated by a mysterious bad CGI creature we saw in the opening sequence.

Stone closes the beach down after another round of bodies (or what's left of them) shows up, much to Jimmy and the Mayor's dismay. Stone calls Dr. Powers (played by the voluptuous Brooke Hogan), who shows up and finds a baby shark tooth that is larger than the palm of her hand.

Meanwhile, Jimmy continues his plans for the party despite the warnings to stay away. He enlists the help of a group of interns and the local electrician, Sparky.

Something takes out the power in town, and the entire cast goes out to see what happened. Powers is on the beach when two large shark fins begin to encircle her, and we then see the sharks in their entirety.

These sharks are Sand Sharks. They have the ability to swim in sand as if it were water, and they are animated by (it looks like) the same people who did the monster in *Vicious.*

In other words: BAD.

The shark is a completely obvious cartoon on a live-action backdrop. The mayor gets chomped, and Sparky wanders off to plug the power back in. Who would have thought that the power for an entire island was connected by a single plug just randomly lying on the beach?

Yeah. Sparky becomes dinner, and the shark explodes when it bites down on the plug. The end.

The movie is only halfway over. Please shoot me.

The Sandman Festival goes into full swing, and Jimmy is on his way to host when his intern shows up and begins kissing him. Brenda, who is Jimmy's ex, sees and runs off. Amanda smirks at her, and then becomes shark food.

Yup. More of them.

Jimmy, with the help of his other interns, covers up the attack so as to not kill the party. Soon sand sharks invade and begin eating partygoers left and right.

Yes, it is very obvious that the director shouted at the extras to just run in all directions randomly.

They are maybe twenty yards from the road, and they just run in circles. No, really.

Jimmy, Sheriff Stone and Dr. Powers escape the beach and are greeted at the police station by Angus. Angus is the local fisherman who knows what the sharks are and knows how to stop them.

Where the hell were you in the opening sequence!?

They return to the beach where Angus has set up shop and rigged a trap for the sharks to melt the sand into a glass cage. The trap backfires, and Jimmy sacrifices himself to get things back on track.

Angus uses a flamethrower to encase the sharks in glass, but Mama Shark shows up and eats him. Stone and Powers escape back into Angus's bunker, but the shark bursts through the floor to come after them.

Stone throws a propane tank in its mouth and jumps out the window while Powers delivers the line of the movie, the one line that the shameless hack of a writer based the whole f**king movie around: "Eat this, you shark of a bitch!"

The explosion killing the shark and raining guts all over the place was drowned out by my agonized groan. Scene change to Jimmy's trailer where one of his interns is about to become sand shark food. The end.

Please do not make a sequel.

VERDICT: Short bus.

This movie was retarded, plain and simple.

What could have been a ridiculous satire on over the top monster movies (such as *Eight Legged Freaks*) was nothing more than an hour and a half of watching a cast of nobodies make complete dumb-asses of themselves on camera.

Here Comes Honey Boo-Boo! makes more sense than this movie. Watching it was like trying to carry on an intelligent conversation with a poodle.

The acting was not bad, but being a complete idiot doesn't take a lot of effort, either. I've seen movies where one character or set of characters is ignorant, but the entire cast!? If sharks ever invaded Jersey Shore, I now know exactly what would happen.

The only thing I got from this movie was a massive headache and a craving for paste.

I would rather lick the floor of the short bus than watch this movie again.

Severed-Forest of the Dead: Can't see the trees for all the dead guys

As I'm sure you're all aware, the zombie movie market is sparse. I mean, really. There are simply not enough zombie movies or television shows out there. And video games? Forget it.

Sarcasm. Gotta love it.

With a zombie-infested market fully accessible 24-7, *good* zombie-related content can begin to get sparse. No one can help but compare every zombie flick they see to *The Walking Dead,* and zombie-based video games are often compared right back to *Resident Evil* even though the zombies in that series games were the least of the player's worries. Breaks were an absolute must.

One can't forget the *Xena* show times for an hour of fapping.

As it is typical of my friggin' luck when searching for a halfway decent zombie flick, I find this festering in the Netflix archives and decide to give it a look.

Lumberjacks and tree-hugging protesters are toe-to-toe in the forest, and the corporation that is ominously known as "The Company" (hello, someone likes *Aliens*) is urging the jacks to press on. Mac and his crew are working when one of the guys cuts into a spiked tree and gets a chainsaw to the chest. Mac and the others tend to him, but he suddenly turns into a zombie and attacks.

Carter and his partner are studying the tree sap for the Company, but their findings are yielding results that they are concerned about. Meanwhile, Rita and her band of hippies are going to drastic measures to stop the lumberjacks from cutting down trees.

Tyler is sent in by his father, who is chairman of the board for the Company, to find out why they lost communications with Mac's camp. He finds a camp swarming with zombies and is attacked. Luke saves him and leads him back to a makeshift shack where Mac, Rita, Carter, and Stacey are hiding.

They decide to make their way to the camp after they wreck Tyler's truck. They clear out the undead and try the radio to no avail. The next plan is to find a vehicle and leave. Luke goes out with Carter to clear out the last group of zombies and is eaten while Carter gets away.

No, this is about as exciting as it gets.

Carter explains that he was head of a research group for the Company developing a mutated hormone that would rapidly increase tree growth and size while reducing the time it takes for a tree to reach full maturity. The side effect, obviously, was not expected.

And, apparently, the writer/director is also a *Resident Evil* fan.

They find Luke's truck and escape the camp but are attacked by Luke who is now a zombie. Rita kills him to save Mac, and the group discovers a nearby encampment of lumberjacks and hunters run by a Hispanic madman named Anderson.

Yeah, sounds familiar to me, too.

The group escapes after Carter lets a horde of zombies in, and Anderson and Mac are eaten. Tyler and Rita escape, but Tyler hears Carter screaming as he is swarmed. He leaves Rita to save Carter and is eaten as well. Rita makes it to the road and begins running.

Meanwhile, Tyler's father is having a drink in the study of his mansion as he broods over the loss of his son. Without a word he gets up and walks out of the room. Credits.

Nope. Credits. Nothing else. Fini.

VERDICT: Huh? Wha?

So if a lumberjack is eaten by a zombie in the woods, and no one is around to see or hear it, it apparently doesn't even matter (ba-dunk, chsh!!). This movie has all of the potential to be a decent zombie movie, but it fails in several areas.

Most notably, it's boring as s**t.

The acting is what it needs to be given the content. The actors portray their characters well, though Rita is almost too much sometimes with her tree hugging. Even in the face of what is going on, she still finds time to protest the destruction of the forest.

B***h, we got zombies. We burnin' this motherf**ker.

The story, as you can see, is weak and drags on like Renee Zellweger at the Oscars. As mentioned before, the writer basically took elements from everywhere else, most obviously *Resident Evil*. There are a ton of nods to video games like *Left 4 Dead, Dead Island,* and *Dead*

Rising (those who know the *Dead Rising* backstory will see it), as well as the famous *The Walking Dead* television show and the movie *Aliens*.

Anderson is totally the Governor.

The zombie makeup is a nod to classic zombie flicks, the skin being yellowed and streaked with purple veins. The zombies are erratic and slow moving but are deadly in swarms.

All in all, it sets up a fair-to-midland zombie flick, and then drowns the viewer in boredom with repetitive dialogue and action.

I'm not going to say that I would cause myself physical pain before watching this movie again, but I will say that there are more interesting things I could watch that are more suspenseful and engaging.

Like a documentary on Swamp-Ass.

Sharknado: A natural DUH-saster

Where the hell do I begin?

Syfy bills itself as home of the sci-fi movie. The Asylum fancies itself a modern-day Toho Studios (the Japanese studio responsible for the *Godzilla* movies).

When these two meet, it's like two completely constipated lovers that discover a way to release all of the crap they've been holding away over the months in one glorious hour and a half long newspaper session on the public toilet.

And Tara Reid? Really?

A hurricane (notice: a movie called *Sharknado*, and we open with a hurricane. Hmmm...) is forming in the pacific ocean as an Asian man in a suit makes his way across the deck of a ship and into the quarters below. He meets with the captain, who is a shifty character. They talk briefly about the Asian paying the captain a large sum of money to capture over 150,000 sharks.

Before their conversation makes any sense whatsoever, the massive storm hits. Suddenly the air is filled with sharks, and the Asian man is eaten. The captain laughs, thinking he has gotten away, but the sharks get him as well.

Cut to Fin and his Aussie buddy, Baz. They are surfing when sharks suddenly attack the beach, one biting Baz on the leg while the others dismember beach goers. Fin rescues Baz, and they go back to the bar Fin owns after getting him patched up.

Nova, Fin's only waitress, expresses concern. George (played by John "If-It's-On-SyFy-I'm-In-It" Heard) is the local drunk who asks about when the beach will be open again. Fin casually explains that they'll reopen once the sharks are cleared out.

Time out.

Lemme make sure I understand this s**t. About a dozen people get mauled on the beach by ravenous insane sharks, and Fin is just "Eh. They reopen when it's clear. It happens." Oh, sure! No problem! You know what else just "happens!?" Plague! Yeah, that s**t just happens, too!

AAAAANYWHO.

Bad Movie Beware!

The storm hits the beach, and sharks begin flying in through the windows, wriggling around on the floor as they scramble for screaming people who are fleeing in terror. Fin suddenly goes into hero-mode and arms Nova and Baz. George opts for his trusty bar stool, and they escape as the waves take out the bar.

The waters flood the streets of L.A., and they realize quickly that the waters are shark-infested. The hurricane is flinging sharks everywhere. Fin wants to go check on his daughter and ex-wife, so they hit the freeway to try and get to them.

On the way, they stop to rescue a group of drivers trapped in the underpass. George saves a woman and her dog but is eaten by a shark as the underpass floods. Fin, Nova, and Baz get back into the Jeep and head off.

As it turns out, April and Claudia live in the snazzy part of L.A., a lifestyle Fin gave up when they divorced. April (Tara Reid) is not thrilled about Fin's arrival, nor is her new live-in boyfriend. Dude-man McFee turns out to be a real slime ball and is eaten by sharks as the waters crash into the house.

Yes. This kind of pattern goes on for a while. A WHILE.

Fin and his group finally end up at the air base where his son, Matt, is learning to fly. This is after about an hour-ish of shenanigans and sharks crashing through windows and eating people. Matt falls hard for Nova, and the group finds out that the hurricane has spawn three tornados loaded with sharks.

And the "Sharknados" are heading right for our group. Yippee.

Matt gets the idea to build bombs to drop into the tornados...wait a damn minute. Okay, I watch some pretty far-fetched crap. Not gonna lie, I LOVE the Freddy and Jason flicks. *Lord of the Rings*? Can't be beat! *Harry Potter*? Yeah, you know you look at Emma Watson. Don't lie.

But dropping bombs into a tornado!? That's a bit much. I mean, what the...nevermind. Let me just wrap this synopsis before I drink more to drown away the stupidity.

Fin, April, and Claudia escape to the nearby retirement home for shelter while Matt and Nova board a chopper and prepare to bomb the sharknados. Baz stays behind, ready to set off his own bomb in case Matt's plan fails.

Baz is eaten, and Matt succeeds in bombing the first tornado. The sharks are blown to bits along with the storm. Nova hurls the second bomb, taking out the next storm. The third is the largest one, and begins its trail towards the retirement home.

Nova tries to kick at a shark that has latched onto the chopper but falls and is swallowed whole. Matt drops the final bomb, but it does nothing. The tornado sucks up Baz's bomb, which explodes and takes it out. Fin rushes outside with his chainsaw only to see a massive great white coming his way. He aims the chainsaw upwards and cuts his way into the shark.

All hope looks dim when Fin suddenly cuts his way out of the giant shark, dragging an unconscious and alive Nova with him. Matt revives her, they hook up, April and Fin get back together. Credits.

Behold, the stereotypical SyFy ending.

VERDICT: Throw it back; it looks weird.

I thought that *Sand Sharks* was, without a doubt, the most ignorant movie I had ever seen. Then, along came *Sharknado* and completely reset the standard. Never before have I watched a movie that gave me such an urge to lick a window.

And yet, it has appeal. Go figure.

If I may, Tara Reid sucks at acting. Every line was delivered as if she was reading directly off of a cue card. Cassie Scerbo (Nova) was decent, but her character really served no other purpose outside of eye-candy.

Fin is Rick Shepherd from *The Walking Dead*. No two cents about it. The lines, the character choices, everything screamed that this guy was this movie's group leader. I mean, really. Just go ahead and give him the hat while you're at it.

The Asylum is not known for their quality films. The CGI in the movie is abysmal, the animation on the sharks not being much better than what we saw in the FMVs on PlayStation One. Then again, what can one expect?

IT'S A MOVIE ABOUT STORMS THAT SPIT SHARKS.

Track of the Moonbeast: I want my intelligence back...

Thanks to everyone for being patient, as you all know how an eventful weekend (such as the Broncos fapping instead of actually playing football at the Super Bowl) tends to slow things down a bit around here. Anyway, onwards to *Track of the Moon Beast!*

Okay, so that intro was about as exciting as this movie gets.

It's not easy writing a review on a movie with a shallow story line. It's even more difficult to write a review on a film with a shallow story line AND a boredom factor that makes amateur golf as exciting as porn.

Even the creature in the poster from the movie looks as if he's reaching to the sky, asking God, "Why? Why must this movie be a reality?"

He needs hug.

Paul is a mineralogist studying under his former teacher and mentor, Johnny Longbow (our token Native American). Johnny tells the students in his class the legend of a rock that strikes a man and turns him into a monster.

That evening, Paul takes his new interest, Kathy, up to a spot in the hills he likes to go to relax. A meteor shower that was predicted earlier begins, and as they watch the sky, a meteor falls and strikes Paul in the head.

Yeah, I know.

He takes it like a man and shakes it off but then spends the next day or so acting lethargic and having blackouts. He takes Kathy to a party one evening, and here we get the musical portion of the movie.

Okay, let's slam on the brakes for a moment here. So most movies have a band playing in the background during a bar, club, or party scene. But the band doesn't get front and center attention, let alone a FULL F**KING MONTAGE.

Oh, yeah! Believe it! The next five minutes of the movie are literally Johnny Longbow and Kathy taking care of Paul as part of a music video for this band that, I guess, was friends with the director or something.

The song was "California Lady." Yeah, I'd never hear of it either.

AAAAAnywho, that night a local man is mauled at his house, and his wife dies of a heart attack. The police chief brings in Johnny Longbow to look at some odd tracks around the house that look to have been made by an upright crocodile.

Okay, at least we might see a cool-looking monster or something.

Paul has his head scanned, and the doctors find a piece of meteorite lodged in his brain. He is held for observation but escapes. A group of people in the woods are killed, and Paul returns to the hospital believing that he is responsible.

Johnny and the chief agree to tie Paul down and watch him for the evening. Kathy comes by to visit, but Paul sends her away as the night approaches. Everyone watches as he shifts into...

Kermit with Downs? What the f**k!!?

Who the hell comes up with this stuff!? Paul turns into what looks like every early concept of Godzilla rejected due to sheer stupidity.

Ever. Combined.

It's like someone took an alligator, then squashed its nose back into its head and filled his underwear with warm Jell-O. This would be because of the unintentional s**t-eating Teenage Mutant Ninja Turtle grin on his face.

Paul breaks free the next night and attacks, but Kathy follows him despite Johnny's warnings to stay away. The doctors discovered that the fragment has shattered, and that all hope is lost for Paul. They corner him on the highway after Kathy finds him, and we get to see the Moon Beast in his full form.

Is that a pocket on the front of the...yeah. That's a mechanic's jumpsuit. Jeez.

Johnny takes an arrow that he made out of a piece of the rock that hit Paul and takes aim while Kathy and the chief watch. He fires, and the monster screams as he dies in a furious display of Technicolor flashes of light. I think I actually saw some flower power there.

The chief gets in his car and drives away. Kathy goes to Johnny Longbow, and they head to the car. Another day done. No, really. They get in the car and drive away like nothing happened.

The end. Why do I do this sober?

VERDICT: Launch it into orbit!!

This movie was a prime example of what happens when you let just anyone make a movie. Not that all indie flicks are bad. I actually have one called *Off Season* that really isn't all that bad, despite a couple of shortcomings.

Let's start with the acting. Donna Drake plays Kathy, well not so much "plays" as "pantomimes human-like gestures while reading a teleprompter." Probably an android like Kevin Costner or Lorenzo Lamas. Paul was no better, though his lines were few and far in between and consisted of not much more than "Something's not right," and "I'm the Moon Beast!"

I think the Terminator had more personality.

The monster suit was God-Awful. It was literally a jumpsuit painted green, a rubber mask, hands and feet. It wasn't one of those scary and lurking costumes. It was more of an "I stole this outfit from a guy named 'Jim' while he changed my oil at Jiffy Lube!" outfit.

And, dear God, the BOREDOM!

In a monster movie, you pretty much have one job: keep the audience entertained with sheer ignorant action and violence. Not a stretch. This movie fails miserably at that. I can actually say that I found watching my bread cook in the toaster was more stimulating than watching this pile of sheep pellets.

It wasn't so boring that I wanted to jump off a roof at least. But it dragged on for so long that I actually began to wonder if I was eligible for retirement and ready to invest in my obligatory Depends for the next twenty years while I waited for Nurse Nasty to bring me my new copy of *Playboy: The Geriatric Playmates Lingerie Edition.*

I'm old. Not dead. Well, *Manos Hands of Fate* almost fixed that.

Vicious: Unrelentingly Craptacular

Yet another that I received when my Aunt lovingly graced me with what I am now referring to as the "Box-O-Turds," *Vicious* fell out into my hands like breakfast at Waffle House an hour after the fact.

Don't let the creature on the cover fool you, nor the fact that it stars the legendary Tom Savini sway you in favor of this film in any way.

I assure you that when it comes to creature-features, this movie is a dirty fart in the genre.

The movie is about a military experiment gone haywire (surprise, surprise), and a monster is on the loose killing people.

Behind the whole bit is Kane, played by Savini, who has lost his marbles and is feeding the monster to watch it hunt. Of course, a group of coeds shows up to fish and are taken out one-by-one by Kane and the beast.

The effects, on the whole, are not much better than the graphics on the Sega CD Game System. It was painful, really, to watch this thing work. The difference between the "CGI" monster and the real world on camera was done way better in *Who Framed Roger Rabbit.*

Also, with a movie that features Tom Savini, one would expect gore. Gallons of guts! No, we get a splatter here, a smudge there. I've seen more blood on a used tampon than I saw during the kill scenes in this movie.

As if the terrible effects and crummy writing weren't enough of a kick to the groin, the director decided that every character should have a theme song.

EVERY CHARACTER!

Now, as much as I love Iron Maiden, I consider my theme song to be "Alive and Amplified" by the Mooney Suzuki. Do I have a ghetto blaster blaring this out everywhere I go?

No.

So why, in the name of all that is holy, would I want to hear a different musical bit for every character!?

I've gotten more entertainment value out of watching the scrolling TV guide on old-school cable television.

The gratuitously long scene where the redneck shows up to fish was almost physically painful to watch. The guy pulls up, country music a-blaring, parks his car on the railroad tracks, gets his gear, walks through the woods, and goes fishing.

It took them twenty minutes to show me this douche prep for a relaxing day of friggin' FISHING! In fact, that's all anyone in the movie does!

I like fishing too, but by the power of Grayskull!

VERDICT: Skeet shooting.

Yup, that's about all this DVD is good for. The only person in the movie with talent is Tom Savini, and his acting clearly shows that he is in the gory equivalent of *Super Mario Bros.*

Well, I say gory, but...ah, hell, you know what I mean.

Bad computer effects that may have been programmed on a Super Nintendo, bad acting done by college students with nothing better to do on the weekend, and a story that has been done more times than Paris Hilton make for a joke of a film that would have ended Tom Savini's career if he were any less awesome than he is.

Hmm...I could watch this oozing pile of elephant diarrhea again, or I could play *E.T.* on the Atari.

Decisions, decisions.

The Wickeds: Zombies, Vampires, Gore...and Ron Jeremy?

So I just tallied things up, and I have watched 96 movies since starting Fail-Flix, this one being 97. (Note: this post is from September of 2013. Obviously, I've added a few atrocities since then.) I have seen movies that should have been commended for their brilliance and artistic expression.

I have mostly seen festering piles of s**t.

This movie falls into the second category and proves that the porn industry is in dire straights. One would think Ron Jeremy would be more selective in what he puts his name on (or in, depending on where your mind is already), but no. Apparently, all I need is a large all-meat pizza and a six-pack of Pabst Blue Ribbon and I'm set.

Five friends go thrill seeking on Halloween to a haunted house where the jokester of the group, Dylan, knows that a horror movie is being filmed. Meanwhile, Gus (Ron Jeremy) and his younger cohort Teufel are grave robbing in a nearby cemetery.

Billy and Alyssa go upstairs in the house to have sex while the others stay downstairs to explore. Yes, I can't tell you how much a run down house that is supposed to be haunted makes me want to screw. Please note the sarcasm.

Gus and Teufel unearth a body that is too fresh to be as old as it is. Gus takes a medallion from the corpse, which turns out to be a zombie vampire. It bites Teufel, who escapes. They run for it as the vamp rises from his grave and summons all of the dead to rise. Gus and Teufel fight for their lives and end up at the house.

Jake, Julie, and the others don't believe the two grave robbers until their friend Richard is dragged out the front door and eaten. Kate, the token black girl in the movie, keeps hearing voices.

They have meds for that, chick.

Upstairs, Alyssa and Billy have what has to be the most inconsistent and awkward non-sex sex scene I have seen. Ever. They are making out heavily. They take off their shirts. She keeps her hands over her breasts, so we never see them. They make out. Camera switch. They are both naked, and he is wearing cowboy boots. Camera switch. His pants are back on, and they are hunching. Camera switch. No pants. Camera switch. Pants.

How the hell did...why the hell did...nevermind. I'd rather not know.

Anyway, Billy gets taken out by the head zombie vamp and Alyssa is sent downstairs screaming. Jake and Dylan rush upstairs after a few more seconds of bad acting and dialogue, save Billy, and bring him back downstairs. Teufel is wounded and lying on the couch, and Gus is running the show from a recliner.

Jake and Billy make an attempt to run for it, and Alyssa follows. Meanwhile, a ghost comes downstairs and possesses Kate. Yeah.

Makes total sense. Why not?

Billy and Alyssa are caught, and Billy is dismembered while Alyssa is turned into a zombie vamp. Jake finds Gus's truck, but a zombie has the keys.

Back to the house.

More bad dialogue and a complete formulaic character freak-out moment where Julie recounts their situation at the top of her lungs...twice. Okay, I get it chick. Move on.

Teufel dies on the couch. Gus mourns him, and Dylan makes a run for it as the house is beset by zombies. He runs into Alyssa, who is now a zombie vamp and seduces him. He gets away and is surrounded. He backs into an open grave with a zombie in it, and we see him thrash around.

Bye Dylan.

Teufel comes back and attacks, and Jake and Julie flee the house after stabbing him as the zombies take Gus. Jake and Julie run back to the house when they figure out that they need the medallion to end it all, but Jake is attacked by zombie-vamp Richard. Who can talk.

Excessively.

Jake and Julie get separated, and Julie finds Kate. She's now a zombie vamp. Julie yanks Kate's eyeballs out while Jake fights off a group of zombies in the living room. Julie grabs the medallion, but the head zombie vamp gets to her and tries to take it from her. She smashes it, and all of the zombies vanish along with the head zombie vamp.

Julie helps Jake to the car, and Jake awakens as a zombie vamp.

VERDICT: Bury it in the cow pasture.

Where, oh where, do I begin? Why do some guys get a camcorder from Best Buy and suddenly think that they're Steven Spielberg? And what's worse, someone knew how to get Ron Jeremy to be in the movie. He must be a hell of a sport. He took time away from doing what...who...he does to do this rancid pile of elephant poo.

As I listen to the thrash metal music during the credits, something sticks out like a salute from the chess team khakis during cheerleading practice...no one actually starred in the movie.

According to the opening credits, the movie starred Ron Jeremy. Yet, the end credits state that he co-starred...ALONG WITH THE ENTIRE CAST. So, what? The opening credits are just a big fat lie?

The acting is abysmal, even for what this skunk fart is. The lines are delivered in a soap-opera manner that would make the cast of *Days of Our Lives* die from hysterical fits of laughter.

The makeup is nice. I can tell that the cashier at Spirit Halloween had a hell of a transaction that day. All of the props and makeup in the film can be found at various Halloween stores, but they were done well.

They were the ONLY thing done right in the film.

The soundtrack is thrash metal, which I found kind of cool, but it had no hope of de-sucking this movie. It's like having Dave Murray stand in as Rebecca Black's lead guitarist for a song. He's awesome, but her music and singing still sucks a camel's sand hose.

The Zombinator: Braaiiins...or the lack thereof

Oh, boy. Another zombie flick.

Jesus.

Don't let the cover fool you; it's not about zombie-robots from the future that have traveled back in time to kill the future leader of the human resistance. There is no way in the world this movie could ever aspire to be that truly awesome.

Also, let's remember that the "Found Footage" film is now actually considered a subgenre. That, itself, is just a sad state of affairs. As much as I love *Paranormal Activity* and *The Blair Witch Project*, found footage is getting kind of stale and, frankly, unbelievable.

This movie does not help the decline.

It hits the f**king gas.

The film opens with no title card, and we discover that we are watching a fashion student shoot a documentary on fashion styles around Youngstown, Ohio. Things go to hell fast when they attend a wake for a friend who died in Afghanistan and are besieged by zombies.

Okay, so getting right into the action. Let's see where this goes.

Straight to Hell, that's where.

The main character, Nina, escapes with her friends and they spend the evening dodging zombies as they make their way to their old school, which is abandoned. Through this, we see clips of a mysterious man in a black trench coat and shades (at night) shooting down hordes of the undead.

Blues Brother with anger issues?

The group meets up with a paranormal research team inside the school, but they all get attacked and separated. Three characters die at that point, but the man in the coat saves the rest of them and takes them to an empty room somewhere in the school.

He explains that they are in the middle of crossfire between him and rogue soldiers who are trying to secure a serum that causes "zombie-ism."

What the hell, dude. Just because you added "ism" doesn't make it legit.

One of the girls tells the trench-coat guy that he looks like the Terminator. I'm sorry, but this dude does not look anything like the Terminator.

Actually, he looks more like that lonely guy that goes to cons dressed as the Terminator because he thinks that the shades hide the fact that he's trying to look up Sailor Moon's skirt.

Anyway, Nina takes the token wimpy dude who loves her and leaves to search for her boyfriend, who got separated from the group. While they're gone, the rest of the characters in the room are attacked and eaten by a horde of zombies.

Nina and skinny kid run into the Colonel, an old guy from the beginning of the film who talks to them during the wake. As it turns out, their buddy who died was part of the team developing the zombie serum. The Colonel is really the bad guy who's trying to turn everyone into zombies so he can sell the vaccine for a fortune.

The Colonel ends up killing both of them as…wait. What the f**k!? Really!? The main characters are killed off? How much longer is this!?

Oh, about fifteen, twenty minutes. No main characters.

WTF.

Okay, at this point all of the fashion designer people are dead except the camera crew, who follow the Zombinator to an old mill. He has his final showdown with the Colonel. They fight, and even though the Colonel stabs our hero about fifteen times, our guy still manages to kill off the bad guy.

The End.

VERDICT: Whaaa…?

Okay, I have to be honest, here. This movie wasn't…terrible. It had flaws, major flaws that needed real attention. The lighting was bad, the camerawork (even for a found-footage film) was awful, and the acting was sub-par at its best.

The movie was shot in four days without a script. No, really. No script. The entire film was just shot and made up as they went along, and it shows.

The makeup wasn't bad, really. For an indie film, they did a decent job making the zombies look good. They also acted like zombies. Not a stretch, but it was still better than the main actors.

Considering that every line in the movie was made up on the fly, they did what they could. But, as a person with a degree in theater, I can tell you that improvisation is drilled into us and is an art. Some are excellent at improv, such as the masters on *Who's Line is it Anyway*. Others, not so much. If these people had actual training in theater, then they have no excuse.

I have one burning question: why didn't the zombies eat the camera guys!? I mean, really! These guys are just standing there filming while hordes of flesh-eaters rush by, and none of the deadheads give them a second's thought. I understand suspending my disbelief, but at some point, I have to call a truckload of horse s**t.

Also, this movie breaks a serious cardinal rule. The main character dies. No, don't give me that "stick to Michael Bay movies" bulls**t. Yes, main characters can die, but not until the end of the film! You don't whack your main ten to fifteen minutes before the credits roll, then finish the movie with a supporting character!

It would be like J.K. Rowling killing off Harry Potter in book six, then writing *The Deathly Hallows* from Ron Weasley's viewpoint.

Yup. Went there, big time.

In truth, this isn't the worst movie I've ever seen. It had a good premise, a decent makeup crew, and a possible storyline that just needed a little tweaking. In truth, calling the movie *The Zombinator* is one of the things that screwed it up. If you want to see a halfway decent indie, give it a try and just be forgiving of A LOT.

Supernatural Silliness

One of my favorite genres! Nothing shakes me up more than things that go bump in the night! That feeling you get when you're just sitting there and the room gets cold, or when you're heading to bed and you wonder if you're alone in the house or not.

These movies are things that fart in the dark.

Most of them are demons.

Amityville 3D: Not 3D and not good

I took a step back and watched *Amityville 3* largely because I have seen parts 1, 2, 4, and the remake.

Imagine my surprise when I am reminded that it is actually *Amityville 3D*!

I grab my 3D shades from the pile I've horded over the years, sit down with my movie breakfast (crockpot oatmeal with bananas, brown sugar, and maple syrup) and press play.

No 3D.

Instead, I get 3D goofs in 2D.

It's the same effect of a lap dance happening across the room, but the chick is looking right at you and making gnarly faces that look like something from the Garbage Pail Kids cards.

A writer moves into the Amityville house to finish his novel (yeah, original). He is divorced, and his daughter comes to stay with him. The daughter is none other than Laurie Loughlin from TV's *Full House.*

Though this was pre-Tanner family and she was friggin' HAWT.

What follows is a series of events that everyone experiences except the writer. By the end, he is a believer and the house is filled with paranormal researchers trying to get the haunts on tape.

Yes, we really are going to see them prove the existence of ghosts by taping the purple orb that isn't really there.

It looks like a fingerprint of Crisco rubbed on the lens of the camera and then illuminated by a bad computer. This was the most expensive shot of the movie, and I could have done it with a VHS camera and editing software.

What got me was that the house never directly killed anyone. It possessed people and made them kill. In this movie, it drowns one guy in flies and blows up the vehicle of another victim while she is still in it.

There were also no monsters actively in the series (you might catch a glimpse, but that's it), yet this does not stop the guy in the rubber demon suit from jumping out of the well of boiling blueberry Kool-Aid to drag a researcher straight to hell.

The house finally destroys itself in an explosion truly intended for 3D audiences. And only intended for them.

There was no reason to destroy the house. Yet there are two movies after the fact.

HOW!?

VERDICT: No.

Do not take this movie any more seriously than you take comments from Sarah Palin. The acting is bad, the story is weak, and the movie makes more random turns and story events than *The Sweetest Thing*.

Not that I would never watch it again in the face of excruciating pain, but I have no desire to be that bored again.

Ever.

Bachelor Party at the Bungalow of the Damned: Cite for stupidity ordinance violation

We've all done it. Admit it or relinquish any self-respect you have left. We've all put our grubby little mitts on a video camera at some point and shot a movie of some kind. Most of us have thought, "Gee, I bet a horror movie would be fun!" Some of us have actually filmed said horror movie and come to one of two conclusions: great idea, just needs Hollywood backing or your mom lied to you. Your movie is just bad. Never do that again. Ever.

I stumbled across this pile of skunk turds whilst perusing Netflix, which seems to be becoming more and more of a Cult-Movie whorehouse and less of a movie-lover's dream come true.

Bachelor Party in the Bungalow of the Damned is a prime example of why college buddies should never, ever, get a Sony Handycam and an animation program into their hands. The results can be dangerous. Just looking at the cover should warn you, provided you can look beyond the hot chick they got to pose for it that makes an appearance nowhere in the film.

As I've stated in the past, I fully accept that student films kind of are what they are, and expecting good production quality is about like expecting a Roland Emmerich movie to last less than three hours and not be a disaster flick.

That being said, I've seen more floaters than sinkers.

ONWARD!!

Sam decides to host a bachelor party for his buddy Chuck at a bungalow in the Hamptons that belongs to their buddy Gordon's uncle. Along for the ride are Paulie and Dan (a.k.a., The Fish). Chuck promises Michelle, his bride to be, that he will not get too crazy during the weekend. Sam arrives and also assures her that he will look out for Chuck. They pick up the other two friends and meet the creepy Gordon at a gas station close to the house. He is irritated with Sam but has an obvious crush on Chuck.

They finally arrive at a home in the middle of the suburbs...wait a minute (checking description and title). The Hamptons? Which Hamptons? I've never been, but the characters keep describing a wild party all weekend in the middle of nowhere. Yet, I see neighbors, cars, kids...what the hell?

Anyway...

Later on that evening, three escorts hired by Sam show up to entertain the boys. One is a chubby redhead, one is a tall brunette, and one is a very muscular and top-heavy black girl with Beyoncé issues. They pole dance for the men, then feed Chuck a variety of potions from bottles that look like they were bought at Dollar Tree during Halloween.

Chuck goes into an alcoholic stupor and is led off by Red for sex while the other two girls take Paulie and the Fish back to their rooms (dorm rooms I think, from the looks of things) for some fun. Sam is left alone to answer a manic call from Michelle telling him that she is on her way over.

The next scene shows us the brunette as a skeletal demon who melts Paulie, and the black girl has demon mouths on her boobs that she uses to devour the Fish. Sam walks in on Chuck and Red and tells Red that she and her friends have to leave before Michelle gets there.

The girls leave (Chuck and Sam are clueless), and the boys ask Gordon to help them clean up. Chuck vomits and passes out, and the three girls return claiming that they are having car trouble. Sam discovers the bodies of Paulie and the Fish, and he takes Chuck and runs just as Michelle arrives. Sam returns for Michelle, and they discover that Chuck is now...a vampire!?

Okay, so I've got 3 succubi, a vampire...what's next!?

Sam and Michelle decide that Red is the Master Vamp and go back to the house after her. Sam succeeds in killing off Brunette and Foxy Brown, but Red is more elusive. He escapes her, and Michelle takes her out. They return to find that Chuck is still a vamp. He attacks and kills Michelle.

Yes, the movie drags on like this for an hour and a half.

Sam runs back to the house to find Gordon, who reveals himself as the Master Vamp, but also tells Sam that he is the one who created the Master when he yanked Gordon's pants down during a photo shoot.

No, I'm not kidding.

Sam kills Gordon, then himself. He wakes up to find time reversed, Chuck and Michelle safe, and Gordon nowhere to be found. Michelle leaves, and Sam and Chuck begin to walk home when a redneck in a truck tries to run them down.

VERDICT: I need heroin after watching this movie.

First off, the director/writer/producer couldn't even rent a real cabin or bungalow for a weekend to film this horrid pile of s**t, so they just go to a buddy's house which is, very obviously, in the middle of suburban America.

Then, they apparently have a buddy who knows a little something about computer animation and film editing, but never finished school because he got booted out for plagiarizing artwork from *Dragonball Z*.

To put icing on the cake, they found three girls willing to get nude in front of the camera even though one of them is built like Kathy Bates in a whore outfit.

The movie is supposed to be a horror comedy in the same vein as *Evil Dead 2*, but the jokes fall flat and are just silly. Many of them were obviously inside jokes between the cast and crew, so who the hell is supposed to understand them anyway?

Even for what it is, this movie stinks like a rancid fart inside a subway car. This movie almost made me kill my Netflix account, but I then remembered that I need it in order to continue my crusade to save everyone from falling victim to underwear skid marks like *Bachelor Party in the Bungalow of the Damned, Troll 2,* and *Sex and the City* to name a few.

This movie is that weird smell in the Netflix archives. Keep scrolling. There are more intellectually stimulating movies to watch, such as *Zack and Miri Make a Porno*.

Book of Shadows-Blair Witch 2: Randomness haunts these woods

Not gonna lie: I love the *Blair Witch Project*.

I love it because it is the first "found footage" film I have ever seen, and the first one to really give me that eerie "what the hell" feeling. Every time I watch it, I catch on to something new. I have a nice sound system, so I am able to pick up on all of the little noises and things that happen in the film.

Too bad the second movie didn't follow the same idea. In fact, it ran screaming from the original concept, turned around, ran back, punched it in the face, and pooped all over its feet.

I felt nothing for any of the characters and was rooting for the witch by the end of it. And a third one, supposedly, is under way.

Just f**king shoot me now.

As if this wasn't bad enough, I get to be kicked in the rocks by another bad sequel? I may be prejudging. I bet y'all are saying, "You haven't even seen the third movie yet." Well, I've seen *Eat, Pray, Love*. Wasn't that enough punishment?

ONWARD.

The movie opens with a small snippet in the beginning to attempt to orient the audiences into Documentary Mode by stating that what we are about to see is a reenactment of the events taking place after the tapes that comprised the first movie were found.

We return to Burkittsville to find the small town in chaos as crazed fans of the original movie try to tour the locations and sites from the film, and even take tours in the woods in an attempt to catch a sighting of the Blair Witch.

Jeff, a small town film maker recently released from the loony bin, heads up his first tour from his Blair Witch Hunt website with a Wiccan named Erica and two tourists named Stephen and Tristan. They also pick up Kim, who is a Goth psychic. Tristan is pregnant, though we don't find out until Kim outs her.

The group stays the night at the ruins of Rustin Parr's house. Parr supposedly killed seven children at the behest of the Blair Witch years ago.

A wild night of partying leaves them all without memory of the night before. The cameras have been smashed, the research documents Stephen had brought along, shredded. They leave after finding the tapes buried where the original tapes from the first movie had been found. Tristan has a miscarriage, and they go to Jeff's place after her night in the hospital.

Jeff lives in an old condemned warehouse, which is the setting for the rest of the movie. In between scenes, and sometimes during dialogue, the camera cuts to an interrogation room where Kim, Stephen, and Jeff are being hammered by the police.

Eerie events begin to happen, but it all blends in after a while because it's the same type of thing over and over again. It was like watching a *Friday the 13th* film, but Jason kills everyone the same way.

The EXACT same way.

The movie ends with a plot twist that is supposed to make you wonder if the Blair Witch is real, or if Jeff, Stephen, and Kim went bananas and killed Erica, Tristan, and another group of tourists. In fact, the entire movie shifts back and forth between the Blair Witch Project being fact or fiction. It's not so much as trying to mess with your head. It's more like the writer couldn't decide which way to go, so he went both.

News flash, dude: this ain't a buffet.

You can have steak and chicken, but you can't push two complete different themes in one movie and think it'll go over well with the audience.

Too bad I can't get those two hours of my life back. Ever. And people wonder why I drink.

VERDICT: Meh.

Truthfully, this movie could have been really good. Decent acting and great ideas for scares do not make up for dialogue that doesn't add up to much more than "What was that!?" "How do we stop it!?"

All of the scares are well done, but the movie was more of a reason to put all of the jump-moments back to back and see how much alike they were. The first one, I think, is a great movie. The second movie (By the way, f**k you, Mr. Title. THERE IS NO BOOK OF SHADOWS!) is an attempt to capitalize.

I won't say that I would rather have my nipples chewed on by a horse on meth, but I wouldn't watch this movie again unless it was a choice between it and *Blood Mania*.

Demonic: Naked chicks with bubba teeth...and Tom Savini.

Tom Savini is a HUGE name in the horror industry, whether anyone wants to admit it or not.

We have him to thank for the original Jason Voorhees concept and makeup effects, all of the gore from series such as *Friday the 13th* and *Creepshow* and many more special effects that give the computerized CGI effects the middle finger and go for good ol' fashioned realistic blood and carnage.

And he likes bit roles as nut-bars with a crazy streak.

Demonic is actually called *Forest of the Damned*, so if you get all curious and stuff on IMDB, you'll end up pulling your hair out trying to find it under *Demonic*. The title was changed once it hit the states.

Five friends embark on a road trip to go camping for the weekend (Wow. How original.) Emilio has brought along his horrendously hateful sister Ally and his friends Molly, Andrew, and Judd (Molly's boyfriend).

The van breaks down in the middle of nowhere after they hit a girl wandering the road. She is in bad shape and needs help, but no one's phone is working. Molly, Judd, and Andrew go off to find help while Emilio and Ally stay behind to watch the girl.

The girl suddenly grabs Emilio's arm and warns him and Ally not to "look into their eyes" before passing back out.

Molly and Judd split up from Andrew to keep looking. Andrew finds a group of naked women bathing in the waterfall and decides to join them. After a few cuts back to Molly and Judd to check and see what they're up to, Andrew goes missing.

Outside of the opening sequence, this is as exciting as it gets so far.

Molly and Judd find a house in the woods but are attacked and knocked out by Tom Savini (Stephen, but we'll call him Tom to keep it all straight).

Come to find out that the nude chicks with Jaws disorder killed his family.

Molly and Judd escape after Judd shoots Tom Savini in the gut with a shotgun. The naked demon-chicks are on their heels after a quick stop at the van to dismember Ally and Emilio.

Bad Movie Beware!

Judd falls down a ravine after another two-minute montage of nothing happening and is disemboweled by the demon girls.

Note: This is about the millionth interlude in the movie. It's like the writer couldn't really get past the attacks, but he needed a movie with some depth. So he paid his emo kid sister to write a story for the characters while they waited for death via naked girl with piranha genes.

Molly returns to the van but is attacked by the blonde demon. She is about to kill Molly, but the cross around Molly's neck repels her. Molly goes crazy and takes Tom Savini's place as film nutbag.

The end.

Yeah, I checked. It's really the end.

VERDICT: Turn over and go to sleep when you're done.

What can I say about this movie? The acting is great. The girls really play up the role of feral demon and get into it, snarling and hunting like wildlings. The meatbags...er, main cast, also do their roles well. In fact, if it hadn't been for the writer (hate to say that...no, no I don't), the movie would have been good.

Ally is overly hateful and needs to be punched in the face. The writer gave her far too many lines, and the viewer (me) actually sighs a "Thank God" when a demon-chick rips her head off and drinks from it.

Emilio comes off as a whiny little girl the whole time, and isn't really missed when he's out of the picture.

The worst thing about this movie is how boring the in-between stuff is. The dialogue was recorded so low that you have to really crank the volume to hear what the actors are saying, but then you get your face melted by monster sounds and effects during the off times something happens.

I mean, really. How in the HELL do you make a movie like this boring!? The entire premise is "Girls, get naked and put in these Bubba teeth! We're makin' a movie!" Who the hell doesn't want to see naked demon chicks!?

Okay, yeah. I'm kinda weird.

It's not a great movie, but it's not an utter fail either. If you want cult indie movies done better than Handycam Cinema tends to put out, give it a look. Just make sure you stock up on Red Bull and Mountain Dew because this film will put you to sleep.

Drag Me to Hell...For watching this stupid movie

I had high expectations for *Drag Me to Hell*, and I was even told that it was a decent flick. I, like so many other moviegoers, actually got suckered in by very cool-looking previews and trailers.

I finally got to watch it, and I have to say that while it had its moments, this movie was clown shoes when it was all said and done.

And I mean that in the nicest way.

Well, not really.

Christine, a loan officer at a bank, is offered a promotion if she can make a tough decision that will net the bank serious money and close a big deal that she is working on. In order to impress her boss, she tells a shambling old woman that she cannot extend her mortgage, and the woman swears vengeance.

After a knock-down drag-out fight in the parking garage, including a bit where the woman's dentures fall out and she tries to gum Christine's face off, she snatches a button from Chris's coat and puts the curse of the Lamia on her.

The Lamia is a goat-shaped demon that tortures souls for three days before literally dragging them to hell.

That's the story.

No, really.

After that, the old woman dies in the hospital. Chris is haunted by both her and the Lamia. Though I almost drew the line at the bit where the woman appears and rams her arm down ol' girl's throat up to the elbow, I believe the sequence where the goat they brought in during a séance punched it over the edge for me.

"you tricked me, you who-o-o-ore!"

The cheap Wal-Mart puppet bleats the line while one of the men at the table tries to kill it.

I mean goat.

Bad effects, Sam Raimi. No cookie for you.

The acting is top-notch stupidity, and the action is as predictable as the lame ending. The ending is meant to be a twist, but the lack of real action up to that point that is saturated in weak dialogue fails to give Christine's fate the shock value that it could have had.

The only thing worse than a movie that has plenty of things to trash in it is a movie that is just BLAH.

Verdict: YAWN.

It was marketed as a scary movie, but ended up trying to be *Evil Dead 2*. The difference?

Alison Lohman is hot. Bruce Campbell can actually act.

Maybe if they hooked up, we might get a decent lead actor/actress out of the union.

Or just a three-eyed mutant that looks like it was conceived in toxic waste.

If you see it in the $4.99 bin at Best Buy and really want to watch it, don't waste your money. See if someone else will buy it for you. After you watch it, remember to shoot speed because you will need it to take that boring hour and a half out of your mind.

Promptly drive down the interstate and throw it at a sign.

The House Where Evil Dwells...And yawns

It's been a while due to a new schedule, but I managed to find another stinker in the depths of the random crap that Netflix throws onto the instant queue.

The House Where Evil Dwells is deceptive, enticing you in with an interesting concept, an awesome and bloody and gruesome opening sequence, and the whole fact that it is set in Japan.

However, once you've obligated to sign away an hour and a half of your life, it delivers an experience that makes watching cheese age look exciting.

Ned and his wife, Laura, are brought to Japan by Ned's best buddy Alex so that Ned can pursue a career as a journalist. They rent a house in the hills and find out (surprise) that the place was cheap because it is haunted.

After a weak attempt at ghostly phenomenon and a pointless sex scene that goes on far too long, we see the manifestation of the three ghosts that haunt the place.

Yes, these are the same three that hacked each other to pieces in the first sequence.

Note that every time one of these clowns appear, no matter what the mood of the scene is, we get bells and chimes as if Tinkerbell is coming to visit.

It gets almost riotous when the ghost chick possesses Laura and has her call Alex to start an affair.

It begins to get more intense when the daughter, Amy, freaks out at dinner because one of the ghosts is in her bowl of soup making faces at her. More chimes. Then Ned is possessed by the killer samurai and forces Amy to drink her soup.

More chimes.

In fact, when these buffoons materialize in every scene, they are less like evil spirits bent on revenge and more like the Three Stooges. The most intense scene comes when Amy and her friend are sleeping and are suddenly attacked by three giant crabs.

Yes, crabs. Big ones.

Let the STD jokes begin.

So preteen Amy jumps out the window to avoid the crabs, climbs a tree, and finds that the crabs can come after her no matter where she is. She falls out of the trees and ends up in the hospital without the crabs (no drugs necessary!).

Ned and Laura go home and have a local Monk conduct an exorcism. Soon Alex shows up, letting the ghosts back in, and he and Ned end up fighting after Laura admits that she has been sleeping with Alex.

The ghosts possess all three of them and they end up repeating history. It all happens with very little dialogue that actually has meaning.

In the end, the credits rolled with me feeling like I asked for the cute waitress starting her freshman year in college and got the fifty-year-old redneck chick that smells like cats and Old Spice.

VERDICT: No.

While it has the potential to be a decent flick, it kicks Mr. Opportunity square in the junk and opts to be another bad haunted house flick.

I got more entertainment value out of my root canal than I did watching this flick.

It wasn't so bad that I would rather inflict excruciating and deforming pain on myself than watch it again, but I think I'd rather watch a mass Sea Sponge migration than this movie.

Lord knows the sponges would have more entertainment value.

In Search of Lovecraft: He's in his grave...spinning

The "Found Footage" genre has really taken off, giving the right movies a realistic and documentary-ish feel. Made famous by such gems as *The Blair Witch Project* and *Paranormal Activity*, many films are starting to use it as a way to break the barrier between the audience and the screen.

Unfortunately, it's also given every a**hole with a digital camcorder, too much time on their hands, and friends outside of their mother's basement the ability to shoot a movie on the cheap.

Rebecca is a rookie (and cute) reporter given a fluff story to do on H.P. Lovecraft for a Halloween piece. Her cameraman, Mike, is coaching her on and trying to get her to be more enthusiastic about the piece. Her intern, Amber, is a dimwit teenager who wants to be an actress and flirts with Mike incessantly.

Yes. She is also cute. Then she speaks. The horror.

After interviewing a crowd of people at a local party who have not one clue about who Lovecraft is, she interviews Professor Sutton. She can't keep a straight face during the interview, and Sutton gives her the name of a local occultist who can prove that Lovecraft's demons, including one call Nyarlathotep, actually exist.

Dr. D'Souza is a creepy dude, but also the best actor in the movie alongside Mike. He tells Rebecca that she is dancing in dangerous waters and assures her that the occult is very real. He talks her into visiting an old woman in the asylum, and they meet only to discover that the woman is almost catatonic, repeating the "Hail Mary" prayer over and over again. D'Souza calms her, and she explains that she was driven mad after watching a video she found at a house.

After a few days of whining about the story and running into dead ends, D'Souza calls Rebecca and Mike to Professor Sutton's apartment. Sutton is dead and barbecued in his kitchen due to a magic spell.

Feel free to begin bashing your head against a wall. It only gets worse.

Mike, Rebecca and Amber take a road trip to the house the old woman talked about...wait a minute. How is Mike filming the car pulling up? He's driving!? Who the...

It's not "Found Footage," and it's not traditional cinema.

It's BOTH.

Amber is yanked out of the car by an unseen monster, and cultists with glowing eyes begin to show up. Mike and Rebecca flee, but return later after mourning Amber's loss. I mourned her too, about as much as one can mourn a possum in heavy traffic. At the house during the daytime hours, they meet Keja, a local witch who also used to be the lover of D'Souza.

Okay, so he's a very LUCKY creepy dude.

Turns out that there is a stone that they need to get to before Nyarlathotep does. Otherwise, he'll be able to come into our world freely and enslave all of humankind.

That night Mike loses his mind and shoots himself after Rebecca and Keja find D'Souza dead in his office chair. Keja makes a circle in the living room to protect them from demonic attack, and James shows up and tells Rebecca that he misses her and should have never left.

...WHO THE F**K IS JAMES!?

After visits from Amber and D'Souza, both now demons, Rebecca is attacked by Zombie Mike. She cuts him down with a sword and takes a blueprint out of his pocket. This breaks the circle, and Keja is dragged off by a squid tentacle.

No, really. No, I'm not joking. Watch it, I got $5 says she was.

Rebecca uses the map to locate the local lighthouse, the location of the rock. She climbs to the top and opens a chest, a golden glow consuming her.

In the next scene, two orderlies are standing above her bed talking about her case. She had been found trying to dig her own eyes out and is expected to remain in the hospital until she gives birth.

The end of what seems like a story told by a hyperactive preschooler on speed.

VERDICT: Banished to the wasteland of Godzilla's lower intestine.

As if the acting, the story, and the writing weren't bad enough, the director just couldn't decide if he wanted to do a "Found Footage" film or a traditional one. So he did both. "Ah, why not. Nobody'll notice."

I DID, YA PUTZ.

Same rule goes for writing. NEVER switch back and forth between first person and third person. It ruins the story and makes you look like an a**hole.

It also helps if you get people who have had acting experience outside of their family reunions at Christmas time as well as writers who can at least write their names and what they want to eat from Pizza Hut in a way that is not random and aimless. Not that Renee Sweet isn't cute and all, but talent goes a long way.

Kind of like dogs with personality.

Night of the Scarecrow: Maybe the wizard will give this movie a brain

This is my last hurrah before the Christmas season starts and y'all bombard me with horrible Christmas movie requests like rounds from the guns of an Apache Helicopter. Of course, I figured I'd go easy on myself since this looked promising.

And, of course, I am beaten into submission by bad writing and drowned in a sea of clichés.

Not even a television cop show is this formulaic. Movies are like a recipe, really. Look at the ingredients, make tweaks and adjustments to make it your own, and spice it up. Otherwise, your movie just turns out to be a carbon copy of Aunt Lily's Blueberry Liver Mush 3-Cheese Casserole topped with Peanut Butter Marshmallows.

ONWARD!!

Claire returns to her small town home after growing up and finds the place ready to land a large land deal thanks to her father, Mayor Goodman. She is the typical "girl next door" and meets up with the dashing young newcomer and construction foreman Dillon. The two hit it off, and it is soon revealed that Dillon recently fired a boy in town who happens to be the son of Mayor Goodman's buddy.

Let's see where we are: five minutes in and we've met the Girl-Next-Door who moved away and came back home, the Good-Hearted Bad Boy who sweeps her off her feet, and the sleazy mayor who also has a secret embarrassment when it comes to his daughter (we never find out the embarrassment, so don't get your hopes up. She's modest...ish).

The cliché continues to dinner where we meet the town reverend Thaddeus (read: stiff), his wife (prude), and his daughter (slut).

What a shocker there.

The sheriff is also kin to Claire, as is Danny the farmer. Yeah, I was thinking inbreeding too. Meanwhile, back at the ranch (literally), Dillon's former employee and his buddy go on a destructive drunken rampage on the construction site that ends up in a cornfield next to a peculiar-looking scarecrow. The shenanigans disturb an ancient tomb, and the scarecrow comes to life. The boys flee, and Uncle Danny returns home from Mayor Goodman's just to be fed to a piece of farm equipment.

The next day...wait a minute. "NIGHT of the Scarecrow." Let me see: *Friday the 13th* (the original) took place on Friday, June 13th. *Night of the Living Dead*...ONE night. Shouldn't this have been "Night, the Next Day, and the Following Night of the Scarecrow?"

Eh, guess the title is too long.

Anyway, the next day the town is in an uproar over Danny's murder. Claire handles it by going out with Dillon. Susie (Reverend Thaddeus's daughter, slut) goes out with ol' drunkman himself: Frank the Former Employee!

They sneak out to go have sex in Frank's van, but he decides to break off for a beer while she waits alone in the van.

ALONE. Yeah. Shocker.

Scarecrow shows up and plants a fungus in her mouth, and when Frank returns, she sprouts and is dragged off by her new roots. Franks is chased and killed off. Next we see Thaddeus, who is ambushed at the church by Scarecrow and has his mouth sewn shut before he is hurled through a window. He shows up at Dillon and Claire's hotel room (another shock) and tells them the legend of the town's deal with the Devil in return for crops. They turn on the warlock that sealed the deal, and he curses them by casting a spell that will reunite him with his bones if he can get his book back from the family of the man who led the revolt. Ready for a twist?

Claire's dad is a direct descendant. I cannot tell you how surprised I was. Golly (said in Ben Stein's voice).

Scarecrow shows up and kills off all of the remaining characters, pretty much at once, and Claire manages to find the book. She and Dillon find the spell to kill Scarecrow once and for all (why the f**k didn't they do that in the first place!?) and they lure him to the corn field. They set him on fire, but to no avail. Scarecrow's coffin is recovered, and his bones are crushed in a pile driver machine.

VERDICT: DROP A HOUSE ON IT!

I understand the clichés of horror movies, but it irks me to no end when I see a movie use them as a cop-out to avoid actually being creative. Plus the little errors like going additional nights outside of what the title suggests and the inconsistencies in the plot just yank at my nose hairs. The acting is about as good as it can get, but anyone can act like a old fart or a slut, so I'm not really willing to say that much was put into the roles.

Let's face it, the last movie that did overblown clichés and got it right was *Scary Movie*, and that series died the day the Waynes Brothers walked away from it. Now there are some good effects in the movie, and a few decent one-liners, but a dress doesn't make an ugly girl pretty.

It just makes a dude in a dress wearing a hippie-wig look fancy.

Nightscape: I no longer believe in anything

What the hell did I do to deserve this?

I was looking forward to this movie. The trailer was fantastic! It was dark, edgy, and atmospheric. It was moody and oppressive. It was…

Well, it wasn't what was shat onto my TV screen.

Let's not go apes**t here. The trailer is in the movie, but it's a dream sequence and has no bearing on the plot whatsoever. As a matter of fact, nothing in this movie has any bearing on the plot. Essentially, there is no plot for any particular action or scene to really relate to. It's more like they just filmed a bunch of disconnected scenes, then spliced them together. Badly. With silly putty.

Okay, I'll back up. I'm probably just irked like hell because I really wanted the movie I saw in the trailer, not the movie I got. It's not really a terrible movie, but it's not fantastic, either.

Emily Galash plays Kat, a lone drifter who is on the road trying to escape her bad luck. When the movie opens, we meet Smoke, who is a racer she has fallen in with. There's no sexual relationship or anything going on. They're simply traveling partners.

They happen across a diner that has been ransacked. The attacker has left all of the customers and help dead. Kat and Smoke find a waitress in the back, but she falls down and begins to transform into a demon. She attacks Smoke and cuts his arm. Before she can finish him off, our duo is saved by Roshak, a Hispanic gunman with a strange handgun and a desire to simply drive around in his black El Camino all day.

Roshak is on the search for a phantom car that brings the demons in people forward. He takes Kat and Smoke to a motel, but Smoke goes demon and kills Kat before escaping.

Hold up. Dammit.

Okay, so they killed the main character again. This time, way early. The movie has been on for about twenty minutes. Dag-nab-it, they pulled this crap in *Zombinator*!

Oh, wait. She comes back to life.

For. No. Reason.

Well, either her luck is turning around and we witnessed a legitimate miracle, or this chick has the deepest sleep EVER. Either way, she and Roshak hit the road to continue the hunt for the phantom car. Their adventures lead them to a revival, where Roshak recovers Smoke and recruits him to help them draw out the phantom car. Roshak and Kat also end up at a poker game where Roshak reveals his demonic hand that he keeps hidden by wearing a single glove.

Once again: WAY out in left field.

The movie ends when the phantom car ambushes the trio, takes Kat, and runs Roshak's El Camino off the road before taking off. Roshak wakes up and is greeted by the car, which now possesses Kat, and bids him a kind of farewell. He makes a call to a mysterious woman and is given another assignment.

Turns out he is an artifact hunter. Like *Warehouse 13,* but violent and stuff.

VERDICT: Confusticated.

Okay, all in all, this movie wasn't absolutely terrible. A lot of people have bashed it, saying that it moves far too slow, and I can see where they're coming from on that one. It tends to drag in areas, particularly in scenes intended to flesh the characters out and give them more substance.

The acting is not the problem in this movie. Emily Galash, in particular, does extremely well given the writing. Her character is believable, though the accent is a bit forced. It was less "Y'all want some sweet tea?" and more "Grab the banjos and lube, paw! We got us another one!" Michael Biesanz pulls off the mysterious Roshak well, making him come off as morose and dangerous.

The sound was also good, for an indie, as were the visual effects. What hurt this movie was the plot. Well, plots. There were a LOT of them.

The writing was the issue, not that it was bad, but in that the writer/director/producer obviously couldn't decide what story he wanted to tell. So, he just told ALL of them. At once. In pieces.

And didn't finish them.

Grr.

I mean, I feel his pain. I did the same thing on a book I spent forever writing. The difference is, I picked one story and focused on it, and things are going much smoother now. The same can't be said for *Nightscape,* which manages to tell about four different stories from multiple genres and only gives the viewer tidbits of each one. It was almost like watching a movie comprised of nothing but clips and trailers.

For example: WHY did Kat come back to life? She was dead. Like, stone cold. And what was the real history between Roshak and the phantom car? Where did this old woman at the end come from? Some things could've been hinted at in the film and been a surprise at the end instead of a kick to the proverbial beanbag.

It was an action/fantasy/sci-fi/horror/monster movie.

Dude, really. Pick one.

Watch it if you're curious, but don't expect anything in particular. It raises a lot of good questions, but answers none of them.

Ever.

Slices of Life: Tales from the dumb side

I can remember Saturday nights as a kid when my family and I would settle down on the couch to watch *Tales from the Dark Side* and *Monsters*. Then *Tales from the Crypt* came out, creating a trifecta of campy television horror mayhem and entertainment. I was a big fan of *Tales from the Dark Side*, in particular.

Apparently, so was this guy.

Slices of Life is proof that, once again, just being a fan with friends and access to cameras and makeup doesn't mean you can write/direct a movie.

Mira is an amnesiac who uses a very macabre-looking sketchbook to remind herself about things in her life when she has spells of memory loss. Her book, entitled "Work Life," is her only key to her memories.

Her boss Irma and Marv the janitor tell her to watch the front desk of the motel they live in while she goes over her book. This is the intro to the first story, "W.O.R.M."

Yeah, I don't know what it stands for, either. The movie didn't elaborate.

William is a lonely Mr. Fix-It that works at Nimrod Corporation. He works in solitude at a desk down in the storage catacombs of the building and is rejected by everyone in the office as he is a socially inept outsider.

He visits an online dating site and is rejected by every woman, including the sixty-year-old hag. While up in the office doing his rounds and getting socially rejected and abused by everyone, he overhears a colleague talking to the boss about a new program that can transmit neural suggestions to people through email, thus making them susceptible to slight mind control.

The boss rejects the idea and throws it in the garbage. Will digs it out and uses it on the dating site.

Of course, he picks the hag.

She has a sudden change of heart and has webcam sex with him. The keyboard becomes skin, and the mouse becomes a vagina.

Yeah, totally would've been better had he not picked Granny Whorebucks.

Suddenly the geriatric ginger turns into a zombie and attacks the webcam, screaming his name. Come to find out he also sent the email all over the office, turning the entire staff into zombies obsessed with him.

Will hides in the parking garage and finds the homely secretary who likes him. She is about to kiss him when a guy in a HAZ-MAT suit shoots her in the head and takes him into custody. Will is locked away, screaming that he doesn't want to be alone anymore.

Really?

NEXT.

Mira sees a newscast that Nimrod Corp. has had a major biohazard outbreak. Whispers suddenly come through telling her it's real…wait a minute.

Okay, so the director thinks that the viewer is dumb as a stump, so he has to broadcast the hidden little hints out where there's no mistake.

Wow.

Mira's sketchbook suddenly changes and is now called "Home Life."

The next tale is called "Amber Alert." It was actually an improvement over "W.O.R.M." but it still had its issues. Fortunately, the issues were technical. It's a story done to death, but still cool either way.

Vonda is a pregnant woman whose husband is a police officer. She is concerned because she is due in a week, and there have been several cases of young girls being kidnapped, killed and tossed into the river. She has a baby shower at her house while her husband is off at work. During the shower, a young girl named Rebecca goes missing. Vonda's friends advise her to get some rest, and she takes a nap while they clean and leave.

When she wakes up, she sees shadows of young girls around the house. One of them is in the back yard, and when Vonda approaches, the girl's face turns demonic and distorted. Vonda runs back into the house just as Lamont comes home from work. She tells him there is a girl in the back yard, but he goes out back and finds nothing. He checks the workshop, then locks it and hangs the key around his neck.

After Lamont is attacked by Ally and carted off, Vonda takes the key and opens the workshop to find a white van inside. Inside the van, she finds Rebecca in a trunk, hungry but alive. Lamont turns back up and attacks, but Ally shows up and turns into a monster. Lamont is thrown back into the wall and a sledgehammer falls on his face crushing his skull. Ally tells Vonda that she is her unborn daughter and that they are free.

Campy, done to death, but I'll take it.

Back at the ranch, Mira gets a visit from a young girl and her mother. The whispers inform me (because I'm so stupid I can't put two and two together) that the girl and the mother are from the story.

The book is now entitled "Sex Life."

Now it gets interesting.

Susan is a young girl living with her brother and uncle in an apartment. Eric, the brother, calls and says that he will be home soon. The uncle, Jack, uses the opportunity to rape Susan (a regular thing, apparently). Eric comes home as Jack is doing the deed and tackles him. Susan knocks Jack out with a large iron skillet, and she and Eric flee.

Meanwhile, a young girl is tied up and locked away by her father in the basement of a house. He then goes upstairs and carves a dead boy in the bathtub into pieces and loads the trash bags into the trunk of his car. He is driving away when he finds a branch lying across the road. He tries to move it but falls and knocks himself out.

Susan and Eric happen across the man and take him to the hospital. According to his I.D., he is Edgar. Susan and Eric go back to the house and find Elizabeth in the basement. They take her upstairs, and she tells them that her aunt showed up and her father went crazy, taking her away from her brother and mother while mumbling something about a family curse.

Elizabeth goes off to take a shower, and she and Eric make eyes at each other as she leaves. Susan and Eric decide to pack a few things for the road.

Edgar wakes up at the hospital and tells the nurse that his son was killed. He gets his clothes and has the nurse arrange a ride home for him.

Eric is in the bedroom getting some sheets when he sees a very naked Elizabeth step out of the shower. She advances on him, seducing him. They fall to the bed and begin to roll around, and he puts his fingers in her. He begins to scream as he pulls his hand back to find that his fingers have been chewed off. Elizabeth flips him over and begins screeching as she straddles him and begins to devour him...with her crotch.

What. The. F**k.

Edgar bursts in and finds Elizabeth on the remains of Eric and shoots her in the head. Susan comes in and kills Edgar with a sledgehammer. She mourns over Eric, then sees Elizabeth's body twitch. The body is dragged to the wall, and a direct rip-off of the *Alien* chestburster shoots out of the dead girl's hoo-haa and flies like a bullet into Susan's hoo-haa.

Wait...what the!?

(Rewinds scene and plays again while peeking between fingers of epic face-palm).

Yup, there goes the Snatch-Maggot flying across the room and up Susan's dress. Didn't dream it. I have now seen it all.

Jesus.

In the next scene, Susan shows up at Jack's place and seduces him. As she forces him back into the apartment and closes the door, we hear the screeching and see blood pool on the floor.

Yeah.

Mira is suddenly approached by a drunk man asking for a room for a few hours. He is followed by Susan, who says that they will definitely need cleanup.

Yes, thank you, whispers. I got that. It's her. Go play in traffic.

Mira then goes into a room and finds Irma and Marv in the middle of a ritual. Irma tells Mira (yeah, it's going where you think it is) that she drew all of the stories, just like she drew Mira. Mira is to be host to a new younger body for Irma. Mira stabs Irma, but electricity shoots from the wound into Mira's mouth.

Mira returns to the front desk, now dressed in a nightgown and obviously inhabited by Irma.

What a shocker. I need a drink.

VERDICT: Throw it into a dark bottomless pit.

It's really sad when movies or stories have potential. It's even worse when that potential is put into the hands of someone who writes with all the finesse of George Lucas. Like I said earlier, I was a big fan of *Tales from the Dark Side,* but not enough to poop on it like an incontinent gorilla with mommy issues.

Though the first segment was bad and the second was only okay, the third segment was the one that raised an eyebrow. A young girl, possessed by the creature of Ridley Scott's nightmares, eats and mutilates a young boy with her vagina.

    Wow, whatcha gettin' at there, Mr. Writer?

    And it's contagious!?

Succubus: They got the "suck" part right

Another for the vault (read: dumpster).

So there's a Horror-Con coming up soon called "Mad Monster Party," and none other than Gary Busey himself will be there signing autographs! Since it's been a while since I've seen a Busey flick, I decided to give *Succubus: Hell-Bent* a try since he supposedly stars in the movie. The girl on the cover also helped the decision.

Yeah, I know. You can't judge a book by its cover.

I'm a sucker for goth chicks.

Adam and his friend Jason head off to Cancun for a weekend of sun, fun, and sex. Their goal: sleep with as many girls as possible. Winner take all.

Jason is up to five by day two, and Adam is only slightly behind until he meets Lilith. Lilith is the most beautiful girl he has ever laid eyes on (guess he's never gotten a good look at Milla Kunis, Melissa George, or Rachel Hurd-Wood), and discovers quickly that she is strong, dark, and sexually vicious.

He sleeps with her, drops the "I love you" bomb to get more, then bails while she is asleep. Back in L.A., he meets up with his girlfriend Heather, who is not happy that he is covered in scratches and bites from his tryst with Lilith.

Heather leaves, and Adam calls Jason to set up a party. The bash is in full swing, and Adam is about to have a threesome when Lilith shows up and has another round of sex with him (looks more like rape).

When Heather shows back up and talks her way into Adam's bed. See a pattern yet? Lilith is not happy and kills Heather in the pool while Adam sleeps. The police blame him but set him free after his very rich and powerful father makes the right phone calls.

Adam and Jason go over the video Adam took of himself sleeping with Lilith and find a frame in which she turns into a demon. They decide to deal with it by going to the bar to get drunk and pick up women.

Because that is the most productive solution.

Adam thinks he sees Lilith, but Jason meets up with her for real in the bathroom where she turns his head completely around, killing him. Adam, after finding his friend, goes home to try and talk to his dad.

Wait…massive police presence, ambulance, yadda-yadda when Heather dies. Not one government employee when Jason dies. So what? You just go to the bar, your best friend gets his head ripped off, and you handle it like your puppy got kicked?

Jesus.

Anyway, Pops blows Adam off, so ol' lover boy decides to call Sentinel, a local Demon Hunter.

NOW we see Gary Busey, the salty Sentinel who hunts all forms of supernatural being. He gives Adam a scroll and a box of goodies to lure Lilith, who Adam has now figured out is a succubus, into his house so he can kill her. Sentinel then gets back into his pickup and speeds off.

Yes. Gary Busey was in this movie for one minute.

Adam summons Lilith, and the last five or ten minutes of the movie are spent watching him prowl around the house while Lilith taunts him and runs by the camera. They fight for all of two seconds, and he stabs her with his old sword from military school.

End of Lilith.

Adam gets arrested for killing an innocent young goth girl in his home.

End of Adam.

Lilith wakes up in the back of the coroner's truck while a necrophiliac driver gropes her.

End of necrophiliac.

End of movie.

End of misery.

VERDICT: Send it back to Hell.

So, apparently the director/writer Kim Bass didn't take into account that some of her audience might be looking for some semblance of a plotline.

She must also have been burned by a yuppie rich boy in college because the only thing the males in the movie do is either think about sex, talk about sex, or have extreme amounts of sex with girls who do not have the brains God gave a beer can.

Plus, she managed to pull off all of the sex with virtually no nudity! You see a quick shot of one of Lilith's nipples. That's it. Might as well have been a dude because the ones she's rockin' on the cover are Photoshop specials.

And when I say that the college girl characters are stupid, I mean that in the most literal and forward way that I can. Watching Adam and his "Wing-Man" Jason hit on girls is about like watching two blind monkeys f**k a football. And the girls eat it up and end up in bed with these two stooges.

The acting is worse than *Brain Twisters* with a hint of *Battlefield Earth* thrown in. The effects are decent since it's all camera tricks, but the end result is just lame.

If I watch a movie about a succubus, I expect nudity, blood, and a lot of disturbing demonic imagery. I got less nudity than one might see in a Victoria's Secret catalog, a smidgen of blood, and the disturbing image of David Keith in bed with Yvonne Maverick.

Didn't really need that one. Didn't need this stinker of a s**tpile, either. Run like hell.

Wishmaster: Genie in the crapper

Number three in the fearsome foursome-pack entitled is *Wishmaster* from renowned horror-master Wes Craven.

Needless to say my expectations were high considering that not only did it come from the mind of the man behind *People Under the Stairs* and *Nightmare on Elm St.*, but also starred (supposedly) the legends of horror: Robert Englund (Freddy Krueger), Kane Hodder (Jason Voorhees), Tony Todd (Candyman), and Angus Scrimm (The Tall Man).

Unfortunately, "starring" for these icons in this movie meant "farted into the script at the last possible second."

Robert Englund has the largest role in the movie (a whole fifteen minutes of screen time combined), Kane Hodder is killed by the Djinn almost instantly during his one-minute scene, Tony Todd is a sucker, and you only hear the voice of Angus Scrimm in the opening dialogue.

So much for an all-star cast.

Ted Raimi also appears but is killed off within thirty seconds of screen time. Oh well, onward to the review.

Screw the opening sequence because the only bearing it has is how the Djinn got trapped into the jewel. It could have been shortened by about five minutes.

Alexandra (Tammy Lauren) is given a jewel to appraise after it is discovered inside a statue that was broken during a tragic dock accident. This awakens the Djinn (genie), a demon that grants wishes to those unfortunate enough to grant him the permission to use his power.

He seeks out Alex, granting wishes and collecting souls along the way. His goal is to have Alex make three wishes so that he can unleash the entire race of Djinn into our world.

The characters in this movie besides Alex are incredibly stupid. I'm sorry, but some creeper walks up to me and wants me to make a wish, I'm gonna raise my eyebrow at him and walk away.

Oddball.

Of course, he finally gets to Alex after a gory rampage of wishes that turn his hopelessly dumb victims into his playthings and corners her into making her first wish.

What would a movie with creature effects ripped from the Sesame Street reject warehouse be without a jaunt through the same hallways and corridors we've seen in every other stinking monster movie?

Alex uses her final wish to undo everything that has been done by the Djinn, right down to the breaking of the statue that revealed his jewel.

Talk about anti-climactic.

I've seen more nail-biting sequences of sphincter-tightening action in *Dora the Explorer*. Remember when Boots lost his balloon?

EDGE OF MY SEAT, MAN!!!

VERDICT: Coaster.

Unless you truly believe that even the greatest horror-master cannot have the creative squirts, this movie is best left a bad memory of the 90's. What's worse, it shat three sequels straight to video!

I cannot believe that the concept of putting together favorites from a beloved genre worked better in *The Expendables* than it did in the world of horror. Mr. Craven, though you have redeemed yourself since this abomination, I have made sure that my Wes Craven toilet target has been ordered and shipped in the name of *Wishmaster*.

I wish for my anal aim to be dead on target!

Wishmaster 2: One was enough. Really...

While battling a losing war with bronchitis, I decided to pick another movie. Much to my surprise (read: dismay), I discovered that I actually own the second *Wishmaster* movie.

My hands shook as I tried to fight them from putting the damned thing into my computer DVD drive. I fought so hard but, in the end, it didn't even matter. In it went, and down went my self-respect as the opening sequence stormed onto screen like an angry bout of diarrhea.

As if the first one wasn't bad enough, I noticed that Wes Craven had nothing to do with this movie. This was my second clue that it was going be about as entertaining as rubber whitey-tighties full of Ben-Gay.

My first clue was the first movie.

Morgana is an art thief who gets caught up in a bad heist and blows away a guard during a gunfight that leaves her boyfriend mortally wounded. One of her bullets grazes a statue, and the blood gem is exposed. She grabs it, tends to her boyfriend, and drops it as the police arrive.

It has split from where it stopped a bullet that should have killed her. She leaves, and who else shows up but ol' Wishy-poo! He claims his first victim by granting the boyfriend's wish that he had never been born. What the police find after the Djinn freezes one of them is Nathaniel Demarest. He claims full guilt for the heist, saying he acted alone.

The next forty-five minutes of the movie might as well be a montage that floats between Morgana and her new priest boyfriend, Gregory, going "What do we do!?" and the Djinn granting wishes from desperate (read: frighteningly stupid) inmates.

After a while, the Djinn decides to go elsewhere and ends up in Las Vegas as the owner of a Casino.

YEAH.

Of course, Morgana and Gregory, after the mandatory love scene, go after him and find the casino in utter gory chaos.

A few wisecracks from the Djinn, and they all end up in his world inside the blood gem. Greg gets nailed to a cross and Morgana gets to girl out and beg for his release.

Wish number two.

She then grabs the gem, chants a spell in another language, and banishes him back to "Wherever-the-f**k." All souls get returned. Everyone killed by the Djinn is back to life. Everyone is happy.

Except me.

VERDICT: WORTHLESS (Iranian for Kanye West)!!!

The only actor in this movie with an actual filmography outside of television cameos and porn is Andrew Divoff. The fact that this sequel spawned two more is just a *Low-Down Dirty Shame*.

While not as bad as *Troll 2*, it ranks up there with *Battlefield Earth* and *Sex and the City*.

Both movies. Sorry, but I don't know whether I should hug Sarah Jessica Parker or feed her a carrot and sugar cubes.

The acting is daytime soap quality at its worst, and the script is more random than a Pee Wee Herman movie. In fact, Pee Wee would have made this movie at least a LITTLE entertaining.

Scientific Stupidity

There's so much that can be done with the Science Fiction genre. Really, as long as you can SOUND like you know exactly what all the bulls**t technology you're making up really does and how it works, you can be looked at as a true Science Fiction geek.

After all, it worked for *Star Trek*.

These buckets of diaper mud, not so much.

The Amazing Transparent Man: More like the lackluster invisible gimp

While this wasn't as boring as *The Ape Man,* it certainly had its yawn moments.

Let's backtrack a little here. Once again, this movie hails from the collection I got from the in-laws (also two of my group of original fans). Yep. Another from *The Best of the Worst.*

And yet it still isn't as bad as *The Star Wars Holiday Special.*

The 1950's and 60's still had their own independent low-budget flicks, though they still managed to crank out memorable movies like...well there's... I mean, just look at...

Ah, shaddap.

Joey Faust breaks out of prison in the middle of the night and is picked up by a strange woman in a convertible. Laura is assistant to "The Major," who has plans for Faust. When they arrive at the house, they are greeted by Julian and Major Krenner.

Faust is aggressive and paranoid, constantly threatening to do harm to the Major and his crew. Krenner takes it all in stride and takes him upstairs to reveal the plans.

Krenner plans to take over the world using an army of invisible soldiers. He has kidnapped a brilliant scientist, Dr. Ulof, and has locked away the doctor's daughter in order to keep him working on the experiments.

Not kidding. Wants to conquer the world. Maniacal laugh optional.

Faust watches as they turn a guinea pig invisible and is astonished when he is able to pet the creature even though he can't see it. His role is to steal whatever Ulof needs to continue the Major's plan.

Faust is next under the ray and soon attacks the Major and demands more money. He wants the ridiculously high sum of $25,000 to do the job.

Yeah, I know. But consider the time period.

Faust steals a small metal container from a lab nearby, though the script doesn't really go into detail as to what it is, exactly. Something to do with nuclear something or other. When he returns, he tries to convince

Laura to join him and double-cross the Major. Julian interrupts and knocks Faust out cold.

The next day Faust is given the new assignment of robbing a bank...in broad daylight. He and Laura set out while Ulof pulls the Major aside to speak to him privately. The guinea pig has died from radiation poisoning, and he explains that Faust does not have long.

The bank heist is going well when Faust begins to randomly go between visible and invisible. He holds the bank up and makes his escape in Laura's car. He tells her to drive back to the house so he can confront Krenner and Ulof and find out what is going on.

Yes, the movie is actually already almost over.

Faust and Laura make it back to the house, but the Major is waiting for them. He shoots and kills Laura after she frees Dr. Ulof and his daughter, and Faust goes after him. They fight in the lab, and the equipment is turned on and overloaded.

As they struggle, the realization comes that the house is about to be destroyed. Major Krenner begins to scream like a b***h as Faust holds him down.

No, really. Like a b***h.

The house explodes like an atomic bomb. The next day we see that Ulof has joined two police officers at the site. The sheriff tells him that a good bit of the county was taken out in the explosion. Ulof contemplates the decisions of an invisible man, then turns to the camera and asks the viewer what they would do.

Credits. 58 minutes later. Really?

VERDICT: A fart in the wind.

Not that I'm complaining that I didn't have to spend a solid three hours in horrendous boredom (lookin' at YOU, *Supernova)*, but it goes by quickly. Still, considering the material, any longer would've been about like trying to eat a frozen jawbreaker.

The acting is the typical 1960's over-the-top, though I tend to like that style from time to time because it kept the fourth wall pretty well intact. Then Ulof, among other characters in other films, has to go and kick the fourth wall down like Godzilla attacking the city.

The directors at the time thought that this was an ingenious way to pull the audience in. News flash, anus-waffles: if you feel the need to do this at the end of your movie, then you already know that the film isn't engaging to begin with.

No bones about it, this movie was boring. The action was almost too fast and often without a whole lot of explanation. Faust is supposed to be the anti-hero, the bad guy with a heart. Instead, he's a creep and a thug. You mean to tell me, Sir Writer/Director, that I'm supposed to relate to this a**tard whose sleazy persona is only matched by the gay dude trying to take over the world?

No, seriously. The Major should've just saved the headache and made out with Faust. The character was obviously into him. I don't know if that was intentional or what, but I could SO see Chris Kattan playing Major Krenner in the reboot.

The story is weak, which is unfortunate since it had real potential. The problem goes back to time, really. To flesh out the story and make it the character study it hinted at being, the film would've had to go on for another hour at least. But, as any indie filmmaker will tell you, time is money, and budgets are tight.

Once again, like *The Ape Man*, not a HORRIBLE movie, but not a great one either. I'd watch it again, but it would take a few beers. Maybe a few more beers.

Where did I put that keg again?

The Ape Man: "Monkey Business" is putting it nicely...

The first movie on disc two of the *Best of the Worst* collection is *The Ape Man*, starring none other than the man who gave us the Dracula persona that has been mimicked untold numbers of times: Bela Lugosi!

Hey, we all screw up from time to time.

Not that I had high hopes that this turd would be good, but at least it was watchable, albeit EXTREMELY boring. Nothing really happens until about halfway through the movie, and I spent most of my time slapping myself like a lunatic to stay awake.

I just tell people I got into a fight at the local Magic: The Gathering tournament.

Lugosi plays Dr. James Brewster, a scientist who has gone missing. His photo is all over every newspaper in the city, and a goofy-looking man in a gray leisure suit directs a reporter to Brewster's sister, Agatha. She is upset by her brother's disappearance and is accompanied by James's colleague and friend Dr. George Randall. George rushes Agatha on, telling her he has something to show her.

Cut to Brewster's house, where Dr. Randall reveals that Dr. Brewster has turned himself into an ape-man. His mannerisms and appearance are that of a gorilla spliced with a human, but he still retains his personality and intelligence.

And a "thing" for bananas. Sorry, couldn't help it.

Beyond this point, it's a lot of back and forth between the reporter, Jeff, and his camerawoman Billie as they make multiple (and pointless) visits to the house trying to catch up on the Galloping Ghost or Dr. Brewster's whereabouts.

They can't really seem to decide.

At some point Dr. Brewster explains that he needs spinal fluid to change back, but it will kill whomever he takes it from. (Yeah, I know. Give 'em a break; it's 1943) Dr. Randall refuses, and Dr. Brewster escapes with his gorilla sidekick to go find a victim. He breaks in to Randall's house and kills the butler, taking his fluid and escapes.

Randall shows up at Brewster's house and unwillingly gives him the injection. It works, but only temporarily. Brewster escapes again with his gorilla and goes on a citywide killing spree.

I might point out that it is now a little ways past the halfway mark.

Note: This movie is *Seinfeld*. Nothing much really happens. In all seriousness, it's not even suspenseful. In fact, I'm tempted to hit YouTube. But, I digress.

A.D.D. Sue me.

Anywho, the goofy man from the beginning continuously shows up in the most random places for no other reason than to guide the characters here and there. It's like Ralph from *Friday the 13th*. You know, the "You're all doomed!" guy.

Just more annoying.

Eh, kick it back. Ralph was THE MAN!!

Brewster eventually kills Randall in a struggle in the basement. Jeff and Billie break into the house after hearing the gorilla in the basement howling and grunting, and Brewster knocks out Jeff.

Brewster takes Billie downstairs and is about to kill her when the gorilla gets loose and attacks him. Brewster struggles with the ape but is strangled.

Billie manages to find the button that opens the door to the basement and flees with the gorilla in pursuit. He is stopped short by a hail of gunfire from the police officers that show up on the scene.

As they are leaving, Jeff and Billie catch the Goofy Dude in the car waiting on them. Jeff asks who he is, and he explains that he's the author of the story.

The End.

VERDICT: Not completely horrible.

Sadly, this is the best movie I've seen in the collection so far. In truth, it's not really TERRIBLE. It's just less interesting that watching paint dry.

Sense and Sensibility had more nail-biting, sphincter-grinding action than *The Ape Man*.

Seeing the iconic Bela Lugosi do a role outside of Dracula was interesting, but it didn't save this movie from being a compete yawner.

It's like sitting in science class in high school.

Bueller...Bueller...

The acting, outside of Lugosi, is bad even for the time. Jeff spends more time belittling Billie for being a woman than he does working on the story about the Galloping Ghost or Dr. Brewster. Funny how he makes snide remarks indicating how stupid women are, but he can't make up his damn mind on what his story is on.

In truth, like I said earlier, the movie isn't catastrophically bad. I can actually recommend it to those who are interested in seeing what Lugosi could do with s**tty writing, bad actors, and pacing that makes a Pinto look like a Ferrari. Would I ever watch it again? Not willingly. Unless there is Dutch Apple Pie involved. Love me some Dutch Apple Pie.

The Atomic Brain: A story that will leave you drooling...

Okay, now *that* sucked.

Back into the *Best of the Worst* collection for yet another ancient independent corn nugget from the 60's. *The Atomic Brain* has it all. Mad scientist bent on proving his genius to the world? Check. Bitter old woman consumed with greed trying to do the impossible? Check. Three women who don't have the sense God gave a beer bottle? Check.

And a narrator. Dear God, the narrator.

I guess the narrator is necessary since, apparently, the average moviegoer in the 60's was so f**king stupid that a narrator was needed to explain what was going on right in front of their faces whenever there was no dialogue.

And I can't use the Sony Handycam crack on this one because, well, it was filmed in the 60's. They used 35mm film on most of the movies shot back then, so the camera would've been large and not exactly portable. Therefore, scenes had static shots instead of today's camera styles that pan in and out and follow the action.

What to do, what to do?

I'll just call it a turd.

Meet Dr. Frank, our resident Mad Scientist. His big idea is that people's brains can be swapped around, thus defying death and age.

The movie opens with Dr. Frank in the cemetery looking for a fresh corpse in the crypt. During this, the narrator explains that he was hired by Ms. March and gives us some backstory. He comes across a gorgeous young woman who has recently died, and he decides to take her body back to the lab. His creature pet, a man with the brain of an animal, kills a security guard and helps the good doctor make off with the corpse.

We then meet Ms. March, and the narrator explains that she plans to have the doc transplant her brain into a young woman's body in order to be young and beautiful again, as well as retain her millions.

The next day, three women from three different countries arrive at the airport to meet Victor, Ms. March's manservant. We have Nina from Argentina (sounds like a cartoon character), Bea from England, and Anita from Spain.

Funny thing is that Anita is the only one with an accent.

Bea sounds like a northerner trying to do a bad southern accent, and Nina just speaks with a normal accent as if she is from the Midwest. It's like *The Man in the Iron Mask*. The only person in the movie with a French accent was Gerard Depardieu, which figures since he's FROM FRANCE. Not that I don't like *The Man in the Iron Mask*, I love it. But let's be real. Leonardo DiCaprio was King Louise the XIV with a California accent.

Now that's just wrong.

The three girls are taken to the house, stripped (sorry guys, no boobies), and inspected for perfection by Ms. March. She chooses Bea and decides to do away with Anita and Nina. Anita is taken first, and her brain is swapped with a cat's brain. She goes feral and claws out Bea's eyes.

Ms. March settles for Nina, who is the only one of the three girls who ends up with an ounce of sense. She goes on the offensive, teaming up with Victor to escape after Vic is shunned by Ms. March. Ms. March kills him, and Nina is taken down to Dr. Frank's lab for the procedure.

Just as things look bleak, Frank turns on Ms. March and puts her brain inside the cat. He helps Nina escape, but Ms. March traps him inside the machine and melts him. Nina flees the house just as it explodes.

The End. Yes, really. That uneventful.

VERDICT: SOMEONE DO SOMETHING.

Hell, do ANYTHING. Not saying boobies would've helped, but that would've at least been more interesting than watching a solid hour of three chicks from different countries with no accents (except for Anita, thank you darlin'!) whine about what they're going to do while an old crone sits around wringing her hands and spying on them like a barracuda in a goldfish pond.

The original title to this movie was *Monstrosity*, though the name got changed for whatever reason. There was also an episode of *Mystery Science Theater 3000* that featured this movie, so you can check it out if you're a fan of the show.

The movie was 66 minutes long, but it felt like three hours of watching paint dry because of the boredom. Nothing really out there happens until the last ten minutes or so. Anita goes nuts and thinks she's a cat after having her brain replaced, and no one seems to consider for a minute how weird this is.

And, strangely, kind of kinky.

Many of the older indies from the 60's seem to have a charm to them. Classics like *The Ape Man* and *The Amazing Transparent Man* tend to have their allure, despite being utter cinematic poo-poo.

This steaming pile of donkey crap, however, misses the whole idea of what makes a Bad Movie. It's just a bad movie (notice the caps, right?). Maybe if the film hadn't tried to take itself so seriously, it might have at least been funny.

The narrator just killed the movie for me and managed to make me want to hunt him down. Here I am, trying to get into the movie, and he starts yapping like a well-spoken pain in the a**. I like to think I'm smarter than the average man-child, so I typically don't have a hard time picking up on what's going on in a movie or on stage when the action has no dialogue. I really don't need some blowhard telling me what's going on.

It's like that one redneck in the theater that talks to the screen.

In truth, the narrator was probably the worst part of this movie. Do away with him, and…well hell. Not even that could save this boring piece of crap. Hurry up and flush it before it stinks up the house.

Battlefield Earth: Travolta must pay...with his career

I have watched some real crap in my day. Between cinematic gems such as *Vacancy* and *Reel Horror*, I'd thought that it could get no worse until I saw *Alice's Adventures in Wonderland*. Then, here comes *Asylum*, and I am promptly kicked in the beans by what I had thought was the worst movie EVER.

As if my scrotum begged for more punishment, I am dared...DARED...to watch what must be the biggest sh*t-stain ever smeared on poor defenseless film like Country Crock on a Ryan's yeast role.

Battlefield Earth is, without any reasonable doubt, the WORST MOVIE EVER MADE! The only person who walked away from this trainwreck of silver-screen fecal matter with a career was John Travolta, and he has *Grease* to thank for that crap. Other than Travoltapants, *Battlefield Earth* stars a cast of absolute NOBODIES as characters that no one with an ounce of intelligence would care about at any given time.

And Forest Whitaker.

Fast-forward to the year 2000, when an alien race called the "Psychlos" (it gets better, trust me) invades and takes over Earth. Yeah, I know. Ten years ago. But let's face it. Never mind, let's not.

The movie picks up in the year 3000. In a literal montage of pointless dialogue and utterly random montages of characters doing nothing, we meet Johnny Goodboy Tyler (see, I told you...), who is a headstrong youth that is captured by the Psychlos and taken to a facility where we meet Terl (AKA Fuzzy-Cone Travoltapants), who is the security chief of an installation that looks like an...installation. Yeah, it really doesn't look like anything, truth be told.

They all work for a corporate group who sends out guys from the home office to check in on Terl from time to time because he did stuff to the senator's daughter. My guess: Travolta probably tried to demonstrate his acting abilities for this movie and offended her so badly that she had to be put on lithium just to handle the depression caused by his overacting.

Oh, and the color scheme? The movie is shot in three primary colors: purple, blue, and beige. F*&;KING BEIGE!!!!

The acting is so bad, I was actually pausing the movie here and there to see if they were holding scripts and doing cold reads. The Psychlos spoke like current day human beings and referred to humans as Man-Animals and Rat-Brains.

Almost every male in the movie, at some point, had an erection. I kid you not. Melissa (the wife) caught that one right before she gave up and turned her back on it to do more interesting things like SLEEP.

The special effects were top-notch garbage that were outdone by anything seen on SyFy, and the storyline was broken and beyond repair. It was as if someone ate the script, then had it extracted from his poo and pieced together to form what we ended up getting.

Yeah, that's right, I know the ending.

By all rights, I ought to make you watch it as payback for having me watch this migraine headache. But I can't do that. My whole purpose is to watch these crappy flicks and review them to save you the pain. Every now and then, I find a gem. Be grateful that I am so noble.

This movie actually got a studio sued, cost Travolta $5 million of his own money, and became the punch line of bad movie jokes to this very day, TEN YEARS LATER!!! I would rather have the hair on my private areas shaved off with an Epilady than watch this movie again. The difference? The pain from the hair-removal would go away.

VERDICT: Burn.

Make it die. If you see it on the shelf at the store, get the children out first, and do not look Fuzzy-Cone Travoltapants directly in the eye. His alien, super-hypnotic Psychlo-stare will turn your bowels and make you poop more bad science fiction movies for him to star in so that he can preach more Scientology to us.

This movie will make you hate puppies. This movie will make you want to feed liver to little kids.

Okay, not really.

But I will tell you anything to keep you from destroying your life by watching this crappy, crappy movie. I would grade it, but F is too high a score, and there is nothing after Z.

The Black Hole: SyFy strikes again

Finally getting around to the SciFi four-pack that came in the box o' crap given to me by my aunt Marjorie about two years ago.

Oh, give me a break. There were 24 DVDs in that box, and I work for a living.

Anyways, as I look on the back of the cover for the first movie, I see two familiar names pop up: Judd Nelson and Kristy Swanson. Granted, these two have done next to nothing since *Breakfast Club* and *Buffy the Vampire Slayer* (respectively), but I was willing to give them a shot in what could have been a low-budget pleasant surprise. Instead, I spend the next hour and a half wishing I had been the one getting shot. In the face. A lot.

Shannon (Swanson) is a scientist at the St. Louis Science Center Planetarium and is working on a project to create and control a black hole so that its power can be harnessed. Of course, everything goes to hell instantly when a black hole opens in the basement and kills four guys just doing their jobs.

An entity (yes, that is what they call this thing the rest of the movie) emerges and begins to siphon electricity to keep itself going.

What's the big plan? Let's go wake up Bryce (Nelson) out of his drunken stupor to solve all of our problems!

The Special Tactics Unit sent in by the government is led by General Ryker, who looks like he should have retired after the Cold War was over. Of course, Bryce knows exactly what is going on, he just doesn't know how to stop it. He calls his ex-wife to warn her to take his daughter and run, but that one ends in failure.

Okay, so I guess all of the looks from Shannon indicate a fling? Nah. She's too hot.

The new idea, after they evacuate and the hole sucks down the Research Center, is to trap the entity. The government just so happens to have a storage container off of a train that is rigged up as a large electromagnetic prison.

Go figure.

The attempt fails, even though the soldiers were armed with hand grenades that looked like tomatoes spray-painted black. Talk about low budget.

The President is talked into a nuclear strike, even though Bryce has informed them that the hole will just swallow the bomb. He makes the obvious observation that the entity is avoiding the hole, so he devises a plan to lure it back into the hole and collapse it in on itself.

In about fifteen minutes, a generator truck is rigged up, and all of the power to the city is cut. Shannon proclaims her love for him, and it comes to light that she was the other woman.

WAIT.

Really? Judd Nelson was awesome as the rebellious John Bender in *The Breakfast Club*, but age has beaten him into the ground like a group of over-zealous cops pulling over Rodney King.

Plus, why do I need to know this ten minutes away from the end credits? The city of St. Louis is about to be destroyed along with the rest of the world, I've had to deal with Judd Nelson and Kristy Swanson wearing the same facial expressions for the past hour and a half, and now I have to live with the image of them boinking seared into my brain with a red hot iron from the fires of Hell!?

Thanks, SyFy! Thanks for being no better than the Nazis!

ANYWHO, after describing what he's doing by directly ripping off Sam Neil from *Event Horizon*, Bryce jumps into the vehicle and races off in a chase oddly familiar to *Back to the Future*.

He lures the entity in, the black hole collapses, and everything is okay. In fact, everything is so "okay," that even after we see shots of what's left of St. Louis in ruins, they find him walking around in the city with no damage to the buildings or streets. Traffic is moving as usual, and people are walking around as if nothing had happened.

Yay! Judd Nelson, the Angry Drunken Geek, is the hero!

Shoot me.

VERDICT: WHY!?

This movie was about as pointless as *Eat, Pray, Love*. Not that I expect much from a SyFy movie, but I have to wonder if the budget wasn't eaten up by Disney for making robots that look like Kristy Swanson and Judd Nelson for the roles. The acting in this movie had more wood than a porno flick.

I have to say that it officially shows your failure as a human being if you have stoop to being in one of these movies just to buy some eggs from

Wal-Mart because your career tanked after *Mannequin*. I had to pause it every now and then so I could hit myself in the head with a sledgehammer to relieve the pain.

It wasn't as bad as *Mutant Chronicles*, but it was definitely worse than the second *Sleepaway Camp* movie and way more random than an EA Game (Gamers will know what I did there). I had no problem watching *Strawberry Shortcake* with my daughter later on because those movies are actually more intelligent than *The Black Hole*.

I am now traumatized and suffer from flashbacks of the laundry room and being assaulted by horny, criminally insane llamas with mommy issues.

The Final Days of Planet Earth...and Daryl Hannah's career

The fourth and final (thank God) movie in the Sci-Fi 4-pack was, arguably, the best one. Does this mean it was good? About as good as the idea of tongue-bathing a sweaty sumo wrestler.

It was the third movie in Hallmark's line of sci-fi action flicks, and another three-hour long waste of brain cells that makes *Mortal Kombat* look like *Dead Poet's Society*. The only headliner was Daryl Hannah, who apparently didn't walk away with much of a career after being completely upstaged by Uma Thurman in *Kill Bill*.

Lloyd Walker is an archaeologist with a curiosity for all things ancient and a mean streak towards other living people. Marianne is an exterminator who also is a specialist in entomology, or the study of all things creepy-crawly.

After an archaeological dig sinks into the Earth and is covered in concrete during a painfully obvious government cover-up, Walker begins to suspect something isn't quite right. He also develops a crush on Liz Quinlin, an assistant at City Hall who shares his suspicions. Walker gets a tidbit from a reporter and is sent to a waiting area in the lower levels of City Hall after telling Liz of his discovery of alien-looking pods beneath the city.

All hell breaks loose when he and a few people from the waiting area escape and ambush the bug-people working in the lab. They are harvesting humans for what they call "jacketing," a method in which they use our skin as a disguise. Walker is poisoned during the escape and goes to find Liz. He passes out on her couch as she tries to find the location of his refugees, and we see in the window reflection that she is all buggy and stuff.

Not only is she a bug, she's the queen.

Walker realizes this when he follows her to City Hall and sees her drinking some sugar-water with her mandibles.

In case you are wondering, by the way, yes, I am skipping a lot of movie time because, frankly, nothing much happens other than repeat incidents up until we find out that Daryl Hannah is a bug. No, I mean in the movie she's a bug. In fact, I swear some of the scenes were shown multiple times and just shot from a different angle with other characters photoshopped in.

I digress.

Walker and his crew decide to go and recruit Phillips, an astronaut who was on the same mission that Quinlin and her cronies were on when the bugs took them and came to Earth. The difference? Phillips is poisonous to them. Therefore, they have been keeping him alive to experiment on him.

Walker then takes the crowd to the hive (Yes, he knows exactly where it is having never been there before! LOOPHOLE!!!!) and confronts the queen. By coincidence, the entire population of alien insects (read: giant praying mantis bugs ripped straight from season one of *Buffy the Vampire Slayer*) is present and tending to the nest. Phillips steps up and Walker rushes his group out as Phillips makes his final stand against the queen and detonates a grenade. The entire bug menace is wiped out.

The end. Fini.

IT TOOK 3 F**KING HOURS TO DO THIS!!!

I have seen crippled turtles in a manic depression mate faster. It was like listening to an overactive kindergartner explain the Theory of Relativity using her own words!

VERDICT: The hell with this movie! The hell with the whole pack!

Usually one of these collections has a decent movie in it while the others carry the value of a bin of used diapers belonging to a gorilla with nuclear bowels. The acting was decent, but how much can you do with a script comprised mostly of "What are we gonna do!?"

Daryl Hannah must have it hard up because she approaches her role with the crazed "I can't get any other work" look in her eye that Jamie Lee Curtis has in her Dannon Yogurt commercials.

The bugs are CG that was actually decent given that it was a low-budget attempt to retell the *Invasion of the Body Snatchers* (badly). While not as bad as the others, it still ranks down there with feeling the revenge of the Mexican dinner you had coming on full force while watching a live production of *The Phantom of the Opera* you paid top dollar for just so you could sit right up front and look up Christine's skirt.

If someone offers you a chance to watch this movie, or this entire collection for that matter, please beat them with the business end of a plastic spoon while bashing them about the head and shoulders with a paper plate.

The Last Sentinel: Apocalyptic Randomness

Sci-Fi Collector's Set.

That's what the four-pack that this misguided shart came in is called. I look at this and instantly wonder what kind of person willingly collects bad movies, particularly in sets of four. Then I look at my movie collection and die a little on the inside as the realization hits me like the aftermath of a meal at Ryan's Steakhouse and Buffet.

Oh well, it happens.

This movie was number two, following *The Black Hole* like a piece of ultra-soft toilet paper stuck in the hair of a fat man's a**. It stars Don "The Dragon" Wilson and Katee Sackhoff: two actors with little to no personality playing characters with little to no personality in a movie that looks like it was written by a depressed shut-in with little to no personality.

Talis (Wilson) is the last surviving member of an elite squad called the EE700 (we don't find this out until halfway in). We hear a constant female voice speaking in monotone, and we soon find out that it is his rifle. It talks to him.

No, I am not making this up. It almost seems to have a thing for him. Dude-man's gun is totally crushing on him.

Might have made the movie better, because LORD KNOWS the story sure as hell didn't!

Anywho, Talis soon meets up with Girl (Sackhoff), and that really is her character's name. Girl. Real creative. They live in a world dominated by the Drone Police—an army made up of clones meant to serve and protect.

Drones...clones...someone is gonna get sued.

The Drones turn on humanity (shock) and Talis and Girl decide to save the world by storming a facility and blowing it up between flashbacks of Talis's background in the EE700.

Yes, I am pretty much telling it the way it plays out. No build-up, not a lot of dialogue.

The Drones nab Girl, and Talis goes to save her by throwing away his humanity (Don Wilson has none to give, so I'm still trying to figure that one out) and embracing his inner killer. He easily defeats the Drone army, including the Master Drone, and Girl emerges from the shadows.

Twist? No.

She and Talis walk off together in the setting sun, the world safe from Drones. The end. I am now less of a human being for watching this crap.

VERDICT: MAKE IT DIE!!

Of all the s**t movies I've seen, this one ranks up there with *Battlefield Earth* and *Dirty Dancing: Havana Nights*.

The acting is wooden, to be kind. Ah, screw kindness. I've seen comatose hippos give a higher caliber performance than these two. Don Wilson and Katee Sackhoff have no chemistry on screen whatsoever. The onscreen kiss between these two is akin to hugging the sweaty fat kid in class that smells like sour milk and practices his Ninja Turtle moves on the playground during lunch, and the Drones took their lessons in firearms from Storm Troopers.

I haven't seen a movie this random since *The Sweetest Thing*. I haven't seen anything this pointless since the notion of a sequel to *Sex and the City*. The mere existence of this movie is proof that anyone can make a movie. It is the smear left by the spot that Hollywood forgot to wipe.

Masters of the Universe: Don't mess with the "do," man...

Let me start by saying that, as a child, I thought this was one of the most awesome movies EVER. A real-live He-Man fighting a real-live Skeletor in a real-live Eternia? How can this go wrong!?

Quickly. And tragically.

Let me start by saying that this movie, while silly at most times, is not really terrible. It has its moments, and though the 80's glam is woefully present right down to the blaring synthesizers to indicate the fantasy realm of Eternia this movie does as it promises: we get to see what He-Man looks like in real life.

So they pick a complete robot to play him.

Not that Dolph Lundgren is a bad actor, it's just that he's not a leading man. Hell, even with that hair, he's not a leading lady either.

In fact, he works best when he has next to no lines and is beating up on Sylvester Stallone.

Castle Grayskull has been laid to siege by Skeletor and his army, and they have captured the Sorceress…wait a sec.

The Sorceress? In the cartoon she's this rockin' hot babe in a bird outfit. In this movie she's a middle-aged woman in a crystal crown and white robes who looks like she just got first class on the menopause train.

What the hell? Already?

Skeletor storms into the throne room to meet with Evil-Lyn and Beast-Man. He has one of two Cosmic Keys, a device that is capable of opening a portal between worlds. It's how he was able to take Grayskull.

Meanwhile He-Man and his friends, Teela and Man-At-Arms, meet up with a dwarven inventor named Gwildor who has the other Cosmic Key. He was the one who invented it and is being pursued by Skeletor in order to make more. The heroes warp to Castle Grayskull but are outnumbered by Skeletor's army.

Gwildor randomly presses buttons on the Cosmic Key and opens a portal to…aw, crap.

A fast food joint in Wittier, California.

This is where the movie begins to dive fast. While I can forgive the absence of Battle Cat, the complete lack of regard that He-Man is actually Prince Adam of Eternia, and the fact that Snake Mountain is merely mentioned in the film and never shown, moving this kind of fantasy realm conflict into our world is a mistake.

Kevin and his girlfriend, Julie (Hey, kids! It's Courtney Cox!), are a couple who stumble upon the Cosmic Key that Gwildor lost during the trip from Eternia. They mistake it for a fancy synthesizer, and Kevin runs off to have a friend look at it while Julie waits at the school.

Karg and his team attack, and Julie barely escapes before being cornered by them. He-Man comes to the rescue and fights them off, saving Julie who doesn't really seem that fazed that a bunch of cosplayers are beating the crap out of each other and shooting off laser guns in an alley…

What the hell? Where is the rest of the population? How do people not notice this!?

Skeletor kills off Saurod and sends Karg and his crew back to Earth with Evil-Lyn in charge to find the key and bring it back along with He-Man. They find Kevin, who is frantically searching for Julie with the aid of Detective Lubic (James Tolkan, for you *Back to the Future* fans). They learn about the location of the Cosmic Key and leave.

Julie and the Eternians find Kevin and discover that Lubic now has the key and is at the music store questioning Kevin's friend. They get there at the same time as Evil-Lyn and are ambushed in a fight that ends with He-Man in shackles, the Cosmic Key destroyed by Skeletor, and a fungus on Julie's leg.

While Lubic, Kevin, and the Eternians try to rebuild the Key and take care of Julie, Skeletor begins the public torture of He-Man to force him to bow to him. He-Man refuses, and Skeletor punishes him worse. As the moon positions itself in the sky, Skeletor absorbs the Power of Grayskull and becomes a demi-god.

Before he can destroy He-Man, our funky bunch from Earth show up at Grayskull after getting the Cosmic Key to work. He-Man uses the distraction to break free and reclaims his sword, his power returning as he raises it and bellows his tagline: "I HAVE THE POWER!"

Or is it "I need a shower?"

He-Man and Skeletor battle, and He-Man manages to break Skeletor's staff and return him to his normal state. Skeletor draws his sword to fight, but He-Man pushes him off into a moat far below, killing him. The rest of Skeletor's army flees, and the heroes reclaim Castle Grayskull.

Gwildor sends Kevin and Julie back to Earth after the newly freed Sorceress heals Julie with something a little better than antibiotics. Julie awakens the day of her parent's death and is able to prevent the event, and she reunites with Kevin and their memories of Eternia.

The End.

VERDICT: Kinda Frustrating.

Why frustrating, you ask? Because it's easier to watch a movie that can't decide if it wants to be a horror movie or a comedy. This movie can't decide if it wants to be a good movie or a bad movie. The scenes in Eternia are fantastic, with effects that really pushed the cinematography of the 80's hard and great acting from Frank Langella (Skeletor).

I mean, if they ever decide to remake this movie and do it correctly (leave out the whole Earth bit), Frank Langella would HAVE to come back as Skeletor even if it might just be his voice. Dolph, on the other hand, quite successfully removes all personality from the He-Man character on the whole. Man-At-Arms and Teela were pretty spot-on, but where the f**k did "Gwildor" come from!?

The movie very much nods to Jack Kirby's *Fourth World* comic book series and also has elements of Thor involved but tends to leave the original source material by the wayside. If anything, the biggest culprit was the glam. Oh dear God, the glam.

The costumes are great, though Karg is the poster boy for the 80's glam in fantasy characters, and you can see the cloth in the nostrils on Skeletor's mask. Not that this diminished the film, really, though Man-At-Arms and Teela could've used a little more flare than the dull outfits they were rocking. Evil-Lyn looked pretty cool, and Beast-Man was the only character that was almost spot-on with the cartoon.

All in all, despite the shortcomings (like no Battle Cat and Dolph's lousy acting), this movie is not terrible. It actually does have some of its fanboy service and charm, though the whole meshing with the Earth Realm thing has to go.

What happens in Eternia stays in Eternia.

If you DO decide to watch it, keep a few things in mind. First, it's the 80's. Technology was limited, so the effects are nowhere NEAR the quality we have today. Second, it's the 80's. If it made money as a toy franchise, there was no question that a movie was going to happen. Lastly, it's the 80's. We just really didn't know any better.

Dedicated, in loving memory, to Collin Gilbert
You will forever be my best fan and my baby brother
September 16th, 1980 - March 19th, 2014

The Phoenix Rises: Not even close

Oh, okay. It's another one of THOSE.

I was told about this movie at work by a fan who's pretty much become one of my distributors. Apparently he wasn't able to finish it, being turned off of the film within the first fifteen minutes.

A movie someone can't finish? I readily accepted the challenge! Granted, I've watched movies I haven't been able to finish, but they were either that awful or had blatant violence against children. Even I have my limits.

I should've told him to use it as an interstate Frisbee.

Oh, well. Let's hit play on yet another dog turd of a movie.

This s**t stain starts with a group of scientists gathered in a command center, presumably at the Pentagon. They are firing a laser beam into the sky when another laser beam comes back and hits the building. The screen begins to distort, as does the sound, and the team hits the floor screaming and covering their ears.

Okay, I'll bite. Another one where things are happening right awa—

Ah, crap.

It's one of THOSE movies. You know the ones, right? The movies that start at the end, then take you back and bring up to that point in time? Yeah, there's a right and wrong way to do that. This movie did it wrong by transitioning EVERY F**KING SCENE with clips and bites of the opening sequence.

Okay, breathe man. Just breathe.

Jack, one of the members of the elite scientific research group known as "Phoenix," is tasked with picking up Tom, a government official, from the airport. After a gunfight with a chick that looks like Richard O'Brian with boobs, the two manage to make it safely back to Phoenix headquarters.

Jan, Jack's girlfriend, is not at all happy about the gunfight. However, her concerns, and the gunfire, are soon forgotten by the entire group as Tom reveals the nature of his visit. Turns out he's part of a team that has helped create "Project Phoenix," a system that controls the ionosphere and can create weather conditions.

Unfortunately, terrorists have gotten a hold of the coding and built their own Project Phoenix. Phoenix…OKAY. Even I'M getting confused. Team Phoenix is now officially known as Team Yawn. Why Yawn? Because the writing is atrocious, and the acting isn't much better! I am SO BORED. WHY ISN'T ANYTHING HAPPENING?

Damn you, bait and hook. Damn you.

The next several scenes are nothing but relationship exposition hell as we watch the group research different ideas on how to combat the terrorist attack on the weather. Strange how they all know EXACTLY when the strike is going to be…

Tom reassures the team with possibly the most epic line in the entire movie. It's the line that keeps me going and makes the group believe in themselves.

"Your country needs you to do this!"

Sorry, I got delirious there. Nothing a few good whacks on the desk with my head didn't fix.

About three-fourths of the way into the movie, Jan and Maryanne, the other girl in the Team Yawn group, are kidnapped by Maxine (Richard O'Brian chick) and Jamal. Maxine speaks only Russian, but Jamal speaks English with a Jamaican accent.

SO WHY DOES HE HAVE SUBTITLES!?

Ugh, this movie is killing me! I can't friggin' do this!

Anyway, Tom assembles a team and goes after Jan and Maryanne. He caps one in Jamal's face, and Maxine escapes. Jack is glad that Jan is back. He and Jan have been having problems because Jan feels like Jack cares more about work than her. Jan and Tom share a kiss and then Tom leaves.

WHO CARES? I want to see some weather disaster, dammit.

More exposition, more whining about interpersonal relationships that just need to end either in bad sex or gunfire, and we get to D-Day. Yup, back at the beginning of the movie. Only now we see that the team survives and has a plan of attack. They fight off the terrorist beam with minimal effort.

That's it. They fight off the beam. Poof. Done.

Jack and Keith show up with rings the next day and propose to Jan and Maryanne. Maryanne is thrilled, Jan not so much. Credits.

No joke. Credits.
VERDICT: SEND IT BACK TO THE ASHES!

What makes a bad movie good, you ask? Charm. Take a dog, for example. You may see a dog that looks like he's been beaten with the ugly stick up one side of his face and down the other, but he's endearing because he's sweet and chill.

Bad movies can be the same way. They're cheesy and campy, but they're endearing because they're just fun to watch.

NOT the case with *The Phoenix Rises*.

This is supposed to be a movie about a team fighting terrorists that can control dangerous weather systems. Why, in the name of Alfred Hitchcock's baggy chin, do I give a crap about watching a group of number crunchers come up with an idea to counter the enemy laser with a laser of their own?

The exposition in the movie isn't even the main problem. First, the writing is awful. Obviously the writer has his DVR set to record anything and everything on SyFy. The plot in this movie has been beaten to death. Instead of a special effects extravaganza, we get eighty minutes of dialogue and about five minutes of actual event. The pink laser column coming out of the top of the building is the heaviest the effects get. The rest is literally all talk.

Speaking of talk, bad acting is next on my attack list. I haven't seen acting this wooden since the Presidential debate, you pick which year. News Anchors have more personality than these people! Their facial expressions look less like they're conveying emotions and more like the entire cast is battling an epidemic of constipation on the set.

The sets, oh God, the sets. The "command center" set has been used in so many different campy SyFy originals that I actually knew where each station was before the characters did. It's the same idea as the one standard house set they use for most sitcoms. Ever notice that? The staircase is in the same spot, relatively. The kitchen is separated from the living room by a swinging door and (at times) a window. The front door has steps leading up to a foyer of some kind.

I could go on and on, but I'm just glad I made it through. I haven't had this hard of a time watching a bad movie since *1313 Cougar Cult*.

Stonados: Rocks in the Gas Tank

How to Make a SyFy Disaster Movie in One Easy Step!
DON'T.

Following the huge success that was *Sharknado,* Syfy decided that they needed this tornado silliness to keep going strong. *Sharknado* came out in July of 2013, so while the fans eagerly await the upcoming *Sharknado 2,* why not give them a swift kick to the sensitive areas with a new original?

Ladies and gentlemen: *Stonados!*

(Crickets.)

Takers? Anyone?

The movie opens with a tour guide leading a group to Plymouth Rock Memorial to view the actual rock. Out of nowhere, a waterspout kicks up, and a tornado forms in the bay. The rock and the tour guide are lifted up and sucked into the storm, along with the tour guide. The storm dissipates.

Meanwhile, the movie goes through a montage of people living their everyday lives. One is a shot of two guys playing basketball. When one of them wins, he stands beneath the goal and delivers the customary smack-talk.

And then he becomes the jelly in a Plymouth Rock-asphalt sandwich.

Joe Randall (Paul Johansson) is a high school science teacher. He is outside conducting class when he gets a call from Maddy (Miranda Frigon), his cop sister, to come look at the Plymouth Rock incident. Joining him on the scene is his old partner, Lee (Sebastian Spence). Turns out these two used to be expert storm chasers.

What are the odds?

Sigh.

Joe decides to head back to Boston to get his kids to safety. Megan (Jessica McLeod) and her brother, Jackson (Dylan Schmid), are walking around the harbor where Megan is supposed to meet a friend. She makes Jackson promise to sit on a bench and not move until she gets back. He is obviously younger sibling (Dude, he's 14 at least).

Bad Movie Beware!

Just as Joe, Maddy, and Lee show up to the harbor, another waterspout kicks up, flinging large rocks and boulders everywhere. People are scrambling for cover as the harbor gets hamme—

Wait a sec. What the f**k?

There are rocks the size of basketballs and larger being hurled from a tornado, and stuff isn't getting demolished. In fact, all of the damage localized for each particular shot. No buildings explode from the impact, no walls collapse, nothing. Given the fact that the rocks also explode, you would think that there would be more carnage.

Nothing.

Yup. Exploding rocks.

(Beats head on desk)

The storm backs off, and Joe is reunited with his kids. Jackson trips out because Megan left him alone even though she was supposed to be watching him.

The kid is obviously fourteen because that's how old the actor was. I guess Jackson is supposed to be like ten or eleven, not really sure. But his voice is deeper than it should be, and he's almost as tall as his sister. It's like if they got Michael Keaton to come play Tiny Tim in *A Christmas Carol* just because he's short.

Suck it up, kid. YOU'RE A TEEN.

Of course, since this is a SyFy flick and there IS a formula to follow, the crew heads to the obligatory government agency to tell them what's going on. The agency follows the formula to the letter and blows them off. Joe stays up for the night and creates a storm simulation that shows that Boston may be wiped off the map.

What a shock. I wonder if he knows this is a disaster movie?

Joe shows the simulation to Lee, and they head off to find Maddy. Megan and Jackson decide to go the football game that is going on that day since the skies are clear and the weather report shows nothing on the radar.

Things go to hell quickly when a gigantic waterspout erupts in the harbor, takes out the local lighthouse, and begins to destroy Boston. Joe, Lee, and Maddy rush to the football game to find the kids. They are reunited, and the group escapes.

Back at Obligatory Government Headquarters, Joe shows Tara (Thea Gill) the simulation. Tara is the head of the agency that blew him off last time, but the latest reports coming in combined with Joe's mock-up make her a believer.

Tara shows the group the solution they have come up with to stop the tornado before it lays Boston to waste. Unbeknownst to our heroes, the government has been working on a top secret "G-14 Classified" (Jackie Chan fans will get the reference) technology to stop extreme storms.

A rocket launcher.

WHAT!? THAT'S IT!? This whole time, all these years, countries have had to endure Mother Nature's struggles with PMS through hurricanes, tornados, monsoons, tsunamis, and the like! All we had to do was target some ICBMs and blow the motherf**ker to Kingdom Come!? WHY DIDN'T I THINK OF THAT!?

Oh yeah. Because I tie my own shoelaces.

The group, including the kids and Tara from the agency, climbs into an SUV and drives to the base of the tornado. As Joe is about to fire the bomb into the storm, Tara jumps in front of him to commend him on how brave he is for risking his life to save so many. Because, you know, that's what you do in these situations. The last second when the fecal material is a'flyin' is always speech time.

She is then deleted by a stone.

And what do Joe and Lee do? They pretty much shrug and say "aaanyway," then go back to prepping the rocket launcher like nothing happened. That moment, that precise moment, was priceless!

I won't say how they eventually get the bomb into the storm, but it's predictable. The storm blows up, everyone's happy, everyone's dreams come true. Happiest of endings all wrapped up in a nice neat little SyFy bow.

VERDICT: DUH!!

I love a good ignorant movie. I'm an OLD SCHOOL *Transformers* fan, and I loved Michael Bay's movies because of what they were. I wanted to sit down with a bucket of popcorn, shut my brain off for a while, and watch robots shoot the s**t out of everything. Bay's *Transformers* movies deliver on this nicely.

Stonados, on the other hand, WAY over-delivers on the stupidity to the point of just plain dumb. The solution to horrific and destructive weather is to blow it up with a bomb. REALLY!?

Well, hey, it worked in *Sharknado,* right?

The acting is laughable, but the script is almost as shallow as the script for the *Super Mario Bros.* movie, so I can kind of cut the actors a break here. You can't really build a mall out of toilet paper and toothpicks, but you sure can shoot a movie with the proper amount of poop and wet wipes.

The only character that really grated on my nerves was Jackson. The actor did what he could with what he had, but the character was the most dependent, needy, whiney little girl of a 14-year-old boy I have seen since Draco Malfoy in the *Harry Potter* series.

The books, people. Read Recklessly.

The characters also do a lot of stupid things without any possible rhyme or reason. Lee is stopped by a large fortuneteller woman during the storm so she can randomly accuse him of being a lousy weather man, Tara likes to make press conference speeches while the city is falling down around her, and the kids just want to go with their daddy into the heart of Armageddon to watch daddy fire a rocket into a tornado.

They missed boatloads of opportunities with the effects. Buildings receive little to no damage from the storms, and every scene has its own set of damage for the shot. I understand that effects cost money, but what the hell. At least TRY. Break out the PS One and at least make the effort. *Vicious* had the WORST effects of any movie I've seen, but at least they tried.

If you want to shut your brain off for a while, and you are a die-hard SyFy fan, go ahead and watch *Stonados.* But be warned! You will probably lose consciousness from the sheer stupidity, and wake up to find that you've spent the past hour and a half licking the windows in your house.

Hours you will never get back.

At least the windows will be clean.

Supernova: The sun is going to blaaaaaahhhhhhh...

Yet another from the good ol' Sci-Fi 4-pack. One would think that when I manage to happen across a collection of copious crap like this that I would watch one, then move on and assume that all of them suck. Alas, I always have hope that at least one will attempt to redeem the collection. Then again, I may be wrong and end up feeling like I have been taken advantage of or cheated because I at least want to be kissed while I'm being...

ONWARD!!

Peter Fonda stars as Dr. Shepherd. Shepherd finds through a mathematical formula figured out by his colleague Chris (Luke Perry) that the sun is actually older than we thought and that it is going to supernova in a matter of days.

Or weeks. Or hours. He really isn't that specific.

In fact, this whole movie isn't that specific. His assistant, Ginny (Clemency Burton-Hill), sets off for the day to see her boyfriend. Meanwhile, Chris returns home to his family only to be told by his wife that she is still having nightmares about the serial killer that came after her and their daughter a year ago. Chris tells her that he has to leave...

WHY, GOD, WHY IS THIS DRAGGING OUT SO LONG!?

I grab the case and look at the running time. One hundred and seventy minutes. Almost three hours long!? Jesus.

Let's skip ahead.

Chris and a team of European scientists are picked up by Agent Delgado (Tia Carrere) and whisked away to an underground facility ruled by Lance Henrickson. Just when I didn't think it would stop, we get more explanations of what is happening on the sun.

Meanwhile, the Earth is getting firebombed as the sun readies itself to explode. Chaos erupts, and the serial killer Grant Cole (who cares?) escapes to come after Chris's family. A British reporter named Laurie Stephenson shows up and has history with Henrickson that dates back to Bosnia. About six scenes later, each one ending with a dramatic gaze into the distance by the character during their close up, we get another explanation of what is going on with the sun.

Bad Movie Beware!

OKAY, I GET IT. THE SUN IS EXPLODING. WE'RE F**KED. MOVE ON.

More chaos, more bad acting, and we get a close up of Ginny with her "Oh, my God" gaze that comes off more like her "Ermahgerd!" face.

Complete with tongue hanging out. I can't make this up.

More chaos, more Cole grunting as he plots his revenge, more explanations of what is happening with the sun, and we get credits! The movie is over!

No, it's not!

WE STILL HAVE PART 2!

The second half of this Hallmark miniseries opens with a thrash-metal theme, and I find myself headbanging while holding up the heavy metal hand. I then apologize to the metal Gods and all that is Iron Maiden and continue my self-inflicted torture.

Guess what? It's another hour and a half of the same friggin' thing that went on in the first half!

It all climaxes in a secret lab with a government plot, Ginny, Laurie, Chris, two never-before-introduced colleagues, and dramatic music. Suddenly, in one sphincter-tightening moment, Chris realizes that he made a mathematical error. He added a plus sign where there should have been a minus.

I hate it when I do that. Psh.

Poof! The sun stops blowing up, everyone is happy, and the Supernova is averted! Yes, it took three hours for Hallmark to tell me that Luke Perry is a complete idiot who made his career by making out with Shannon Doherty and should have stopped with his bit role in the *Fifth Element*.

But WAIT!! It's not over! Suddenly, someone decided to inject *Friday the 13th* DNA into the script, and Grant Cole shows up to butcher Chris's wife for sending him to prison. Chris is almost killed by Cole when his wife shoots him. Then end. No, really.

Christ.

VERDICT: DRAINED.

Watching this movie was about as fun as having shishkabob skewers rammed under my toenails. What's sad is that this might be the good movie on the 4-pack, making the whole collection an utter failure (in case you haven't guessed, I'm SO optimistic about the final movie in the collection).

Peter Fonda may have been great in his younger days, but it looks like Kevin Costner got ahold of him and retrained him to have less personality than the Terminator.

Yes, I mean the Governor of California, not the cool robot from the movie.

Tia Carrere's acting was better in *Wayne's World*, and don't even go there with Luke Perry. Dude, you are not Justin Timberlake, so stop trying to act like him.

I have also determined that the Sci-Fi community hates the Saint Louis Arch because this is the third movie in a row that I have seen its destruction. I thought it was established by *Planet of the Apes* that we hated the Statue of Liberty, but I guess that just goes to show what an out-of-date nerd I am.

I have seen Do-It-Yourself videos on how to properly use a commode that are more interesting than this movie. Ben Stein ("Bueller...Bueller...") would have made this movie more fun to watch. Hell, watching reruns of *The Facts of Life* on Lifetime (read: The Ovary Channel) would be more intellectually stimulating than this pile of goat poo.

Teenagers from Outer Space: In space no one can see you drool...

...what the hell...

Okay, I'll start by saying that this isn't the worst movie I've ever seen. By no means is it good. In fact, it rates right down there with *Battlefield Earth*. The difference: I didn't feel like my soul was being sucked out of my body through my eyeballs the entire time I was watching it.

Travolta can have that effect on people.

It's black-and-white, and it's an indie, circa 1959. Why is this significant? The last skid mark in Hollywood's underpants I watched tried like hell to recreate the 1950's styles and slang. But badly. I equated watching *Eegah: The Name Written in Blood* to having my nose hairs trimmed with an Epilady. This movie isn't painful so much as it is just boring.

A ship lands in the desert, and the hatch opens just as a dog runs up and starts barking at the man climbing out. He fires a ray gun at the pup, reducing him to a skeleton. The gunman removes his mask, as do his comrades, and we meet the only two who seem to have names: Derek and Thor. Derek is a quiet, mild-mannered young man while Thor is a sadist and kills for the sake of killing.

It was at this moment that I began looking for heroin.

The group is on Earth to drop off a gargon: an animal that they breed on their planet for food. Derek turns on the crew and flees. Thor is sent after him with instructions to kill without prejudice.

Derek ends up at the home of Betty and Grandpa (yeah, the names were really creative). Betty and Grandpa show him around, and soon Derek inadvertently becomes their tenant in a room in the house. Thor follows Derek into town, killing people along the way with his ray gun. Betty and Derek elude him consistently but are finally captured by Thor when Thor is shot in the shoulder. He forces them to take him in for medical attention.

Meanwhile, Reporter Joe and a random cop are exploring the desert and come across the cave where the gargon was left. The gargon has grown gigantic and devours the cop as Joe flees. Derek and Betty face off with

Thor in a car chase that ends with Thor driving over a cliff and getting arrested.

Wait, it gets better. No, I'm lying. It doesn't.

Derek and Betty return to the desert to find the gargon...WHAT IN THE NAME OF OPRAH'S FAT A** ON TOAST IS THAT!? No, seriously. I'm really seeing this! The gargon is the shadow of a lobster superimposed onto the screen and put into slow motion to create the effect of being gigantic. I know the 50's were a bit limited, but c'mon!

Betty and Derek connect the power lines nearby to Thor's broken ray gun and kill the gargon, but it's too late. A full-scale invasion from Derek's home world is on its way. Derek reunites with his father, the leader of the Space Teens, and orders the legion to approach at too great a speed.

A giant explosion borrowed from some other movie claims the lives of all of the space people. Betty, Grandpa, and Joe walk away with their heads down as Derek's last words echo something about never leaving Earth.

Except for the pieces that got launched into orbit.

VERDICT: Golly-Gee! Shoot me now!

Not that I take issue with the 50's, but I have to know if it really was that...MaGoo...back then. Anyone?

I'll start with the acting. I guess Skynet found a way to send a Terminator back to the 50's with the purpose of opening an acting school. The acting is, literally, mechanical. Derek shows no emotion, and Betty is mechanical and overacted at the same time. Wrap your head around that one.

I've already gone over the effects on the gargon, but the cost-cutting costumes and props bear mentioning. The spacesuits were second-hand jumpsuits with masking tape and flight helmets, and their space boots were tennis shoes covered with white socks. No, really.

The writing, while atrocious, had its moments and is what feebly attempts to save this movie. Granted, the dialogue is the same vernacular as *Troll 2* (pidgin English), but there are some key points that help move things along. Unfortunately, this didn't really make me care much as to what was going on, and I ended up watching the movie with the same energy and excitement as I show when I am drugged, drunk, and asleep.

Holiday Hoopla

The holidays are a time of year for giving, being good to others, and spending time with family. What better way to ring in the season than subjecting your loved ones to ocular rape by forcing them at gun point to watch these acts of abuse on the intelligence of the average viewer?

Easter Bunny, Kill! Kill!: Grindhouse at its finest

Back in the 70's a form of burlesque dubbed "Grindhouse" hit the drive-ins and movie theaters around the country. Grindhouse films were exploitation films that played on large amounts of violence, sex, and drug-use mixed with absurdity. The plotlines were thin at best, and the characters were more caricatures of your basic horror film stereotypes. Bad guys weren't just bad guys; they were sleezoids. The good guys were sappy and wholesome almost to faultlessness, and the others were just fodder for the serial killer in the movie.

Grindhouse movies, as bad as they were, did not lie about what they were and what they represented. Thus, the cult following is huge. Even after the death of the genre, the movies are hailed as Trash Theater Masterpieces. The problem is that many young filmmakers of the current generation do not simply nod to Grindhouse.

They try to recreate it.

Easter Bunny, Kill! Kill! isn't the worst movie I've ever seen, but it's bad even for what it is. Still, the director did his research and came up with a Grindhouse film that would have nestled in just fine with the others back in the 70's. The characters are way overdone, and the movie is unforgivably violent and exploitative. Bear in mind that this movie is meant to be what it is: rough, over-the-top, and gritty.

And stupid. Very, very stupid.

The movie opens during a robbery in a convenience store at the hands of a man wearing a very goofy-looking Easter Bunny mask. He shoots the clerk in the mouth with the shotgun, then heads off after stealing a few chocolate rabbits. Scene change to Nicholas, a retarded teen living with his single mother who works the night shift at the hospital.

Enter Remington, the new sleaze-bag boyfriend who is also, very obviously, the killer from the opening sequence. Meanwhile, Nicholas takes out the trash and is given a live bunny rabbit by a strange hobo. Remington is very affectionate and caring to Nicholas's mother, Mindy. But when she is out of sight, he is abusive to Nicholas and plays on his weakness caused by his mental disability. See, I was being real there. Lenny from *Of Mice and Men* retarded, not Nikki Haley retarded.

Mindy is unaware of the abuse and leaves for work after Remington promises her that he will take care of Nicholas.

She leaves, and he immediately calls his pedophile associate to come over and keep Nicholas "occupied" while Remington goes out on the town to pick up hookers and drugs. Remington leaves, and the pervert is slaughtered by a killer wearing the Easter Bunny mask from earlier.

The two Mexican helpers from an earlier scene arrive to sneak into the house and collect some things along with a giant brute of a bodyguard, and all three are slaughtered by the bunny killer.

Remington returns with his whore in tow, and the two girls are killed within minutes of being in the house. Remington catches the killer cutting up the last girl, and the killer is wearing the mask backwards. I won't spoil the ending for you, since I know some of you are into the Grindhouse thing, but it ends pretty neatly for what it is. It almost reminded me of the television show *Monsters*.

VERDICT: Meh.

Truthfully, I'm not into the Grindhouse thing. But, I was willing to give this one a look. It was an art film, but there were too many issues that seemed to plague the movie (such as the green light on the entire project). Grindhouse began in the 1970's, and ended in the 1980's, roughly. It really needs to stay dead. With the birth of the internet, there is nothing really shocking about them anymore. Watch it if you're a fan of the genre, or if you feel like being really ignorant for an hour and a half.

Jack Frost: Awkward. That's all I've got. Awkward.

With Christmas right around the corner and a compulsive need to watch horror movies (particularly utter s**t), I stumbled across this waste of time from 1997.

Keep in mind that a family-friendly movie starring Michael Keaton came out under the same title, and that really sent video stores into a frenzy as horrified parents returned this pile a crap because they had rented it thinking they were in for the feel-good movie of the season and not a reject from Santa's septic tank.

This movie, thankfully, recognizes itself as a comedy. The one-liners get classic sometimes, but some of the sequences are poorly written and Jack's jokes fall a little...melted.

Jack Frost, notorious serial killer, is on a prison transport during the Christmas season. The transport crashes into a tanker truck carrying a genetic material. Jack is doused in the acidic material and is transformed into a maniacal killer snowman.

Yes, I'm telling the truth. Killer snowman. Look it up.

Anyway, small town Sheriff Sam is the reason Jack was put away, and he is still haunted by Jack's threats to come back after him and his family. A giant snowman suddenly appears in his yard, though he writes it off as a creation of the neighborhood kids since his own son, Tommy, denies building it. Tommy is portrayed as the sweetest kid ever, even baking horrific cookies for daddy.

Soon the neighborhood bully is mysteriously decapitated by his own sleigh. Then his father and mother are killed. Enter Shannon Elizabeth. Many of you don't know that she was in this movie. Solid proof that every actor/actress has that one flick that they deny hands down.

Moving along, we find Jack on a rampage as the townsfolk begin to panic. Two Feds show up, both of them having a mysterious connection to the killings. Come to find out that one of them made the genetic goop that transformed Jack into Frosty Krueger.

Meanwhile, Shannon Elizabeth and her boyfriend break into Sam's empty house to have sex. She goes off to get ready, and he hunts down some champagne. Enter Jack, who uses icicles to impale him to the door. Shannon gets gratuitously naked and gets into the bathtub, and we get to see Jack's ability to morph into water as he freezes the tub, assumes his snowman form, and proceeds with the most uncomfortable scene in cinematic history, after which Shannon Elizabeth falls dead and Jack laughs. "Christmas came a little early this year!"

Yeah, use your imagination.

Back at the ranch, Sam and the Feds determine that Jack Frost has somehow returned and soon have an encounter with him when they go to a local home and find him chasing them as running water. With all else failing, Sam panics and uses a hair dryer on Frost, who howls in pain. Realizing Jack's weakness, Sam and the townspeople arm themselves with blow dryers and extension cords.

They force Jack into the furnace in the basement of the church and torch him, but he returns as steam and regains form from the moisture. He corners the science Fed and takes him. In the next scene, Dr. Science is walking by Sam, then suddenly begins to vomit massive amounts of snow. Jack emerges, and Sam panics and throws the cookies at him. Jack screams as the cookie melts half of his head.

Turns out, Tommy put antifreeze in the cookies so his dad wouldn't get cold. So be paranoid when your kids make food for you.

Sam gets the bright idea to have a pick-up truck bed filled to the brim with antifreeze and ends the final confrontation by catapulting Jack into the bed of the truck and killing him.

VERDICT: Okay, FINE.

Okay, so it was a little bit entertaining. Frankly, had the writers tried to take it at all seriously, this movie would have sucked massive donkey balls. As it stands, it's nothing more than a live-action horror/comedy cartoon. The characters are over the top, with the hero being annoyingly heroic and the dimwits being utterly stupid to the point of drooling.

It's difficult not to laugh at the slapstick humor and irony of a snowman that kills people, and many of the one-liners hit the mark even if they do get excessive.

I'd watch it again, but I'd have to be drunk off cheap beer and someone would have to pay me in Krispy-Creme donuts. Warm ones. Glazed only, please.

Krampus, The Christmas Devil: Awkward. SO awkward.

Another one for the compost.

This one came out of left field and is about a character widely ignored during the Christmas season. And for good reason. Who the hell wants to think that Santa has a counterpart that kills off the children who are naughty rather than just let Santa give them a lump of coal?

And why a lump of coal? A more effective present to punish the naughty kids would be something like mowing the lawn while wearing a tutu or having to watch *Manos: The Hands of Fate.*

I know the latter shaped me up pretty good.

Krampus is actually old news. He originated in European lore, mostly in Austria and Germany. The idea is that Santa doesn't just give the bad kids a lump of coal. While St. Nick is out rewarding the kids who were good for the year, Krampus goes house to house and punishes the kids who were naughty.

While this might've been an effective tool to scare kids into behaving back in the day, modern-day kids would be more likely to act up just to see the cool monster.

The movie opens with Krampus dragging a kid wrapped up in a burlap sack across a snowy field. He drops the kid into a hole in the ice covering a lake then leaves. The kid manages to escape and get home, and Krampus runs out of time before he can retrieve the child and punish him.

Fast forward to present day. Jeremy Duffin, the kid from the beginning, is now an adult and a detective with the local police. He's called into work, and his first line in the movie is where the whole damn thing begins the first stages of the flushing process.

Kids have been turning up missing all over town, and Jeremy is juggling his investigation with his personal search for his own childhood abductor. He takes his slack-ass acting skills to the chief, who approves his request to assemble a team and go after the culprit.

Okay, we're ten minutes into the movie, and he already has a bead on the bad guy and a plan of action? Sweet! The pain will be brief on this one...

Oh, God, it's an hour and a half long.

S**t.

Meanwhile, a surly redneck in a Santa outfit storms through the dark like a disgruntled *Hee-Haw* actor and approaches Krampus. Turns out this is "jolly" ol' St. Nick. Father Christmas is deer-huntin' good ol' boy with a mean streak as wide as the Confederacy and the mouth of a sailor.

I half-expected to smell the beer and Copenhagen on his breath through my TV screen.

He tells Krampus to remember that he only has until midnight on Christmas Eve to complete his work and that the naughty children must be punished. He gives a short lecture on how important the work is. Krampus nods and the scene ends.

No, really. That's it.

Jeremy and his crack (head) team of two extras, I mean meatbags for Krampus, hit the woods the next morning armed with automatic rifles and camouflage to find Krampus and save the kidnapped children.

I get it. Totally. With no leads, no info that we know of, and no transition whatsoever, we're just to assume that Jeremy felt a disturbance in the Force and followed it to the woods. Either that, or someone (Jason Hull, writer/director) is a huge *Call of Duty* fan.

Anywho, Krampus takes out the two squad members, killing one and knocking out the other. Jeremy shows up, and Krampus knocks him out as well, then drags the living back to his lair.

There's a young kid, maybe ten, locked up in a chicken wire cage, and there's a girl tied up in a corner wearing nothing but her panties.

Jeremy's partner wakes up, and Krampus kills him. Jeremy wakes up while Krampus is busy fondling the girl and escapes.

Could've freed the boy at least.

Dick.

Santa shows up and frees the girl and boy, then sets Krampus straight and tells him to focus on Jeremy's daughter, Heather.

Jeremy shows back up to the station a mess and is suspended so that they can investigate the murders of the two other officers. In the meantime, Jeremy goes to the local bar to get drunk and ends up in a bar fight with a few of the other cops out there who are angry with him over four other officers who have died during his investigation.

Okay…this would've been good to know in the beginning. Not asking for an entire scene of exposition, but just a line would've been nice.

OH! That's right! MOST OF THE MOVIE IS IMPROV.

Cut to Jeremy's house, where his wife and daughter are besieged by a group of convicts with a vendetta against Jeremy. The leader ties up the wife while one of his thugs chases Heather up to her room.

Keep in mind, this girl is supposed to be like fourteen or fifteen. Obviously she isn't, but we all know how that goes. She easily convinces the thug that she wants to ride him on her bedroom floor, then she stabs him to death with a knife that she just so happened to have in her room.

The leader interrogates Mom in the kitchen, but she doesn't have any idea where Jeremy is. The only question he didn't ask her was WHAT IN THE NAME OF ZEUS'S BUTTHOLE DOES THIS HAVE TO DO WITH KRAMPUS!?

Dude goes outside when he hears a noise, thinking that it might be Jeremy. Krampus shows up in full light, and we see his face as he growls at the criminal and kills him off. Jeremy shows up, sees the carnage in the yard, and finds Heather wandering the yard. He goes in and kills off the last thug, then sends Heather up to her room to hide.

Jeremy frees his wife, then says that Krampus is here and that she needs to get out. I guess it was his Spidey-sense tingling because nothing happens to indicate that Krampus is nearby.

Krampus knocks him down, kills the wife, and leaves with Heather. While the cops storm the house, we cut to the cave where Krampus has Heather tied up and is about to have some holiday fun with her.

Fini.

VERDICT: Santa left a turd in my stocking.

Dear God, this was bad.

It goes back to the fact that, despite what people think, I actually do enjoy a good indie film. Note the operative word there. Budget is an issue, but talent doesn't need financial backing, and improv is just f**king hard to pull off convincingly. I have to give it to the actors in *The Blair Witch Project* because they managed to come off real.

Not these guys!

While it may have been written by Jason Hull, the story seems to be made up by the actors on the fly. They often add in elements during the dialogue that end up being pointless and lead nowhere in the story.

Even entire scenes happen for no real reason, at least not initially. There is no transitioning from scene to scene, so a lot of events that may (or may not) have been built up earlier are seem to come way out of left field because any possible build-up has been forgotten by that point.

The acting, of course, ends up coming off wooden and unrealistic. The actors often repeat the same line over and over while they try to come up with another line that will move the scene along, and a lot of it just ends up being an endless word vomit.

The only saving grace is the costume on Krampus, which is where most of the budget probably went. Now, if only the storyline stuck to that character instead of wandering like a mental patient on thorazine. Though it may try to tell an intense and deep story, the movie is really just one massive SQUIRREL! moment.

Do yourself a favor if you plan on watching *Krampus The Christmas Devil*...ask Santa to bring some morphine and a bottle of whiskey to wash it down. It'll at least cover the smell of Santa's chew.

Leprechaun: The dog turd in the clover patch.

Onward to movie number two in the infamous four-pack I got from the in-laws this Christmas. *Leprechaun* is, without a doubt, one of the worst excuses for a horror/comedy I have seen since *Thelma and Louise*.

Evil Dead 2: Epic!

Beetlejuice: Epic!

And my thought was that, with a young and über-fine Jennifer Aniston running around in shorts, this movie couldn't be all that bad. Top it off with Warwick "I played Willow" Davis, and it could have been at least entertaining.

WRONG!

It felt more like I was having my colon cleansed with dry Lucky Charms.

Warwick Davis plays the Leprechaun, which you can feel free to read as "close family relative to that mean little door greeter at Wal-Mart." His gold is stolen by an Irishman who ends up locking the little booger up for ten years under the spell of a four-leaf clover.

Tori (Jennifer Aniston) moves in with her dad, who now owns the house, and one of the painters unwittingly unleashes the ankle-biter from hell. The Leprechaun goes on a murderous rampage searching for his stolen pot of gold.

Oh, get your fingers off your temples. I'm not done yet.

Tori, Nathan and his brother Alex, and Ozzy (not Osbourne) are trapped in the house by the homicidal Leprechaun. They soon figure out that a four-leaf clover can kill him, and after about a half-hour of Loony-Toons shenanigans, they off the little guy.

The end. Thank God.

Not that I'm trying to make this short and sweet, that's not it at all. That description is literally how the movie plays out. It moves quickly, which is about the only good thing I can say about it. In fact, I had to check my clock to make sure that it wasn't only about thirty minutes long.

The makeup on the Leprechaun hid Warwick's "I'm-desperate-for-work" expression quite well, and Jennifer Aniston was very much Rachel from *Friends*.

The scenes that were supposed to be humorous came off as blatantly stupid as if the writers were too busy telling inside jokes in the script rather than writing jokes anyone would get.

Of course, where would we be without the famous line: "F**k you, Lucky Charms!"? Makes me wonder how much General Mills paid for that little piece of advertising.

VERDICT: Set it on fire!!!

This movie deserves a spot in the archives of films we want to forget right next to *Battlefield Earth* and anything made by Uwe Boll.

The acting was decent given the writing, the effects were good, but the movie was a floater in the public swimming pool. Any movie that makes my head hurt because of the lame attempts at humor and horror, a thing that cannot be pulled off easily, needs to be banned from existence and the people who were involved need their memories of the film wiped.

It actually spawned several sequels, all of which can be bought in a pack inside the port-a-john at the end of the brown rainbow.

Santa Claus: I want what Santa's smoking for Christmas, Mommy!

...um, mark this day on your calendar.

I don't know where to begin.

I have just watched, hands down, the most messed up and disturbing Christmas movie ever. Throw in some blatant inconsistency, pile on the bad writing with a side of pig dung, and you MIGHT have the ingredients needed to describe this movie.

Santa Claus was filmed in 1959 by a Latino production company and is a Latino production. However, the director felt that it was necessary to dub it in English as well so that Americans could enjoy it.

Instead, everyone who saw it was left drooling and wondering when the next commercials would come on to give them a break from the visual lobotomy screen-raping their poor defenseless television sets.

Okay, so forget everything you know about jolly ol' St. Nick. He doesn't live in a workshop in the North Pole. He actually lives in a set of castles floating in the clouds. The film opens with him laughing like a pervert impersonating James Earl Jones as he tries out random toys around his sh—

THERE'S A F**KING NARRATOR!

Why in the hell does this movie need a narrator!? Thank you, Mr. Narrator! I wouldn't know anything about what is happening in the scene without you telling me every step of the way! Even though I can plainly see what's going on, I NEED A NARRATOR!

About like I need a second anus.

At least it's not a variety show. I hate variety shows.

ANYWHO, Santa goes to his piano, which is also a telecommunications center so that he can use the cameras to see the children making toys. That's right. Elves? No. He brings in special children to help him make the toys. He closes in on each group as the narrator announces them. Each group does a musical...number...

Oh s**t.

It's a variety show. Shoot me.

Each group of kids sings a song from their respective culture. We see the kids each time, except for the ones from England because, I guess, they're harder to come by. Yet they managed to find a group from America.

Figure that one out.

Every group sings beautifully and professionally except the American kids, who sing "Mary Had a Little Lamb" both out of tone and out of sync. So, I'm to guess that being American makes you a crappy singer. Or, maybe, it was done on purpose to be "cute." Either way, the entire sequence was so bad it actually gave me the sensation of rats clawing the inside of my skull.

Scene change, and we're in Hell. No, I mean really. Not just because I'm watching the movie, the scene ACTUALLY shifts to Hell. Did you know that devils pirouette while planning their evil deeds? Satan calls on Pitch the Devil to go to Earth and stop Santa from spreading cheer.

Yes. The Devil is targeting Santa.

Back at the North Pole, I mean Santa's castle, Santa visits Merlin the Magician to get a supply of magical items he'll need during his trip.

Yes. Merlin.

Merlin, it turns out, is whacked out of his skull. Either he's lost his marbles completely, or he's on some greeeaaat s**t and isn't sharing. He dotters around his lab singing to himself and gallops like he's on a horse everywhere he goes while he sings. He gives Santa a flower that will turn him invisible if he huffs it and magical powder to make all the children of the world sleep.

Santa heads to the observatory, where the movie just becomes a straight acid trip. The telescope can see the Earth and pinpoint the exact location of every child so that he can watch to make sure they're behaving. It does this by spinning the colander that they attached to a metal pole while picking up the radio frequencies with the spatula sticking out of the middle of the colander.

Not making it up.

He also has a communication center that is a giant computer with a massive mouth where the monitor should be. When someone calls out to Santa's castle, the lips move and speak in that person's voice. It's actually downright f**king creepy. The lips look like someone took the singing lips from *Rocky Horror Picture Show* and fed them shellfish just so they could see the allergic reaction.

Pitch manages to get three boys to act up, and Santa puts them on the Naughty List before he heads out. Pitch also finds a little girl, Lupita, and tries to get her to steal a doll. She refuses, and Santa praises her and promises her a visit this year. He heads out to his sleigh to get his reindeer ready. His reindeer are actually toys that he has to wind up.

Also creepy.

Santa takes off for Earth, stopping first in Mexico because, well, this IS a Mexican movie dubbed in English. He drops off presents at each house but has to thwart Pitch at every turn. Pitch tries everything to get rid of Santa, including lighting a fire in the fireplace while Santa is climbing down.

Santa manages, though, until the last house. Pitch steals Santa's magic items and sics a dog on him. Santa is trapped, and it's up to Merlin to rescue him. Merlin tells Santa to use a toy cat to distract the dog.

Absurdly, this works.

Santa manages to set Pitch on fire somehow (can't remember, I was too busy beating my head on my desk to distract myself from the pain), and Pitch runs off. Merlin tells Santa to head back to the North Pole because it'll be daylight soon. Santa refuses, saying that he has one more house to visit.

Lupita awakens to find a large doll outside her house. She brings it in, and everyone is happy and in wonder. We all finally believe in Santa Claus, and Christmas is saved from Satan. Yay.

The End.

VERDICT: BAD TRIP FROM HELL.

This, hands down, was the most bizarre movie I have ever watched in my entire life. Considering the line-up I've got on the site, that says fathoms. I left out a lot because, frankly, it wasn't pertinent. Let's remember:

IT'S A GOD-FORSAKEN VARIETY PIECE.

Probably the most disturbing bit was Lupita's dream. Pitch infiltrates and tries to convince her to steal. Several adults dressed as dolls with faces on both sides of the heads come out of caskets and dance around the little girl while shouting at her to steal and lie.

I almost woke up screaming for my mommy.

Really, Lupita and Santa are the two most enjoyable and down to Earth characters in the entire movie. Everyone else is either a ham, overacting every line, or a complete psycho and acting like that weird guy that hangs out at the park and stares at people.

The acting is atrocious, and the voice work is a complete mess. They managed to sync things correctly, and everything tech-wise is good, but the acting itself is awful. The writing also fails simply because the plot is laid out like a hippopotamus shart on a white wall.

I wish I could be forgiving since it was made in 1959, but *A Christmas Carol* starring Alastair Sim came out in 1951, and it is still an amazing film in every way.

All in all, I can promise you that your kids did nothing bad enough to warrant sitting them down in front of this s**t stain of a movie. I guarantee you that if you make them watch it, they will beg you to take them outside and pelt them with lumps of coal.

This movie was hailed as a classic, and it probably is to someone out there. But, like the fruitcake that gets mailed to every house in America every year, it's that one turd log that just won't flush.

Santa Claus Conquers the Martians: Please shoot me.

A big thanks to my mother, who has an eye for utter s**t.

I hoped that Santa was thinking *Gears of War* and going after Martian bastards with a chainsaw bayonet on his assault rifle, but no. I figure I'm in store for some utter crap, but little did I know that Christmas would actually turn around and s**t in my face.

The Martians, led by Kimar (King Martian, yeah), are worried because their children spend too much time watching Earth television. The favorite, of course, is anything to do with Santa Claus. Kimar assembles his group and they visit Chochen in the forest.

This dude is so old that he owes Moses five bucks.

The "forest" is Styrofoam rock and Martian trees, which is a far cry from the wooden and cardboard sets used for the Martian home.

Chochen tells them that Mars needs their own Santa, so Kimar gets the bright idea to go nab Santa Claus from Earth and haul him back to Mars. He and his men depart in a spaceship that looks like it was made out of a paper towel tube and toothpicks. The control room consists of a plywood box that is the "Radar Box" and a kitchen table with various screens that might actually be old school fish finders.

The turbulence of hitting Earth's atmosphere is not much more than an epileptic jerk performed by the green men.

Well, kind of green.

They're seemingly working with papier-mâché helmets and makeup that fades to the point that you can tell they're pasty-white dudes desperate for money.

They nab Santa with the help of a cardboard robot and two children they run into, and they haul Santa and the kids back to Mars. Meanwhile, Voldar, the bad guy, tries to kill Santa and the kids.

He's classic, sporting a walrus mustache and a scheming eye. Kimar beats the crap out of him in a fight scene ripped from the archives of the old Batman series.

The group lands on Mars, build Santa a shop, and begin work. Voldar cooks up a plan to sabotage Santa but is foiled when he gets the crap kicked out of him by four kids while Santa watches and laughs.

So, Santa basically won and got to go back to Earth by spreading cheer.

Yeah, no bullets. Just happiness.

If it wasn't the bad acting, it was the bad sets. I should have known that I was in for hell when the opening theme spun, starring kids singing about "Santy Claus."

Maybe the fact that the guy starring as Kimar was taking his role as seriously as Russell Crowe in *Gladiator* should have been a hint that this movie was gonna blow chunks because Lord knows I sure didn't take the hint from the f**king TITLE!!

VERDICT: Gag.

Even for a family flick in the 60's, it's cat vomit. Made for TV with no other purpose than to torture families trying to enjoy their f**king Christmas, this movie remains the hideously deformed stepchild that stays locked in the attic until the holidays when some alcoholic intern at the TV station with enough booger-sugar in his system to bake a wedding cake for the Mexican Cartel decides he wants to cause the mass destruction of the Christmas spirit by airing this post-incontinence underwear for the entire world to smell.

It's bad enough that we have to sit through holiday specials that are generally a crapshoot as it is, but we also get to look at this wet fart that sits in the annals of television history like spatter material on the back of the toilet bowl.

If the guy who created/pooed this movie is out there, damn you for ruining Christmas on television!

Santa Claws: The litter box smells weird.

DEAR GOD.

What better way to wrap the 2014 season than with a movie that dishes out the cute with all the grace of a Super Soaker filled with napalm?

And it sucks at doing even that.

As if *Santa Paws* wasn't groan-inducing enough, here comes The Asylum's *Santa Claws* like a high-speed glob of gelatinous rotten buffalo poo flung at the screen by an angry gorilla. I knew I was in for a ration of s**t the minute I saw The Asylum's logo stain the screen like an unwiped tucous.

Now that the s**t imagery is fully implemented, let's talk background. The Asylum is a small production company that does knock-offs of major blockbuster films. They are responsible for such underwear nuggets as *Transmorphers* (based on *Transformers), Paranormal Entity* (obviously off of *Paranormal Activity*), and *Snakes on a Train* (if you don't get that one, you need to get out more). They also brought us the *Megashark* franchise.

Onwards with the annual Christmas family fun.

The film opens with Santa appearing in a house to drop off Christmas presents. He goes home to home, then finally settles in on a place that has cats for pets. He is allergic to cats and gets startled while delivering a 45 (that's a small record to all you young bucks) and sneezes like crazy, falling backwards and breaking the record.

A young girl named Julia comes downstairs and finds him lying on the floor. Santa panics and zaps himself back to his sleigh, taking off as the boy next door, Marcus, takes his picture. Julia and Marcus nod to each other, and they both now know that Santa is real.

Fast forward thirty years…wait the hell up. Thirty years!? That would put these two kids in their forties!

Anywho, Julia now has a son named Tommy who is desperate to celebrate Christmas like all of the other kids. Julia forbids it, telling him that Christmas and Santa were invented by corporations to make money off of the general consumer.

What the hell? Okay, so we're trying to make a political social statement about anti-consumerism?

They live in the house with four cats. Maisy, an orange tabby, is mother to three roly-poly mischievous kittens. They go by Hairball, Mittens, and Patches. These three live for trouble and are always finding ways to drive Julia insane.

Marcus and Julia still live in the same houses they lived in thirty years ago, though it is never explained why or what happened to the parents. So, I guess I'm just to assume that I watched two completely self-sufficient kids grow up alone in these houses and one of them procreated at some point.

Either that or Tommy came via UPS.

Marcus is now the creepy guy next door who over-decorates for Christmas in hopes that Santa will reappear to him after all these years. Marcus and Julia have a tense relationship, and he spends a fair amount of time complaining about the kittens tromping through his yard whenever they get out.

That night, Tommy and Julia have an argument when Julia discovers that Tommy has purchased a small tabletop Christmas tree for his room. She confiscates the tree but can't bring herself to toss it.

Meanwhile, the kittens fret over the fact that Julia is about to put them up for adoption. While they brainstorm a way to stay with their mother, Tommy comes out with a box and packs them up with a note to Santa. He figures that giving them to Santa would be better than letting them get adopted by another family.

Santa shows up and takes the box up the chimney with him. He opens the box and sneezes himself off the top of the house, knocking himself out. The reindeer and sleigh GPS system (yes, it has GPS) convince the kittens that it's up to them to deliver the presents since Santa is incapacitated.

What the...how many movies are they going to knock off here!?

While the kittens take off in the sleigh, Tommy comes out and finds Santa sprawled out in the back yard. He gets Santa into the house while Marcus devises a plan to get the cats and attract Santa to his place for proof of existence.

The kittens go house-to-house, stopping off and encountering problems at every turn. One place is home to a psychotic little girl who may, or may not, have pigtails (depending on the shot) and a slight need of prescription lithium. She almost has them trapped, but they manage to escape and continue delivering presents around the world.

Meanwhile, back at the ranch, Santa tells Tommy that he needs to get going. Julia hears Santa and comes downstairs to ward him off because she thinks he's an intruder. Santa convinces her that he's the real deal by performing different magic tricks until she finally believes.

Shot of the exterior of the house, then back to the scene as Tommy explains that the kittens have the sleigh. Santa trips out, saying that we are looking at a "Cat-tastrophe" (not kidding). Shot of the exterior of the house, then back to the hallway where Santa tells Tommy and Julia that he needs "brain food."

Exterior shot.

Tommy and Julia give Santa some cookies, but Santa is allergic to peanuts and goes into anaphylactic shock. Julia happens to keep an epi-pen in the first aid kit and sticks Santa to save him from suffocating.

Exterior shot.

WHAT THE F**K? Why on God's green earth do we have to see constant random shots of the outside of the house IN THE MIDDLE OF THE SCENE!?

Cut to the kittens, who are lost on a snowy plain made of bed sheets and fake snow. The reindeer have abandoned them for no reason whatsoever, and they are trapped with no way to get home. Marcus hacks into the Santa Network and tells them that he will activate the onboard rockets to get them home, but they have to steer.

Dear God. It has rockets.

Long story short, the kittens make it back in the nick of time, and Santa is reunited with the reindeer while Marcus and Julia reconcile. Marcus agrees to keep the kittens so that Maisy can come by and visit any time she wants. All is well and Santa returns to the North Pole.

The glorious end.

VERDICT: Eternal pain.

Ah, Christmas. Cute kittens with zero personality and a cheeseburger fetish.

This movie is a disaster from the opening credits on. It's sad that I can actually say that the Buddies film *Santa Paws* was a much higher quality film than this pile of rhino dung.

I usually like to start with the acting because, frankly, it's an easy target. The acting is horrendous, even by the standards set by this genre of movie. The voice work is a lamentable mess, made worse by the improvisation the actors have to do because the animals in this film were not trained.

The CGI in the film is cheap with the mouths and snouts on the cats often staying static while the rest of the cat's face moves around in the shot. The one shot of the reindeer pulling the sleigh looks like a cinematic off of an old video game.

Santa Claus, as a character, is a train-wreck of a human being. He is allergic to everything under the sun and panics at the drop of a hat, often screaming like an ugly old woman when things get hairy. Apparently he missed his Xanax pills before leaving the North Pole and is having a very un-medicated Christmas.

The Asylum steps outside of their norm with this family-friendly flick, but ends up just creating a dog turd steaming in the yard instead. It's bad enough that the movie even attempts the level of cute that *Buddies* conveys, but failing miserably at it just makes things ten times worse. Combine it all with the slack-assed production value, and you have a large warm donkey log for the fire.

Santa's Slay: Ho, Ho, DIE.

Bill Goldberg as Santa Claus.

Yeah, when I saw the cover to this bundle of Christmas cheer, I knew what I was in for. Only one wrestler, to my knowledge, ever made the transition from the ring to Hollywood successfully, and that was Dwayne "The Rock" Johnson. And even then he struggled because the movies they typecast him for sucked.

Walking Tall was a stinker.

There, I said it.

Who would've thought that his real niche was family flicks? *Game Plan* was fantastic!

Okay, I'll give you the *Tooth Fairy* business. You win.

The movie opens with a family at Christmas dinner bickering over their differences. Enter Santa Claus, who hangs his hat and proceeds to slaughter them like the Polar Express gone haywire.

The opener is all-star: Chris Kattan, Fran Drescher, James Caan, Rebecca Gayheart, and Alicia Loren. Santa makes quick work of the family, bashing Gayheart's head in with a table leg after pinning Caan's hands to the table with knives. Chris Kattan gets ninja kicked into a shelf and dies, and Alicia Loren is victim to Santa's wicked throwing star skills.

Wait a minute…really? He sets Fran Drescher on fire!?

WHO THE HELL HASN'T WANTED TO DO THAT!?

Fast forward to Hell Township, where sixteen-year-old Nicholas is being told the truth about Christmas by his crazy grandpa. Turns out that Santa was the product of a virgin birth seeded by Satan at the same time Jesus was born. Years after he is grown, an angel appears in the guise of an old man and makes a bet with Santa. Santa loses, and the result is 1,000 years of joy and gift giving.

Needless to say, Santa's 1K is up, and he is pissed.

He begins to mow through anyone that gets in his way, including a stop at the local titty bar where he uses a stripper pole (of course, after sanitizing it) to kill the bouncers before burning the place to the ground. Christmas morning finds the town in havoc as Santa continues his rampage. Nicholas and his girlfriend Mac take refuge in Grandpa's basement, but

Santa finds them. They escape on snowmobiles after Santa runs Grandpa over with his rein...buffalo?

Okaaaaay...moving along.

Nick and Mac realize that Christmas is over in a few hours and decide to hide out in the school (of course). Santa traps them in the ice skating ring and tells them that Christmas is over when he says it is over. Grandpa reappears, and we find out that he was the angel who defeated Santa in the first place. Santa escapes, and Grandpa sends Nick and Mac after him. Nick finds the local hunting club, and they all open fire as Santa descends upon the town. Suddenly, he is shot out of the sky by Mac's father and his trusty bazooka.

I can't make this up.

VERDICT: Uh...

I have no words. The sad part is that I actually found this movie somewhat entertaining, which tells me I need to drink more. The comical bits were good, and Goldberg really hammed it up as Santa.

But the story was meandering with key twists and events happening for no other reason than to shove the action onward blindly in a direction that makes even less sense than the previous scene.

It's worth the watch if you're feeling that ignorant, but you have to realize that you cannot take this movie seriously at all. If you think you are watching a redemption of *Silent Night Deadly Night*, you are in for a really crappy evening.

If you are looking for a simple plot, campy one-liners and live-action cartoonish horror comedy then I can safely say that you should give this a look. The big name players (Dave Thomas, Saul Rubinek, and Tiny Lister to name a few) really speak to the fact that this movie is meant for nothing more than just plain fun.

Just don't eat anything first. Santa likes his gore.

The Search for Santa Paws: Assaulted by warm and fuzzy.

Okay, so before you start reading you need to know two things.

A) I do actually like some family movies. *Gameplan* was excellent, and I am actually trying to find *Ramona and Beezus* because I grew up on those books (I like Ramona more than Junie B. Jones). And if you say *The Goonies* was a bad flick, I will report you to the Feds for treason.

B) I am not above bashing a family flick if it is downright bad, though I do draw the line at slinging vulgarities and s**t jokes at movies with precious little girls suffering abuse from a hateful nanny while keeping their belief that something better is out there for them.

That being said, this movie was a constant reminder that Disney still has the power to force "cute" on us with all of the grace of a hyper-active serial killer wielding a blood-soaked chainsaw while in the throes of 'Roid Rage.

Keep in mind, also, that this is a prequel to *Christmas Buddies*, hence it is a "Buddies" movie. Right. Talking puppies.

Blech.

Quinn is a young girl of about four who is sent to an orphanage to live under the care of Ms. Stout. As it turns out, Ms. Stout is absolutely despicable to the point of pure evil and abuses the girls verbally and emotionally.

Meanwhile, at the North Pole, Santa, Mrs. Claus and Eli the Elf celebrate Santa's birthday along with all the other elves. Eli gives Santa a plush dog. They go to a massive ice cavern, and Eli gives the pup a magic crystal like the one around Santa and Mrs. Claus's necks. The pup comes to life, and Santa names him Paws.

Cue montage of cute (hang on, I just threw up a little in my mouth). Santa grieves at the death of Mr. Hucklebuckle, a toy shop owner who sold only classic toys that required imagination and whose only purpose was to keep the Christmas spirit alive by being an ambassador for the Santa Cause. Hucklebuckle is survived by his grandson James and James's wife Kate. James and Kate have shortened the name to Huckle, embarrassed by Grampy's lack of "real-world" business knowledge and the fact that the toy store only generated $0.01 profit annually. The stipulation of the will? They have to open it and run the place for one Christmas season.

Bad Movie Beware!

Santa and Paws travel to New York to find a new ambassador for the Santa Cause, but when Paws runs out into traffic to save a stranger's hat, Santa saves his life and is hit by a car in the process.

Yes. A movie aimed at very small children shows Santa get slammed into by the side of a taxi.

A bum robs Santa of his magic crystal and tote bag, and Santa is left alive but with no memory. Paws takes off to find help but gets lost in the city.

Back at the orphanage, we find Ms. Stout burning toys in the incinerator that she has confiscated from the girls. Wilhelmina, played by Madison Pettis, is the oldest girl there and has lost hope. She cares for the girls as sisters, being particularly partial to Quinn.

Quinn awakens one night and finds Paws in the ally and brings him in only to be busted by Will. The girls take Paws upstairs and break out into song while the pup tries to convince Will to believe. By this time, the musical numbers begin to go back to back.

Santa, who has been working as "Bud" playing the role of Santa at Hucklebuckle toys, has fallen ill and is rushed to the hospital. Paws, Will, Quinn, the Huckles, Eli, and the now friendly bum Gus rush to Santa's aid and return his crystal to him.

Paws gives Santa his crystal as well, ending up paying the ultimate sacrifice as Santa resurrects and Paws is turned back into a toy. Santa rushes him back to the North Pole and takes him to the life crystal, but the cyrstal's power is spread thin due to the holiday season. A tear from Santa revives Paws, who is transformed into an adult dog and renamed "Santa Paws."

The Huckles return Will and Quinn to the orphanage, where DSS has toppled Ms. Stout and ousted her, freeing the girls. The Huckles make the choice to adopt both Quinn and Will, and apparently adopting a child in this movie is as easy as picking out a puppy at the pet store.

Santa and Paws make a return visit and thank the Huckles, who have changed their names back to Hucklebuckle and have decided to keep the store. Gus becomes a surrogate dad for the girls at the orphanage and a helper to their new nanny who is the lady from DSS. Everyone is okay, happy ending.

Everyone all together now: "Awwww."
VERDICT: Gag.

As much as Disney wants to inject feel-good movie into my spine, at the end of the day it's a friggin' Buddies movie. Yes, I understand the age group it is aimed at, but even my seven-year-old daughter said Buddies movies are way too sappy.

Madison Pettis is super-talented, and her performance along with Mill Cobbs and Katherine Kirkpatrick are about the only thing in the movie not over-doing the warm hugs that the writers loaded into the rail gun of an Apache chopper and unloaded onto audiences.

The sweetness of this movie does not warm your heart; it grabs you by the groin and holds you down while it forces its way into your body like an alien parasite that will erupt from your chest during your spaghetti dinner and soak your family in blood as it scurries off only to later kill them off one by one until you man up and blow it out of the airlock. It wasn't as bad as *Santa Claus Conquers the Martians*, but I found myself in dire need of some mindless violence, blood and gore after I got done watching it.

REALITY CHECK: I like dogs, but hell no. A dog starts talking to me and I'm hauling a** out of there. No "Oooo, it talks! I DO believe in Christmas!" More like: "Oh, S**T! A talking dog! AAAAAAAHHHHHH!!!"

I would rather be beaten over the head with a Belkie Bear than watch this movie again. I understand Sappy Cinema, but Buddies movies are just too much.

Silent Night: Santa's off his meds.

It's Christmas time again in Movieland!

That's right! Tis the season to eat, drink, be merry, give to your fellow man, and deck the halls with cinematic poo-poo!

This year I started off with something a little rare. *Silent Night* is actually billed as a remake, or reimagining, of the original *Silent Night, Deadly Night* 1984 film, which featured a serial-killing Santa Claus.

The original film was panned by critics and banned in several cities because of the shocking and offensive idea of taking the season's most beloved character and making him into a bloodthirsty, homicidal maniac.

Why not? He's already got felony B&E on his rap sheet.

The 2012 film *Silent Night* wasn't given the same treatment as the original, which may or may not speak well for today's society. Hell, I think being completely bat guano is kind of expected these days, anyway.

No, this movie was panned because it just sucked.

We open with a nutcase making what ends up being the most disturbing Santa mask ever. He has two people tied up in a house. The woman is lying on the bed upstairs with her hands and feet bound, and the man is down in the basement tied to a chair with Christmas lights.

Santa walks in and the man pleads for his life, claiming that he didn't know that the woman was married. Santa is wielding a double-bladed axe, so we're already set for some chop 'em up action.

No.

Wyle E. Santa flips a switch and electrocutes the man with the Christmas lights. What the hell? Dude, how long did THAT take to set up? Kris Kringle has way more patience than I ever would.

Anywho, scene shift to Aubrey, who gets a call from HOLY S**TBEANS, IT'S MALCOLM FREAKIN' MCDOWELL PLAYING THE SHERIFF! THIS MOVIE IS GOING TO ROCK!

The sheriff tells Aubrey to come in and act as deputy for the day because Deputy Jordan hasn't shown up to work. She reluctantly agrees, has a pleasant stereotypical interaction with her parents (She still lives at home? What the...?), and heads out to the office.

Meanwhile, a bratty fourteen-year-old girl is screaming torrents of profanity at her mother. Mom leaves the room, and the girl answers a knock at the door to find Serial Santa looming over her. He takes a cattle prod and zaps her with it, then runs her through with a poker.

This scene bugged me a little (OK, a lot) because I'm not really down with violence towards kids. However, I'm to understand that I would find the scene quite cathartic if I were to spend a quality amount of time with a fourteen-year-old girl.

I'll pass.

Aubrey spends her day chasing pithy little complaints and arguments around town and ends up discovering the body of Deputy Jordan. Turns out he's the man from the beginning scene, and the woman he was with was married, and her husband is at the station filing a missing persons report.

Enter the sheriff with more inane bravado and macho writing. Malcolm McDowell does what he can with what he has to work with, but damn.

Santa happens across a motel room where a group is filming a soft-core porn. Santa kills off the cameraman and the assistant, and the topless starlet goes running out the door.

Yup, you guessed it. Christmas boobies bringing yuletide cheer!

Note: the chick looks like Danielle Harris, though she actually is credited as Cortney Palm, so I don't really know what's going on now. I hit IMDB, and they both have separate profiles, but they look like the same person.

The film industry is so confusing.

AAAAAAANYWHO, Santa chases her into a Christmas tree lot and chops her leg off with his trusty axe. He picks her up and performs the tour-de-force kill that had everyone in the blogging community a-buzz: he feeds her into a wood chipper.

That's it. It doesn't get any better than that. The rest of the kills in the film are anti-climatic, and the movie meanders on through a series of "OH MY GOD!" "We'll get the bastard!" and the occasional "What does he want?"

Most of the script is pretty much made up of those three phrases. Through the confusion we figure out that Santa is only killing off the "naughty." He goes after the perverted town reverend, the corrupt mayor, and the mayor's tramp daughter.

Fast-forward through some more irrelevant dialogue and scenes, and the movie climaxes at the police station after Aubrey finds her father butchered in his house. Santa kills off the sheriff, the other male officer that doesn't contribute anything to the film, and the bad Santa locked up in the cell.

Aubrey shows up and goes after him with a fire axe. They have an "axe fight," which is supposed to be like a sword fight...but with axes...I guess.

Aubrey succeeds in using Santa's flamethrower to catch him on fire and burn him alive. The camera pulls back dramatically on the Santa mask burning slowly on the floor but no sign of the Santa Claus Killer.

Scene change. We find out that Santa was actually the child of a man who was gunned down by Aubrey's father years ago. The kid's dad dressed as Santa and burned several people alive with a flamethrower before getting shot and killed while the kid watched.

The End. Please, no sequels. Jesus.

VERDICT: Ho-Ho-NO.

Wow.

I'd say it's been a while since I watched something this bad, but that would be a bold-faced lie. I can say that it's been a while since I watched something so blatantly irrelevant.

The acting is subpar at best, but let's do some real talk: you can only do so much when the script was obviously written by a middle school boy who watches too many slasher flicks.

Not to say that the movie was lacking in any of the typical slasher categories, that's far from true. You had your gratuitous boobies scene that actually lasted longer because Santa chased her all the way from the hotel room to the wood chipper, and the puppies were everywhere and in slow motion no less!

You had the over-the-top gore as well. I mean they may have used up their entire budget just on blood and gore makeup because it sure as hell didn't go to training the actors or editing the script.

Honestly, the wood chipper kill was the centerpiece of the entire movie. As much as I try to stay away from processed foods, there's just something about a heaping serving of mechanically separated naked chick. I wonder if she comes with fries.

See what I did there?

Outside the gore and kill creativity, the movie was really just a forgettable mess. It was touted as a reimagining of *Silent Night, Deadly Night,* and it nodded to the original in a few scenes, but it ultimately had NOTHING to do with the original other than a guy in a Santa suit killing off the a**holes in town.

If you're looking for a montage of blood, gore, and gleefully overdone Wyle E. Coyote-style kills, give it a look (providing you can find this rare…gem. Yeah, we'll just say "gem.") Otherwise, look away. Far away. In fact, if you have a choice between watching this movie and having someone pluck the hair out of your armpits, the tweezers are in the bathroom upstairs. Second shelf.

Silent Night, Deadly Night: Ho! Ho! Ho! Who wants a bloodbath for Christmas?

The pic I found on the website was, unfortunately, really bad. Sadly, it's the best one I could find. It was the original banned cover for this movie. Parents took real issue with Santa going down the chimney carrying an ax. What if he was just chopping firewood? Or maybe he was cosplaying as Paul Bunyan.

Haters.

Silent Night, Deadly Night piqued my curiosity for years as a kid, but also scared the hell out of me because of the idea that Santa would be coming into my house Christmas Eve for more than just dropping off presents. I was too young to rent it, and it became too obscure to find by the time I was old enough to indulge.

A five-year-old-Billy is on his way to the old folks' home with his parents for a Christmas visit with Grandpa. His baby brother, Ricky, is also along for the ride. Grandpa is a vegetable and simply stares off into space. Billy's parents leave him alone with Grandpa to go and sign some paperwork.

Wha...?

That's a great f**kin' idea! Let's leave the toddler alone with the lump! Nothing ever went wrong with a decision like that! (This message brought to you by "Sarcasm!" Making the dumb feel dumber since the dawn of man!)

Grandpa suddenly becomes lucid and goofy, giggling at Billy and telling him that Santa brings presents to good little children and severely punishes the naughty, implying he murders them. Oh, that wacky Grandpa!

Meanwhile, a robber dressed as Santa Claus guns down a store clerk during a robbery. He escapes and drives off into the night.

Billy's family happens upon the Killer Santa and stop despite Billy's warnings that Santa is after him. The Santa kills Billy's dad and mom while Billy watches from the trees.

Skip forward three years, and we find Billy and Ricky in an orphanage run by the nuns and a harsh Mother Superior. Billy is reprimanded for drawing Santa with a bloody knife and a decapitated reindeer (I thought the drawing was cool, myself). He is also punished by Mother Superior after witnessing two of the older kids having sex.

Well, it's not like he has a Playboy subscription, people!

The next morning Santa Claus shows up. Billy goes absolutely bat guano and punches St. Nick in the face. Mother Superior finds him cowering in his room pleading for forgiveness for being naughty.

Ten years later, an 18-year-old Billy lands a job at a toy store thanks to Sister Margaret, the only nun at the orphanage sympathetic to his fear of Santa. As the Christmas season approaches, Billy becomes more antsy, especially when Santa appears at the store to take photos with the kids.

The next day the Santa calls out sick, and Billy is made to wear the outfit. He threatens the children that misbehave by saying that he punishes naughty children, which frightens them into submission.

That night Billy gets drunk and wanders into the warehouse where he sees Pamela, a clerk he is taken with, and finds her being raped by the stockroom supervisor. Billy screams "NAUGHTY!" at the top of his lungs and kills the both of them, then kills off the store manager and assistant manager as well before heading out into the night.

So far we have a body count of four. Average for an 80's slasher flick, so we're off to a good start.

And three scenes of gratuitous boobies. Yup. It's the 80's.

Enter Sister Margaret, now older and wiser but still under the thumb of Mother Superior. She catches wind of Billy being dressed as Santa and knows what's coming. She arrives too late, and finds the massacre at the toy store.

Scene change to two teens getting ready to have sex on a pool table (like I said, it's the 80's). Now, outside of setting up for what's next, these two horn-dogs have nothing to do with the plot. Zero. So watching Billy get creative actually gets a bit fun.

Billy hangs Denise from the antlers of a deer head, and her boyfriend gets tossed out a window. Denise's little sister wanders in, oblivious to the carnage, and thinks Billy is Santa. It's a tense moment when Billy asks if she's been good or naughty. She assures him that she's been good, and he gives her the box cutter he used on Pamela in the store and leaves.

In the next scene, two bullies steal sleds from two younger kids and proceed to sled down the hill. The first one makes it, but the second one is attacked after Billy's trademark "NAUGHTY!!" He rides down the hill headless with his head bounding behind him.

Sister Margaret and the sheriff figure out that Billy is on his way back to the orphanage. An officer is dispatched and sees a Santa approaching. He guns down the Santa only to find out that it is the old deaf priest that helps the nuns at the home.

Billy shows up and takes out the officer. He gets into the orphanage and goes after the wheel-chaired Mother Superior shouting "NAUGHTY!" when he is shot several times in the back by the sheriff. Billy dies, whispering that they are all safe now. Billy's brother, Ricky, glares at Mother Superior and mutters "Naughty."

VERDICT: Eh. I'll take it.

Okay, so this movie was panned by critics and parents alike for the obvious: Santa kills people, particularly people having sex. It was banned in numerous countries and even banned in cities here in the U.S. In reality it's campy with a thin storyline that isn't much more than an excuse to get Billy to start killing.

And boobies. Four scenes with boobies. Ah, the 80's.

The truth is, this movie isn't really as bad as it's hyped up to be. Okay, yeah, it's got its shortcomings. The only actor in the movie worth a damn is the guy playing Billy. He conveys Billy's fear of Santa and his plummet into insanity very well, and he doesn't over-do it.

The other characters in the movie who play his victims are there for no reason other than meatbags for Billy to hack up. They offer no value to the story whatsoever beyond the toy store, and even those characters are debatable.

The setup is a little boring in the beginning, and I found Billy to be a little whiny even for a 5-year-old. The grandpa was out there and way overdone, but it was humorous because I would totally do that to my grandkids as a goof.

Yeah, I know. I'm an a**hole.

All in all, I'd watch it again. I'd even say give it a look if you're that curious. It's hardcore 80's slasher fun for the whole family! Okay, maybe not the whole family. I'd probably send Granny into the next room, but it's never too late to completely destroy your kids' mental stability.

Cheers!

Silent Night, Deadly Night 2: Death by over-acting.

Over the past three years, I've gotten multiple requests from people to review *Silent Night, Deadly Night*. I was actually surprised by the movie, as I was expecting something worthy of wiping the inside of the toilet with. *Silent Night, Deadly Night* is reputed to be one of the worst movies ever filmed: a reputation I happen to disagree with.

That one would be *Silent Night, Deadly Night 2*.

By no means was the first movie a masterpiece. It had its flaws, but they didn't make it un-watchable. However, some raging douche rocket thought that it merited a sequel.

So who wrote this movie? Jerry Seinfeld?

IT'S ABOUT NOTHING.

Baby Ricky from the first film is all grown up now and incarcerated in the local nuthouse for the criminally insane. Dr. Henry shows up to interview Ricky and try to get a sense as to why he committed multiple murders.

Ricky is absolutely bat guano, which is conveyed by the actor about as subtly as an elephant shart. This guy, Eric Freeman, portrays Ricky to the extreme. He talks with a constant snark, is loud, overly intense, and sarcastic.

At first, Ricky is hostile towards the doctor. But he soon begins to recount his childhood. We begin to see flashbacks of the first movie. These flashbacks continue, occasionally being interrupted by snippets of Ricky's interview.

In fact, minus a few basic scenes, they present the entirety of the first *Silent Night, Deadly Night* film. This monotony encompasses, literally, half of the movie. Yes. You can basically fast forward to the mid-point because if you have seen the first film, you have already seen the first half of the second film minus Ricky's intense and sinister bad acting.

Please shoot me.

After that monotony is over, we see Ricky's time before being locked up. He begins to kill those who are bad, shouting "Naughty!" or "Punish!" like his brother before finishing off his victims. He is actually able to land himself a girlfriend but ends up killing her when she trips out because Ricky killed her ex-boyfriend after he admitted to having sex with her before she and Ricky met.

Okay, back-pedaling. How in the name of Kirstie Alley's fat a** on wheat did Ricky have intimate details of Billy's doings while he was locked up and Billy was miles away in town!? I mean, I get it. He keeps saying, "Billy told me." When a**hole!? While he was laying on the floor full of bullet holes!? Because that was the only other time you saw him the whole friggin' movie!

Rant complete. For now.

After killing his girlfriend, Billy goes on a rampage and shoots multiple people in the street. In fact, he shoots more people than he stabs or cuts up. For a slasher flick, the low amounts of boobies and blood are quite unusual. It's as if they decided to just take the Slasher Film Handbook and completely disregard the chapter on appropriate amounts of gore and topless girls for a successful slasher movie.

We come back to "Present Day" to find that Billy has murdered Dr. Henry and escaped. Cut to Mother Superior's house. She is now retired, in a wheelchair, and-WHAT THE RAIN FOREST MONKEY-F**K HAPPENED TO HER FACE!?

Instead of getting the original actress to play Mother Superior, they got some other stand in to do it and made her face look like she forgot herself one evening and had a few shots down at the Zombie Stomp Bar and STD Factory.

Aaaaanway. They fight, and Sister Mary arrives just in time to find Mother Superior sitting at the table. Mother Superior's head topples off, and Ricky emerges from the shadows only to be gunned down by a group of cops. Sister Mary awakens from a faint and screams at the sight of Mother Superior's head. Ricky opens his eyes and grins. Even though he took a slug to the chest. Go figure.

VERDICT: Coal in your fking stocking.**

What. The. Hell.

Sometimes sequels should never be made. Let's look at *The Matrix*. Prime example. I was done with the first film. It had a solid ending, and it was understood that Neo was going to bring down the Matrix. It could've done without a sequel; it could've had a sequel. They went with the latter and made two movies that were considered, by most, to be world-class toilet bowl mold.

Silent Night, Deadly Night was a movie that could've stood on its own. It needed to stand on its own. Hell, take it or leave it. The movie isn't fantastic anyway. But *Silent Night, Deadly Night 2* is a weird streak on the men's restroom mirror at the Gentleman's Club.

This movie was an effort to cash in on the cult following from the first film. Problem is this: cult film fans are fanatical. They have certain expectations that must be met. This film didn't even come close.

Eric Freeman couldn't act his way into the Kevin Costner School of Bad Acting. He portrays Ricky's insanity in a way that makes him a BGB (Big Goofy Ba***rd). He twitches his face incessantly, I guess because some pompous, donut-munching, has-been acting coach told him it made the character look more intense.

Bulls**t, Eric. It makes you look like you're having a grand mal seizure exclusively in your face. His eyebrows give away his real age as they are so large they look like they might come to life and eat his face.

But no. That would've made the movie interesting.

The chick that played his girlfriend also played Robin in *Friday the 13th Part 7: A New Blood* and wasn't much better in that one either. The rest of the cast was no-names. In fact, all of them were no-names. Everything they've done since then has just been more obscure movies and voice-work.

It's considered a slasher film even though Ricky shoots most of his victims and runs one over with a Jeep. When I hear the term "Slasher Movie," I think three things: Blood, Carnage, and Boobies. This had melee, vehicles, and guns.

So it was *Halo* on the 8-Bit NES! I get it now!!

I think I'd rather have Santa fart in my face than watch this movie again.

Thankskilling: Turkey stuffed with s**t

I got this suggestion from a fan on the Facebook page whilst at a Girl Scout tour of the police station (and hoping that the cops forgot that little incident with the fountain and the pineapple bra...long story.)

This movie is a gem.

MADE ENTIRELY OUT OF POO.

This s**t-stain opens with a screen-filling shot of a nipple. We pan out and find that (surprise!) said nipple is attached to a breast. Keep panning out, and we get a topless pilgrim running for her life through the woods.

Hey, kids! It's Wanda Lust!

By the way, this is the boob shot in the movie. The entire movie.

She backs into a tree as a ball of feathers with a nasty-looking skin tag approaches. Yes, it is Turkey: the most vicious Muppet ever to be created. And the cheapest. Ah hell, it looks like someone took a feather duster, inverted a mutated rubber vagina, glued a beak and eyeballs onto it, then smacked it together, and rammed a hand up its a**.

Yes. I went there.

Turkey expresses his approval of the Pilgrim's breasts then hacks her up with an ax. The opening credits begin with a bass line, some keyboard and guitar, and a turkey-gobble in the background. I begin mainlining heroin just so I can make it through this atrocity.

The heroin has no effect. This movie still hurts.

Five college buddies get together after class lets out to discuss their Thanksgiving vacation. We have Johnny (The Jock), Kristen (The Good Girl), Darren (The Nerd), Billy (The Morbidly Obese Hick), and Ali (The SLUT). Yeah, all caps. She makes Madonna look like a prude.

They set off to Kristen's house to meet up with her redneck, backwoods, inbred father who sports a personality best suited for *Hee-Haw!* and a mustache that is as fake as the hair on William Shatner's head. He is an idiot.

Yup, that about covers it for him. No, really.

The kids run into car trouble and decide to camp for the night and continue on tomorrow. Darren recognizes the area as the site of an ancient curse that was cast by an Indian Witch Doctor centuries ago. On a certain night (tonight) at a certain time (now) under certain conditions (like the old nameless redneck's dog urinating on a totem pole the size of a tube of Neosporin) a vengeful and murderous turkey will rise and kill everyone it comes across.

Oh, the dog thing. Right. Yeah, I can't make this up. Apparently all Turkey needed was a little dog pee, and he's up and killing in no time, starting with the dog. The old man vows vengeance.

I vow to find out how many headache pills I can take without dying.

Turkey surprises Kristen while she is making a call to her father, and she tries to warn the others. Of course, no one believes her. Johnny tries, but backs off to flirt with Ali.

The next day, they head into town. Ali is dropped off at her house for her family Thanksgiving, and the others split up to do the same, though it's not really clear where Kristen, Darren, and Billy go. Johnny comes home and is visited by Turkey, who kills both of his parents and tosses Dad's head at Johnny. Johnny escapes and calls the others. They hurry to Ali's house, but she is preoccupied while they scramble across town.

She's having fully clothed sex with her cousin.

This goes back to what I screamed about in *Dreamaniac*. Screwing up fake sex is one thing, but this tops the cake. Both have their pants on, she's on all fours, and her skirt isn't pulled up. The director didn't even try. Oh, wait a minute. I forgot.

THERE'S ONLY SO MUCH A CAMCORDER CAN DO.

Turkey kills the cousin/boyfriend, then finishes the deed on Ali (yes, it is as gross and repugnant as it sounds). He then breaks her neck and leaves.

He next shows up at Kristen's house in disguise. He is wearing a Groucho Marx glasses and nose. Kristen's dad answers the door wearing a chicken suit and invites Turkey in thinking that he's a friend of Kristen's.

Wow.

They have an awkward discussion about the weather, then Turkey kills him off and puts on his face just as Kristen and her friends arrive.

Kristen, upon seeing her father's face on Turkey, reacts true to the retarded nature of this movie: "Daddy!"

WHAT THE F**K!?

Wait a minute, wait just one damn minute. You mean to tell me that this b***h is so stupid that she actually fails to notice that her dad is now two feet tall, has feathers and plumage, and f**king stitches in his face!? Oh, her friends are just as stupid. "Hi, Sheriff Roud!"

GOD HELP ME.

The four friends find a book in the sheriff's library that details how to kill Turkey. Turkey wanders by, still dressed in Sheriff Roud's face, and checks in on them. They tell him that they are fine, and Kristen thanks him for having them over.

Billy attempts to leave and catches Turkey dragging Sheriff Roud's body through the house. He calls to the others, and they tackle Turkey and steal his talisman. Turkey is now defenseless against the spell they need to chant to rid him of his invincibility.

Billy says he quits and leaves but is ambushed outside by Turkey and killed after eating a cartoon hallucination of a turkey.

Darren runs to Billy's body, and there is of full montage indicating that Darren had a gay thing for Billy. Nope. Sorry, man. Straight dudes do not hold hands and frolic in flower fields while chasing birds. You're a bottom.

The three corner Turkey at his teepee (Yes, there just so happens to be a teepee pitched in the front yard of Suburban America). They cast the demonic spell, and then try to kill him. Before Turkey can escape, the old redneck shows up and shoots him in the face, sending him flying into a dumpster.

The kids thank the man, then decide to go to Kristen's house to watch movies for the evening. No, seriously. Kristen and Johnny become boyfriend and guh...girlfriend, and Darren goes to the kitchen.

BUT WAIT.

That dumpster, that curbside green residential dumpster in the middle of Suburbia, JUST SO HAPPENS TO BE A BIO-HAZARDOUS WASTE DISPOSAL UNIT!!! The toxic waste brings Turkey back to life as Kristen suddenly remembers that Turkey is supposed to be burned at the stake. Darren opens the fridge and is attacked by the now chemically charged, mutated Turkey. Johnny enters, but Turkey stabs him in the gut and leaves him to die.

Kristen vows vengeance for Johnny's death and goes outside to find that there JUST SO HAPPENS to be a pile of wood set up in the yard like a scene from the Salem Witch Trials. She lights it, and Turkey appears. She punt-kicks Turkey into the fire and he burns to death, flinging a random perfectly-cooked drumstick into the yard. Kristen picks it up and begins to eat as the old redneck comes back and tells her good job.

As if I haven't suffered enough...

Scene change to a family having dinner. The cooked turkey on the table begins to rumble, and Turkey's voice echoes in the house. "Do I smell a sequel!?"

To be continued...in space...

VERDICT: My brain hates me.

The director/writer figured that he could market this movie if he promised a porn star topless in the opening shot. This weird brown stain in cinema's underwear was shat onto film on a meager budget of $3,500. I have no doubt in my mind that $3,000 of it went to Wanda Lust and $499 was spent on a keg of beer and huge amounts of pizza for the cast and crew.

$1 went to the feather duster to create Turkey. Yes, this means that some idiot was brave enough to put his hand in some other dude's rubber vagina to help bring Turkey to life for the screen.

The Sony Handycam was a Christmas present from Mom.

"Don't film anything perverted or f**ked up, honey!"

"I won't, Mom! Instead I'll make a movie with a bunch of my friends who have ZERO personality! We'll make it about a serial killing turkey!"

"That's nice, honey."

The acting is absolutely horrid. The "guh...girlfriend" bit is how she actually says the line. Chick, did ya even memorize them, or are you reading a teleprompter!? Each character is cast in a stereotype, but Billy seems to be the only one who actually gets it right, and he still screws it up.

DEAR GOD, THERE ARE SEQUELS...

The Star Wars Holiday Special: I watched a wookie do bad things...

I consider myself a HUGE *Star Wars* fan. Hell, I even have my own Lightsaber (Anakin model). So, of course, as soon as I learned of the fabled long-lost *Star Wars Holiday Special*, I immediately thought, "Jesus, this can't be good."

See, I'm one of those who can be a die-hard fan but not think that any particular series or focus of my fandom can do no wrong. No, I admit that this TV special from 1978 does wrong on a MASSIVE scale. I'm sorry; did a game show host announcer just rehash the moving words?

Bea Arthur!? Dihanne Carroll?

Oh, hell.

One thing I hate more than anything is a variety show. I have a hard enough time paying attention as it is, and these a**holes want me to keep up while they jump from one entertainment genre to a completely different one!?

They also managed to get the entire cast from the first movie in to do this 97-minute long embarrassment, and none of them will discuss it in interviews to this day!

Han and Chewbacca are evading Imperial Star Destroyers while Chewie (according to Han) is worried that he will not make it back to his home planet Kyshyyk in time to celebrate "Life Day" with his family.

In the next scene, we meet Chewie's wife Malla, his father Itchy, and his son Lumpy.

Yes. Much thought into these names there was.

The rest of the show...movie...thing is almost entirely in Wookie with some one-sided conversations from human characters. Chewie's family is waiting for his return. To keep Lumpy occupied, Itchy puts a card into the chess hologram board.

Well, at least we get to see some Star Wars che...oh God. Acrobats? WTF!?

Lumpy eats it up like a fly on a fresh pile of...stuff. We move on to another segment where we see Darth Vader storming through the starship demanding all rebel forces rounded up.

This is the ONLY time we see Vader in live action form.

We next see a cooking show hosted by a four-armed alien Paula Dean dressed like Lady Tremaine from *Cinderella*. Luke Skywalker makes his thirty-second appearance reassuring Malla that Chewie and Han are safe. Princess Leia and C-3PO also call in to check on Chewie's family. A friendly shopkeeper and friend of the family shows up bearing gifts, including a new disk for Grandpa Itchy.

Itchy sits back, and we are bombarded by colors, water, and Dihanne Carroll. Itchy soon starts cooing and grunting while she sings about being his fantasy. The scene ends, and Itchy looks satisfied.

Yes. I watched a Wookie crank it to a black chick in a white dress.

I am scarred.

Before Chewie and Han can get to Kyshyyk, Imperials invade Chewie's house and hold Malla, Itchy, and Lumpy hostage while they search the place. Lumpy is put in front of a cartoon to distract him, and we get a ten-minute *Star Wars* toon introducing Boba Fett into the Star Wars universe. The toon isn't bad, minus a few technical details that can be chalked up to being dated.

Suddenly, for no reason whatsoever, we cut to a cantina on Tatooine being run by Bea Arthur. A Golden Girl in a bar. Go figure. The Empire calls in and decrees a curfew that shuts the place down. Bea then breaks into a song...

SUNG TO THE CANTINA MUSIC FROM STAR WARS.

As if this couldn't get any worse! She probably spun seven times in her grave just because I watched this horror.

Meanwhile, back at the ranch, one of the Imperials finds a holographic television that shows a rock group. Note: this is the only entertaining part of the movie. The group is actually pretty cool.

Then back to the lameness of bad acting being reacted to in Wookie-speak. I swear, for the first ten minutes I seriously thought the plotline was "Aaaaauuuuggh! Honk-burf!"

Lumpy goes upstairs and assembles a communicator while watching yet another skit about how to operate the thing. He sends a fake message, and the Imperials leave except for one Stormtrooper. Han and Chewie arrive just in time and dispatch the Trooper. Hugs, family moment, lots of grunting.

In the next scene, we see the celebration of Life Day. A dozen Wookies are gathered around wearing red robes. Han, Leia, and Luke show up as well as C-3PO and R2D2. Leia begins to sing a song...

TO THE TUNE OF THE STAR WARS THEME!
OUT OF TUNE!

At this point, my ears are bleeding. Carrie Fisher is one thing; Carrie Fisher singing is a threat of nuclear war.

This travesty ends, though not soon enough, and I am left wondering what the hell I had just finished watching. It may have had the pretty shine of *Star Wars*, but it had the texture of rotten baked beans and the stench of Bantha poodoo.

VERDICT: Into the Sarlac pit!

I am going to hell just for watching this crap. My IQ dropped fifty-seven points as soon as the opening sequence started. If I had wanted to watch a television show almost entirely in Wookie-speak, I would have watched *Jersey Shore*.

This gigantic failure was splattered onto the network time slot like a dirty wet fart. ONE time. EVER. After its run, George Lucas ordered all prints destroyed in an effort to wipe it from history. It worked.

Until the internet.

Now it is being viewed again to pretty much the same criticism as before. ANYTHING Snooki has said is more intelligent than this nightmare. The only thing that could have made it any worse was Barbara Streisand.

Actually, she may have been the alien with the...oh, never mind.

This special is hailed as the biggest embarrassment in the history of CBS and for good reason. IT IS A TURD!

George Lucas himself couldn't have made it any more painful!

This movie is not the cool guy in the game store that knows all games and gives you free time on *Star Wars: The Old Republic* so you can raid with him. This movie is the disgusting fat sh*t that smells like sour milk and hot garbage and just slapped your girlfriend on the a**. Do not let curiosity get the best of you. Curiosity is a vicious, life-sucking b***h from which there is no escape.

What the Hell?

Everyone's seen one of those. You know, the movie that just makes you pull your hair out and scream because your mind is so blown at the fact that this steaming pile of dogs**t even got funded. Some just befuddle you to the point of drooling; others just crush whatever faith you have left in humanity. Most contain s**t you JUST DIDN'T NEED IN YOUR LIFE.

Yeah, ALL of these qualify.

1313 Cougar Cult: Old Chicks and half-naked college boys. Jesus...

Yeah, there's just no way to make that sound right. I mean, I could add "mutha f**ka" at the end of it in an attempt to let my inner gangsta run free, but even that can't make what this movie is about sound any less uncomfortable or awkward.

What a hell of a way to ring in the New Year!

Games and a countdown with friends, a nice quiet New Year's Day at home, and this God-awful pile of donkey nuts staring at me from Netflix like a pervert at a bowling alley.

The film opens with a pool boy finishing up his shift at the lavish mansion that serves as a home for three scantly-clad midlife crisis victims who apparently had careers back in the 80's as scream queens. He goes into the shower to rinse off before leaving, and we get a montage of about eight minutes of him rubbing himself down in the shower while the ladies creep toward him.

Okay, we all know how much can happen in a minute during a film. Imagine eight minutes of bad horror music, some dude in a shower rubbing himself like a super model gone wrong, and three slutty grandmas walking.

Yeah, it got old fast.

Dude is chased by what sounds like a monster, and the camera cuts back to a shot of the house as we hear him get mauled by the creature. The scene shifts back to the interior, and we see him on the floor WITHOUT A SCRATCH.

The ladies approach, and the blonde (Linnea Quigley) complains about them killing a boy on the new floor. They decide to claim mates and eat the boy to hide the evidence. They make their transformation into cou-OH DEAR GOD!!!!

What. The. Hell.

They turn into cougar-women. NO. You don't...understand. I am not usually taken aback. I typically don't do double takes, or even triple takes, since I am rarely shocked. It's too much.

They were too cheap to even look into masks or something for the cougar monster transformation, so they SUPERIMPOSED a cartoon pic of a cougar's head onto the women's faces. A STATIC pic, so they didn't even TRY to animate!

I may have found the successor to *Troll 2*.

Enter three young college boys. They are Coopersmith, Darwin, and Henry. They're three losers looking for summer work and have answered an ad to work as servants to three rich women for the summer. Clara (Linnea Quigley) answers the door and brings them in to introduce them to her sisters Victoria (Michelle Bauer) and Edwina (Brinke Stevens).

Yeah, I drew a blank on them too.

They hire the boys on the spot and thus begins a montage of the guys sleeping while they rub themselves. Yes, I can't make this up. I ended up fast forwarding through about a total of thirty minutes or more of this crap because A) Not my thing and B) EW.

Darwin begins to notice the strange goings on in the house (the guys that come and never go, the strange noises, the reruns of *Space Ghost*) and brings the weird dreams (read: self rub-downs) to the attention of Coopersmith and Henry. He tells them that he recognizes the amulet around Clara's neck as the same amulet worn by witches eons ago that eat young men to achieve immortality.

Coincidence? Nope. Internet said so. It's TRUE!!

Henry and Coopersmith are entranced by the trio of cougar-women, and Darwin races aimlessly for his life around the house just to be cornered by Clara. He grabs the amulet and presses it to her head, killing her and her sisters in a hail of superimposed cartoon lightening.

He and his friends walk out the front door and reflect on the past few days. They have a final laugh and head off as the credits roll.

Yes, a final laugh. Scooby-Doo style. Shoot me.

VERDICT: FILLED THE BEDPAN!!!

Next time anyone happens to go to the store, please grab me some bleach, a brill-o pad, and a wire brush to scrub the memory of this movie from my mind. At least *The House That Screamed* ATTEMPTED to use actual special effects.

This movie is a prime example of what happens to has-been B-movie actors who just don't know when to say, "You know, I've had a good run. Time to retire and tour with Nerd Con so Mama's-Basement-Dwellers can take pictures of me and fap in their hotel rooms later."

The acting is absolutely horrible. These three ladies decided to be nice and help out the guy making this movie. Either that or he promised a celebrity caller at the next bingo night. The guys are no better, having obviously studied Kevin Costner and William Shatner as role models for their acting careers.

The special effects were...well, they were special. Not "special" because your mom told you that you were but "special" as in I suddenly have the urge to lick windows, watch *Barney*, and bark at people I see in the street. I mean REALLY!? I have a friend who went to animation school, and he once complained to me that some of the work there was just indicative of people who were floating.

This animation was just a floater, period.

The story is weak, but what do I expect? Look at the crap I watch! What was I thinking!? That I would watch something in depth with a massive social impact on today's movie-going audience? Something that makes my mind work and my outlook on life change for the better? Something to give me faith in my fellow man!?

NO.

I expected a movie with slack acting, a sub-par plot, bad writing, and lame effects. I got what I expected.

IN ABUNDANCE.

Alien vs. Ninja: I'm sorry, what?

Alien vs. Ninja first caught my eye about a year ago, though I put it off because of all of the other garbage out there to watch and rip apart. I read up on it before I watched it, though Wikipedia didn't give me much more than "an action comedy set in ancient Japan."

I figured "Why not?"

The Japanese have a very cartoonish sense of humor, and their live-action comedies generally are live-action anime. *Onechanbara: Bikini Samurai Squad* was entertaining crap.

Alien vs. Ninja was BEYOND crap.

It was the fungus that grows on the bottom of a public toilet.

A group of ninjas are out...ninja-ing, I guess...when a UFO crashes. Aliens emerge, looking like the Peanuts versions of H.R. Giger's biomechanoids.

The fight scenes are awesome, but once the aliens enter the picture, the movie spirals downwards faster than Eddie Furlong's acting career after *Terminator 2*. The aliens kill everyone in their sight and birth babies from the holes in their heads.

The choreography quickly changes over, and it looks more like I'm watching a very gross episode of the *Mighty Morphin' Power Rangers*. Not that the ninjas in the film do kung fu while they talk, but I was waiting for it.

The alien costumes were abysmal, complete with scenes where it's painfully obvious that the feet are tennis shoes made up like alien feet. The effects were almost as bad as the carnage that was *Battlefield Earth*.

The worst was the sequence where the alien knocks the head off of a ninja, bounces it off of about fifty trees, then sticks it to a limb. A plastic bird with its wings glued to its sides shows up and pecks at the head.

You can actually see the hand of the dude holding the bird for the camera.

WHAT THE HELL.

I'll admit, *Santa Clause Conquers the Martians* was bad, *Momma Mia* was bad, but this movie was a turd. I should have known something was up when I hit play and heard the toilet flushing in the next room. The torture doesn't end until the head ninja fights the lead alien in space, then enters the atmosphere as he plummets towards the Earth, doesn't burn up, and lands on his feet without turning into a human accordion.

At least THAT would have been funny.

VERDICT: WHY!?

This movie is not even remotely funny. In fact, I've not been this offended by pointless camp since *Sex and the City*. Of all the crap I've seen, this one turns the bathroom into a bio-hazardous accident and then wipes itself with the good bath towels.

Another Gay Movie: I AM SCARRED FOR LIFE.

As if having the screaming s**ts wasn't bad enough, I decide to torture myself with this week's load of donkey stool while laid up on the couch waiting for my next nuclear deposit into the porcelain vault.

One of my good friends is gay and enjoyed my review on *The Gay Bed and Breakfast of Terror* so much that he suggested that I seek out another gay film to review.

I WILL GET HIM FOR THIS.

Four friends, gay of course, decide that if their lesbian friend Muffler can sleep with half the cheerleading squad, then they can manage to get laid over the summer. They make a pact to lose their virginity before summer is over...wait a f**king minute.

Oh God, it's *American Pie.*

Yes, friends! After watching half of the movie, this is a scene-for-scene remake of *American Pie,* right down to sex with a pastry. The difference? Everyone is gay or has homosexual tendencies.

I have to know what the hell the writers think when they are penning this crap. I mean, I know my thought process and my writing process. Not once has a gay little gremlin sat on my shoulder and whispered in my ear: "Do this, it'll be *fabulous!*"

Now I'm not knocking the gay community. I am so pro-equality it's not even funny. But what the hell is wrong with you people!? All I ask for is ONE DECENT MOVIE.

ONE.

Muffler, the lesbian version of Stiffler, is the only character that makes this weird underwear stain watchable, and I still only made it halfway before I finally had to call it quits. I'm secure in my manhood and all, but the last thing I want to see in f**king HD is some dude's bare sausage. Let alone in a close-up.

I consider it an achievement that I actually made it beyond getting eyeball-raped by rainbows and flowers during the opening credits.

Let's be real for a minute: I can generally sit through anything. I sat through *Troll 2* AND *Battlefield Earth.* But if I can't even get halfway through your movie, you've either offended me (and that is a hell of an accomplishment) or your movie is so bad it's actually making me consider giving up on film altogether and joining a monastery just so I never again have to be subjected to the drivel that you unceremoniously shat onto that poor innocent film that did nothing but love you and hope to be the tapestry upon which you paint your masterpiece.

Not the toilet paper you used to wipe your a**.

VERDICT: BAN-HAMMER!!!!

This movie is a prime example as to what happens when you green-light projects while high on crack. Seriously, why has no one been sued? And there are sequels! Yes, ladies and gentlemen, SEQUELS. I guess the first one wasn't bad enough, so they had to emphasize it by spending money and time on making a continuation of the horror.

Do I regret watching it? Do I wish I had never come across it? At this point, I only wish that I could un-see things that have caused me pain and suffering.

Barbarian Queen: In a time of ancient Gods, warlords, and boobies...

Okaaaay...

No secret to anyone who has known me most of my life: I am a HUGE *Xena: Warrior Princess* fan. *Hercules: The Legendary Journeys* was good too, but Xena took the cake and had a lot more of the characters my best bud and I loved: Xena and Gabrielle (of course), Joxer the Mighty, Ares, Aphrodite and Autolycus, King of Thieves.

So imagine what I'm thinking when I delve into the fantasy flicks of the eighties and discover this...gem.

The cover looks great: a group of half-naked warrior chicks ready to kick the hell out of an army of thugs and goofballs who want nothing more than an evening alone with these beauties, and film promised to be loaded with more topless fun than a buffet at the Men's Club.

What I got was a cheap burrito packed full of s**t from the back of a pickup truck.

A young barbarian girl is picking flowers by the river when she is attacked and raped by a group of Roman soldiers and their leader. Turns out, she is Taramis (Dawn Dunlap), the sister of Amethea the Barbarian Queen (Lana Clarkson).

The village is raided by the Roman troops, and most of the people are killed off. Amethea escapes and watches as her husband-to-be, Argan (Frank Zagarino), is hauled off to be a gladiator in the city. Amethea, joined by her two best warriors, vows vengeance and to save Taramis and Argan from the Roman leader.

Okay, a combat sequence. Let's see if it's better than the acting and dialogue.

Nope.

I've seen kids with sticks and garbage can lids do better choreography than this mess. It literally looks like a self-defense class in an old-folks home full of retired cosplayers. It's bad when I can sit there and watch them break character to think about the next move.

Just to bring you up to speed, I've now seen Dawn Dunlap, Lana Clarkson, and Susana Traverso topless. Not complaining! But, just so you're aware, even in 1985, there were movies with more nudity than friggin' *True Blood*.

There's even a drinking game. Awesome.

Aaaanyway, our three stooges...I mean, "Warrior Women of Great Valor" set off to the Roman encampment to see if Taramis and Argan are being held there before they are sent to the city. They find a topless girl tied to a pile of brush being raped by a goon. They save her.

The guards in the camp attack with powerful, gut-wrenching lines like, "Wanna fight? Alright!" More bad dialogue, more gore, and more boobies later, the girl dies and our trio searches the camp.

They manage to find that Taramis is still there, but Argan has been carted off to the Roman city to be a slave for the gladiator circuit. Taramis is out of it and acts like she's about ten years old, even though she was twenty-four when the movie was filmed.

In fact, that's how she acts the entire movie. Kinda creepy. WTF.

Onward!

The group finds themselves in the Roman city (not Rome, the Roman city...Jesus) after meeting a young boy...well they keep calling it a girl. But it...I mean he...but she...

Let me back up here.

The group finds themselves in the Roman city after meeting a young transgender who is the son/daughter hybrid of the rebel leader. The leader is reluctant to allow them to enter their ranks but is convinced when Amethea explains their cause.

More violence and bad acting later, the group is captured after Taramis runs off and pulls Stockholm with the Roman leader. Amethea is put on the rack, which is supposed to be the prime reason for watching this movie at all since she spends the next chunk of the movie topless while being tortured by a one-eyed pervert.

Didn't we see this in *The Walking Dead?*

After several attempts by the Roman Leader to make her disclose the location of the rebel base (I guess Howard R. Cohen was a *Star Wars* nut), the torture chamber dude begins to rape Amethea. She quickly takes advantage and traps him with her...

She locks down on his member with her vagina.

Where does a guy sign up for that?

The torturer begs her to let him go (wimp), releases her, then screams as she lets him go and kicks him into a tub of acid.

The Roman Leader has organized a gladiator battle in the city square, not knowing that Argan has recruited his fellow slaves as rebels against the tyranny. One of them turns, and Amethea shows up with the other rebels and signals all-out combat.

Remember when you were kids, and you would get your group of friends who liked sword fighting to charge on your other group of friends who like sword fighting? And you would have a battle in the back yard that had the same epic scale as the Battle of Minas Tirith from *Lord of the Rings* (read: a bunch of kids spouting off the same bulls**t they heard in the latest episode of *He-Man* and swinging sticks because the school football jocks weren't there to slap them around)?

This grand finale Battle Royale is the same thing, but with half-naked women.

Amethea fights the Roman Leader but doesn't realize that he has had actual stage combat training. He is about to kill her when Taramis runs up behind him screaming and stabs him in the back with a knife that is bigger than her.

The scene is actually reminiscent of the scene in *Austin Powers: International Man of Mystery* when he runs over the dude with the Zamboni.

The rebels rejoice in their victory, and the credits roll...wait, what!?

VERDICT: Brain...is...rotting.

So I guess the guys behind this movie decided that a Victoria's Secret Catalog or a subscription to *Playboy* wasn't enough for their 15-year-old sons, who were too busy with *Dungeons and Dragons* anyway, so they made a movie set in ancient times and filled to the brim with naked chicks.

First thing you'll notice, if you choose to ignore my warnings and watch this turd nugget, is that that acting AND the dialogue are absolutely horrendous. Yup, this is one of those movies where you get a two-fer. Typically, the somewhat lacking dialogue causes the bad acting. But when the dialogue is utter gar-b**ch you can't help but wonder if maybe the actors are also substandard since most would've looked at the script and laughed.

They're called "contractions," Howard R. Cohen. Use them.

While I'm not complaining in the slightest about the level of nudity in the movie, it does get to a point where all the movie is about is putting the girls in situations that will render them topless. Some of the situations get downright laughable, and I actually began to liken them to the death traps in the original *Batman* series from the 1960s.

The costumes weren't bad, though some of them were a little half-a**ed. More efforts were put into the costumes that were easily removable than the more complex stuff. Frankly, there was better costuming in the failed *Mortal Kombat* television series.

Not to say that this was a bad movie, it wasn't. IT WAS AN AWFUL MOVIE. But, apparently, it's part of an entire subgenre of 1980s fantasy movies that feature pretty much the same thing: ancient times, ancient creatures (in some cases), and boobies galore.

Sure, I'd watch it again. I'd have to take about three Tramadol with a beer or twelve, but I think I could manage.

Birdemic 2-The Resurrection: Oh, the f**king PAIN...

...I think I'm gonna be sick.

For a long time, I swore by *Troll 2* as the worst movie ever made. Then, there was *Manos: The Hands of Fate*, dethroning *Troll 2* in all of the explosive crappy glory that can generally only be witnessed during the aftermath of binge-eating Taco Bell.

I looked everywhere for the first *Birdemic*, but I had no luck. Apparently it's a cult phenomenon, which should've been my first clue that I was in for hell. Not that I don't like or respect cult movies, but I'm realistic. Most of the time a cult movie is gonna be bad.

Charming, but bad.

Onward!

Birdemic 2: The Resurrection opens with a young man walking down the street in Hollywood with some hokey seventies music playing in the background. As he turns the corner, I brace myself for something to happen.

I mean, really! It's not an unrealistic expectation for things to go to hell quickly in an action/creature flick. I lean forward, bracing myself to see people torn apart by angry crazed birds.

Wait for it. Wait for it.

...still waiting...

What the f**k?

For five minutes straight, I watch a dude walk down the street from every angle known to man while listening to peppy, poppy seventies elevator metal.

Dude, who we soon find out is named Bill, meets Gloria in a local dive that's obviously a closed-down diner used as the "restaurant" setting for the film. They stare awkwardly at each other, then the boom mic turns on with a loud static hiss, and we hear the first epic line of this masterpiece...

"Hi!"

Let's skip ahead because the next six minutes are spent watching Bill talk about his movie with Nathalie and Rod, the survivors of the first *Birdemic*. Bill is doing a new movie that he's written, and he needs a million

Bad Movie Beware!

dollars to fund it. Rod immediately writes him a check for $100,000 to get him going.

WTF does he do for a living? Can I have some!?

Hey, Rod! Buy me a house! With a pool that someone else takes care of!

What's sad is that the entire movie plays out like this. I haven't seen this much exposition in a film since *Sense and Sensibility*. F**king GOLF has more action and excitement than this massive Arnold Palmer turd.

The rest of the movie is Bill getting an endorsement for his movie, his relationship with Gloria developing, and the two of them hanging out with Rod and Nathalie. The producers at the studio are hesitant to fund Bill's movie.

"Where are the topless chicks? Where are the sex scenes? No blood? No guts?"

No s**t, guys.

Let me make sure you understand that I am not exaggerating: we are now fifteen minutes into this movie, and nothing has happened yet.

Let's fast-forward because there is more nothing to come. No, really, nothing. We meet Nathalie's young cousin, or brother, or son, or something at the local museum when they go to look at the bird exhibit, but he goes away after the scene is over.

Okay, so he was a figment of everyone's imagination?

About twenty-five minutes in, a girl is attacked in the ocean. She runs ashore and is rescued by our fabulous four. She tells them that a "Giant Jumbo Jellyfish" attacked her.

Take note that this is what everyone in the movie calls it throughout the rest of the scene.

At least we're finally getting some action (and alliteration).

The scene ends, and the event is never mentioned again in the movie. Ever. What the hell is with this movie? It's like an un-medicated ADD Vietnamese guy with no experience or training wrote it!

Oh, wait.

Skipping…skipping…okay, I'm sparing you. No, really. I could sit here and write 5,000 words on the story, or I could just skip to the F**KING 45 MINUTE MARK WHERE WE FINALLY GET WHAT THE ENTIRE F**KING MOVIE IS SUPPOSED TO BE ABOUT!!

The rain turns red, and Hollywood is attacked by thousands of birds animated courtesy of...a hacked Sega CD? WTF did they use? The special effects are GIF images overlaid onto the shot like plastic wrap on moldy leftovers from Thanksgiving.

Our heroes escape the set with the sound and camera guys just as the birds kill everyone else. Nathalie screams for them to grab a...hanger? Okay, so hangers are super-weapons in this movie? Apparently they were in the first film, but they don't help this time.

Eventually Gloria and Nathalie forgo weaponry and break out the martial arts. Yes, they actually go hand-to-wing combat with the pissed-off fowl like a round of *Mortal Kombat.* Note: neither one of them have martial arts choreography here, so it looks more like the local nerdy fat kid trying to do karate in his back yard.

The crew finds a cemetery where a few people are walking around and stop to check on them. Yeah, they aren't people.

Zombies. F**king ZOMBIES.

"I made a movie about killer birds, and decided: HEY! What the hell? Let's put zombies in it! That'll work!"

Not.

After a few more shenanigans, the gang ends up at a local zoo. The zookeeper, obviously a Mr. Miyagi fan, explains that the birds are attacking those who do not live a green lifestyle. They are reacting to global warming and will leave if everyone starts living a green way of life.

...oh, my God. I'm watching an environmental statement.

Sigh.

A final attack from the birds kills off the last stagehand, and the four main characters in the movie stand over his corpse floating in a swimming pool as the birds turn and fly away.

I guess they swore to leave a small environmental footprint?

The End. Credits. That's it. Fini.

VERDICT: BURY IT IN A LANDFILL, COVER IT IN OIL, AND BURN.

Not that I'm against watching a movie that makes a statement, but there are ways to go about it. Take *Wall-E,* for example. Right away, as soon as the film opens, it's pretty obvious that the world is f**ked up because of us and what we did. It takes on the issue of pollution by going deeper and showing how it's not that simple. It looks at over-consumption, consumerism, and control.

However, *Birdemic 2* tries to focus on the fact that we pollute, and nature is pissed about it. But what else is new? Should we pollute? Hell no, and we suck for it. But give me more, Mr. Nguyen, and don't stuff it into a large wad and cram it directly up my a** in the last ten minutes of the movie.

Let's look at the mechanics.

The acting was horrific to the point of being described as putrid. I don't know if they actors were doing it on purpose, or if they're just that bad. The script has the same awkward dialogue style as seen in *Troll 2*, and moments that are dragged out to the point where the actors are visibly ready to stop rolling that particular scene and are just improvising (badly) until the director yells cut.

The first forty-five minutes of the movie have nothing to do with the premise of the film and play out like a romantic Hollywood movie after a night of binge-drinking cheap malt liquor. I am watching a movie about birds killing people, but I've got forty-five minutes of exposition to get through first?

Excuse me while I beat my head on my desk.

In writing, there is this thing we like to call "Bait and Hook." You show the conflict early on to draw the reader in, then pan things out from there. Movies follow that same formula, more or less. Even *The Lord of the Rings* opens with the conflict before dropping you down into Hobbiton for some fun with Frodo.

The music is unbearable, yet it fits the feel of the first part of the film. It's hokey, upbeat, and badly chosen. I'm not saying they should've gone with John Williams or Iron Maiden, but damn. Really, it's difficult to figure out what music to use anywhere because the movie is such a hot mess. It's hard to put the right music to your movie if you don't really know what it's about.

This movie, like its predecessor, has a huge cult following of bad movie lovers, and I can't figure out why. As a fellow lover of le Suck Cinema, I'm floored by how bad this particular bad movie is. I'm surprised it got green-lighted at all considering the damning technical issues with it, most notably the writing.

Yes. I am saying that this is a BAD bad movie.

It's available on DVD and Blu-Ray, but why the hell would you do that to yourself? Save your money, and buy something more valuable. What household doesn't need a banana hammock or a collection of rubber duckies?

Blood Mania: For the love of sweet Jesus...

I got a movie pack from my wife for Christmas entitled *Gorehouse Greats*. It's supposed to be a collection of some of the greatest cult gore flicks of the sixties, seventies, and whenever-the-hell.

One stuck out in particular: *Blood Mania*.

I know what you're thinking: gore-galore! Serial killers and gruesomeness and naked chicks, oh my! Well, one of those is right. When I watch porn, I know what I'm walking into. They don't lie about what they are doing with some inane title like *Blood Mania*.

After all, it's freaking porn!

The story opens with some chick running through a garden while some dude is chasing her, intent on killing her. He catches her, sexually assaults her, and cuts her up.

Things are going great so far!

Then, we suddenly plunge into a twisted murder mystery that isn't much of a mystery with story points that lead nowhere and so many booby-shots that after about the twentieth in the first fifteen minutes, it actually gets boring.

Yes, I actually got tired of seeing naked chicks.

Some rich dude who isn't even memorable is sick and dying while his nurse, Ms. Turner (read: dude with a hippie-wig) and his psychopathic nymphoid daughter, Victoria, take care of him and his estate.

The good doctor, Brian, is as much of a whore as Vic. He lives with a girl, who is hotter by far, and is boning Vic on the side. He also owes some dude $50K of hush money about something sinister that went down in med school. There are allusions that the sicko in the opening sequence is the doc, but this movie also has allusions of not being fecal matter, so take that for what it's worth.

Vic promises Brian the cash and offs daddykins. Enter little sis, Gail, who ends up getting everything in the will while Victoria is left the house and $250 a week. Vic goes nutbags and ends up under treatment of Brian while he begins boning Gail for the money.

Meanwhile, back at the ranch, Brian's live-in girlfriend bones blackmail dude to keep him off Brian's back. He gets the goods and walks away, saying that she's not worth $50K. We never see her again.

By the end, Vic has killed Gail, Brian is hiding the body and hooking back up with Vic, and Mr. Creepy McCreeperson shows up with Gail's body and a smirk.

Notice something? NO F**KING BLOOD!!!

The movie is called BLOOD MANIA, but it might as well be an episode of *Murder, She Wrote* with mild violence and enough nudity to edit together panty-porn!

Verdict: Call in a nationwide manhunt for the ahole who wrote and made this movie.**

Yeah, I get it. Women have boobs. Can I please get some kind of cohesive plot out of this mess?

Watching this movie with any expectations other than the possibility of drooling at the end because of the lobotomy you gave yourself to escape this wreck is like trying to hook up with the girl next door. Just when you think...nah. That's too good for it.

It's like feeling like you have to take a crap so large you swear if you lie on your side or sit down that a watermelon will come out of your butt. You sit, and all you get is a nugget. Nothing else.

Ever.

This is not a movie. It is an awkward stain on the underwear of the same industry that crapped *Battlefield Earth* onto film.

Only this time, it forgot to wipe.

Bloodrayne-The Third Reich: Utter shiesse.

I have always had a very strict "No Uwe Boll" rule. I am an old-school *Bloodrayne* fan, having played both games (The original *Bloodrayne* on GameCube and *Bloodrayne 2* on the original XBOX), and I was STOKED that a movie was being made.

Until I found out that it was basically shot with a camera phone.

And Kristanna Loken. Eek.

Ever since then, coupled with Boll's rendition of *House of the Dead*, which actually tossed up high scores during combat sequences, I have always turned my nose up at his crap. NEVER have I seen a good credible review for one of his movies.

Apparently, he also knows that his movies suck and just refuses to admit so. It shows in this, the third installment of his highly loathed *Bloodrayne* series. The dialogue was recorded so low that I actually had to turn the sound all the way up, and it was still hard to understand.

Ah. That could be a reason.

NONE OF THE GERMANS HAVE A GERMAN ACCENT.

Now, I forgave the half-and-half French accents in *Man in the Iron Mask* because it was actually a fun movie to watch. Not great but still a favorite of mine. But when even the director is German, I expect some German-speaking Nazis. I mean, really.

Anywho, Rayne spends her days hunting Nazis for the Brimstone Society. She encounters a train taking a shipment of Jews to a camp and hijacks it along with a group of rebels trying to hijack the same train. She bites the Commandant, and he turns into a Damphir: a half-human, half-vampire like her.

Later, after some brief and pointless damn-near silent dialogue, Rayne visits a brothel for some fun while a German Mad Scientist devises a plan to take her blood and give it to Hitler so that he can live forever.

Meanwhile, after Rayne's gratuitous girl-on-girl scene, she leaves her room and fights all of the Nazis who are inside the bordello. No, there is no real reason. As far as I can tell from the body language, one of the ladies tattled that she was there.

The entire movie plays out like this, feeling less like a film and more like in-game cinema sequences. The scenes are all chopped up and haphazardly spliced back together, and Boll's obsession with seeing the sultry video game character do dirty things on both sides of the field is painfully obvious. I mean, come on, man.

The sex scenes in the *Friday the 13th* movies were more pertinent than this.

The acting is bad...really bad. How hard is it to drop f-bombs on camera? Hell, Boll and his minions even screw that one up. Also, the little details nag at me...

LIKE THE FACT THAT RAYNE'S SWORDS ARE SUPPOSED TO BE ATTACHED TO HER ARMS, YOU DOUCHE.

Has he even PLAYED the games? *Silent Hill*: great game to film movie! *Resident Evil*: not bad at all! *Assassin's Creed*: VERY slick short film! But NO. Boll fought hard and won the rights to do a *Bloodrayne* film, and he's been screwing the pooch ever since.

Anyway, Rayne and the rebels eventually get into a battle with the bad guys, and all of the bad guys die. Yeah, really. That nice and neat. You know, with all of the mythology surrounding the character, one would think that the director (a.k.a. Uwe Boll of Stinking S**T) would have at least done some research.

Negative.

Turns out, he just wanted to make video game porn.

VERDICT: DETONATE.

When studios started really pumping out the video game movies, guess who placed a bid on EVERY LAST STINKING ONE OF THEM!?

You guessed it. Boll.

This is a man who should be barred from ever making a movie. But no. Somewhere out there are enough people who actually like this crap (damned masochists, I reckon) enough to merit him making more crap.

It's almost like the DVD shelf is a wastewater storage area, and he's just adding to the smell. When I saw the cover, I had to take a second look because it almost looked like he had cast a drag queen as Rayne. The jaw on that chick would make a T-Rex blush!

The story was incredibly weak with holes in it as big as the Grand Canyon. It probably would've helped if I could actually have heard the dialogue, but I guess that's too much to ask.

I dare say that *Super Mario Bros.* was better than this movie.

Brain Twisters: Mental Status-Retarded.

Once again I look to the *Gorehouse Greats*: a collection of films given to me by my in-laws from the depths of the $5 bin at Best Buy. Twelve movies guaranteed to chill my bones.

More like guaranteed to give myself a concussion from the atomic face-palm every time I watch one.

Usually these collections have at least one good movie in the mix. *Brain Twisters* was not it. In fact, even though it was the most recent movie in the box (filmed circa 1991), it was still just as goofy and repugnant as the older cult movies. On top of that, the writer and director made their points so painfully obvious that it was less like watching a movie and more like watching someone whine on their Facebook wall.

Dr. Phillip Rothman is a professor of neuroscience at a prestigious university. Laurie and her friends are his students. Unbeknownst to them, he is also part of a project run by a major corporation studying various methods of mind control using a sealed booth with a television and what looks like an Atari 2600 flashing colors onto the screen. The end result is his experiments turning into murders when his students start killing each other after seeing flashing lights or hearing certain sounds.

Of course, enter the debonair Detective Frank Turi.

Turi and Laurie form a fast romantic relationship, and Rothman realizes that he is causing damage at the hands of the corporation. He tries to call it off, but the corporation puts him under mind control. Things begin to go haywire when Michelle, one of Laurie's friends (and the token slut in the movie) gets into the machine and overdoes things. She is turned into a hideous hissing, serial killing hag. Dr. Rothman is shot to death by a corporate henchman who is later run over by Turi. Michelle kills her boyfriend and the CEO of the corporation. Laurie and Turi barely escape Michelle, and the scene fades as they watch her try to reach them through a broken window.

The colors return, this time accompanied by a digital man with a gun dancing around the screen. The camera pans back, and we see a young boy playing a video game on his Atari (have these people not gotten a Super Nintendo yet!?) His mother calls for him, and he bellows back in an insane rage. The end.

Yeah.

What sucks the most is that I actually covered the big points of this crap-noir. It took them ninety-two minutes to tell me a story that could have been told more effectively in less than five minutes. It was like listening to a second-grader tell me about *War and Peace*.

Or watching *Vacancy*. Same difference.

VERDICT: LOBOTOMY.

This movie made *Sense and Sensibility* look like a Bruce Willis action movie. I generally watch this crap in the mornings while eating breakfast, and I actually almost nodded off a few times on my feet while watching this. The acting is poor at best, with the only headliner being the fabulously hot Farrah Forke from *Wings*. No, she does not get naked. In fact, that probably wouldn't have salvaged this boring ninety-two-minute yawn-fest anyway. Yes, I am saying that *boobies* would not have helped keep this ship from sinking.

Also, I understand completely that this pile of poo-poo is an indictment of Corporate America. Fine, I get it. But the entire flick is saturated with evil corporate moguls being behind the whole thing. The CEO might as well be wringing his hands incessantly while asking Mr. Smithers to get him another round of Scotch. Then what's this!? They change gears at the end and make the statement that our minds are being controlled by video games!

ABSURD.

Look, guys, pick a topic and stay with it. This is why *They Live* worked so well.

I would rather eat a cake iced with whipped lard from a drunken camel than watch this movie again. Now, if you don't mind, I have to get the oil changed in my Puma before going out on a hooker-killing rampage so I can have mob bosses send me on menial errands that make no sense but grant me cash out of thin air every time I complete one or score a wicked jump (gamers will get the reference).

Double Dragon: Double crap on toast

I finally got a chance to view this oldie, and I must say I was surprised. It's surprising to me that anyone who was in this movie still has a career.

It's also surprising to me how cheap Robert Patrick and Alyssa Milano work.

If anyone has ever played the game, oh well. The storyline hasn't much to do with it other than that the main characters are Billy and Jimmy Lee, twin brothers (not really, Billy is obviously American and Jimmy is obviously not) who fight in an underground circuit to raise money and pay the bills.

The city of New Angeles is under curfew at night after a truce is made between the city gangs and the police. The gangs are made up of neo-punks in outfits that scream Goodwill last minute shopping.

Marion heads up the good guys of the underworld and rocks a crew cut from hell, which is a far cry from the long red locks she sported in the game. As if the premise wasn't bad enough (find both halves of the Double Dragon Medallion before KokoShuko does), the script was way worse.

Every line is either a bad elementary school joke or a reference of self-representation. I had to groan in physical pain when Alyssa Milano was asked, "Who's the boss, now?" by "Lash," played by the chick from *General Hospital*.

By the way, there is a cheesy line to that one, too.

Abobo, the fearsome giant from the game, is now a walking flesh tank that looks like a mutated Stay-Puft Marshmallow man, and Robert Patrick (read: "T-1000") plays a whiny excuse for a Shadow Boss.

Never mind, his name in the movie is KokoShuko.

Of course, the famous bit between the brothers that will live on in horrific infamy put a different twist on it.

Billy: "Sorry I had to kick your butt so bad, Bro."

Jimmy: "You didn't kick my butt, you kicked KokoPUKE-o's butt."

They both then giggle like a couple of schoolgirls in the sandbox talking about what's under the skirt.

VERDICT: THING IN THE ATTIC.

This movie was all but forgotten for good reason. A script written by a ten-year-old boy and painfully obvious choreographed fights make this gem tarnished as if it had been living in the rectum of a dragon for years before it was excavated. The archeologists who found it probably cried when they discovered that no matter how deep they buried it, the gem would haunt them into madness and despair. I would require a coma induced by a helluva lot of drugs and alcohol to sit down to this donkey turd again, and I would still fight.

The Garbage Pail Kids Movie: Hollywood resorts to dumpster-diving.

I'm about to take you back hardcore!

Okay, maybe "hardcore" is a little much. Maybe medium-core. Anyway, any kid who grew up in the 80's remembers the Garbage Pail Kids cards. You know, the knock against Cabbage Patch Kids that ran like hell from cute and sweet and embraced vulgar and disgusting like the school slut at a party.

Hell, just the thought of some of them still makes me a little queasy.

Well, if you don't remember them then you were both blessed and deprived as a child. What the hell did you do with yourself anyway?

Read? Play outside?

So I'm also sure you all remember how stoked we were when they announced a movie. That's right! A full-fledged Garbage Pail Kids movie!! We flocked to the movie theaters to watch what could've been the most epic kid/nerd flick EVER.

Then we ran like hell when we saw the truth.

The movie opens with a garbage can/rocket ship moving through space. The credits open by introducing the cast via their very own Garbage Pail card. So we have Mackenzie Astin as "Douglas." Yeah, that kid from *The Facts of Life*.

This can't be good.

The story then opens with Doug, aka "The Creep," running from the local bully Juice and his gang. Along for the ride is Juice's fashion-designer wannabe girlfriend Tangerine. It comes to light quickly that Doug has a thing for Tangerine, which gets creepy later on when she supposedly returns his affections. Also, he's fourteen and hasn't even had his voice change yet, and she's old enough to drive.

And maybe attend her freshman year in college.

Aaaaanyway, Tangerine wanders into Captain Manzini's relic shop where Doug works and is followed by Juice and his crew. They rough up Doug again, and the scuffle results in the garbage can we saw in space earlier getting knocked over. The Garbage Pail Kids emerge and are introduced.

Now, for those who were avid collectors of the cards (even when they began to really suck), you might recognize some of the names. We have Valerie Vomit, Messy Tessie, Foul Phil, Greaser Greg, Windy Winston, Nat Nerd and Ali Gator.

Where, oh where do I begin on how BAD the Kids look!? In an effort to make them look like they do on the cards, the engineers forgot along the way that the characters actually have lines.

That's right, Doogie McPuppeteer, the mouths on the kids might actually have to move.

Moving forward (albeit in agonizing neurological pain), we find out that the Kids are not only f**king disgusting, but they are also gifted fashion designers and can make the coolest clothing the 80's has ever seen.

No, I did not mistype. Clothes.

Doug gets the idea to impress Tangerine by having the kids make clothes for her to sell as her own. He convinces them to do it, and they decide to help after a musical number that just makes you want to claw your ears out.

As it turns out, the Garbage Pail Kids just want to wander around and get into trouble. So, after finishing Doug and Tangerine's most recent order, they go out on the town for some mischief. Ali and Windy get into a bar fight at "The World's Toughest Bar."

No, really, that's the name of the place.

The rest of the kids go to the movies and cause mayhem. Shortly after, they are rounded up by Doug and locked back away in the shop basement just as Juice and his goons wander by to talk to Tangerine. After a few more incidents, Tangerine finds out about the Kids and decides to play sweet on Doug so the Kids will make clothes for her upcoming fashion show.

Is this making sense yet? No, it never does.

Tangerine locks the Kids in the basement when she finds out that they plan to go to the show, and Juice arrives later on and has them carted off by the State Home for the Ugly, passing by the Sweat Shop and The World's Toughest Bar along the way.

Real creative with the business names, right?

Doug finds out and leaves the show. He storms the State Home for the Ugly along with Captain Manzini and the bikers from the World's

Toughest Bar and frees the Kids. They all decide to crash the fashion show and give Tangerine and Juice some payback.

The fashion show is quickly reduced to chaos as the Kids stage a full-scale assault. Windy farts all over Tangerine's audience, Nat Nerd pees everywhere, Ali Gator munches on toes, Foul Phil incapacitates people with his breath, Greaser Greg gets hair grease on people, Messy Tessie blows snot all over Juice's goons, and Valarie Vomits covers them in puke.

Doug takes on Juice directly. Okay, people. Doug is VERY obviously a fourteen-year-old kid, and Juice looks to be in his twenties. Yet, they fight *mano-a-mano* and Doug whoops Juice's a** all over the stage.

Anyone else see a problem here?

To end it off, Tangerine tries to talk to Doug later in front of Manzini's shop in order to make amends. She sees the error of her ways and figures out that Doug is a nice guy (even though he is too young to drive and she is a good foot taller than he is complete with deeper voice). Doug blows her off and tells her that he's not interested anymore.

Captain Manzini thinks he may have found a spell to get the Kids back into the garbage pail. He plays their song (the same f**king theme you hear repeatedly throughout the entire blasted movie), then plays it backwards to lure them into the can. They leave the shop and ride off into the night on ATVs.

The End.

VERDICT: This has got to be an achievement of some kind.

Before *Troll 2*, this was considered the worst movie ever made, and for good reason. IT SUCKED GARGANTUAN BOVINE NUTS.

This movie sucked worse than the job of the guy who tongue-cleans sumo wrestlers before and after matches. It sucked worse than eating brussel sprouts with a side of cat poo and extra ammonia dip. Where do I begin, you ask?

The Garbage Pail Kids were awful. The outfits were tailored to look as much like the cards as possible, so the masks not only didn't have movable jaws and lips when the characters spoke, but they also stayed frozen in the same expression the entire movie. The eyes moved, and that was all.

Not to mention creepy.

Bad Movie Beware!

Even though the source material was lacking, the acting could've been better. The only actor who seemed to take it seriously was the late Anthony Newley, who played Captain Manzini. Why does this matter, you ask? Because if the actors take it seriously, then the movie at least has a chance of having SOME redeeming value.

I had to draw the line at the song. Really? And it's an ear bug, to boot. Jesus, make it stop. The cover states that this movie is "Gross-Out Fun for the Whole Family." Why in the name on Oprah Winfrey's fat a** on a biscuit would I subject my family to this!?

Makenzie Aston? Really? You take the good, you take the bad, you take 'em both and there you have a gigantic turd steaming on the video store shelves. Oh yeah, that's right! The video store era is over. As if watching this unholy mule turd wasn't enough to ruin my childhood, I get to watch the one haven I had go up in smoke.

So long, video stores. So long.

I digress. They say that looking back on older movies from the past gives one an appreciation for classic cinema. I say that if it was a roasted manatee intestinal pickle when I was a kid, then it will probably be a roasted manatee intestinal pickle ON TOAST now that I am an adult.

Kind of an adult.

Ah, shaddap.

The Gay Bed and Breakfast of Terror: Yes, I've sunk that low...

Where the hell do I begin?

This two-hour long anal exam (sans the lube) was recommended to me by a friend who happens to swing for the other team. He told me once that being a gay man trying not to be an easy target for jokes was about as easy as going to Chick-fil-A and not eating any chicken.

Possible, but not likely.

The Gay Bed and Breakfast of Terror was so bad that I considered shooting heroin just to escape the ocular agony. If you thought *Brokeback Mountain* was awkward, you have seen nothing. It was only made worse by the fact that my schedule is so hectic that it takes me a week to watch a movie, especially if it is a three-hour s**tbag like *Supernova*.

This cinematic apocalypse opens with Chubbett the Marshmallow Girl running through the Nevada desert waving her arms around her head like she's trying to take off to monitor traffic for the radio station updates. As the screen goes black, she is knocked down and slaughtered. Suddenly, a jaunty show tune begins, and a transvestite go-go dancer warning us about straights serenades us.

Yes. A slasher flick opened by a transvestite go-go dancer.

I have entered the depths of hell.

Welcome, five gay/lesbian couples and "fag-hag," to the Sahara Salvation Bed and Breakfast!

The bed and breakfast is owned and operated by Helen and Luella. Helen is a homophobic religious fanatic, and Luella is her socially tragic lesbian daughter. Helen's sole purpose is to find a husband for Luella and convert both the gay man she finds and Luella to a blissfully straight God-fearing lifestyle.

First to arrive are Dom and Alex, two performers. Dom is the male-dominatrix, and Alex is the drag queen in the show.

Then there are Deborah and Gabby, well-to-do lesbians with likable personalities and a party to attend that evening.

Mike and Eric are the upscale yuppie couple who bring along their friend Lizzette. Star and Brenda also arrive, with the story looking more like Star will be our heroine.

Rodney and Todd end it out with a very odd personal-trainer/trainee relationship.

The men in the movie all decided that they wanted the role of "Bitchy Cheerleader," so the whining and snide remarks predominantly come from them. It gets old quickly as the movie tries (unsuccessfully) to be a gay horror film.

The difference? *A Nightmare on Elm St. Part 2* was actually good.

Helen soon begins her rampage, going room to room and stabbing each character to death as she picks a suitable husband for Luella. There is also a vicious man-thing roaming around killing them off, his bottom-half a sack of putrid mutation (read: badly made-up sleeping bag).

Alex, Star, Deborah, Gabby, and Eric showdown with Helen for a final confrontation, and the movie quickly changes gears.

Apparently, the writers and director figured out that this movie was sucking worse than a bullet entry hole and decided to make it a horror-comedy instead.

Helen reveals that she attended a Republican convention and ended up the centerpiece of an orgy, the product of which Manfred was born.

Yes. You read it correctly. Manfred, according to Helen, is the bastard child of 100 Republican conventioneers.

It gets worse.

Manfred shows up and kills Eric, and Luella kills Gabby. Alex and Star go nuts, and Alex kills off Helen and Dom, who left and came back to rescue him. Deborah kills Luella, and Alex and Star assume Helen's identity and kill off Deborah to take over the Bed and Breakfast. A new gay couple arrives to find Alex in full drag and Star as the redneck caretaker of Manfred.

The end. If I could make this stuff up, I would be on much better medication than I already am.

VERDICT: WHAT THE F**K!!???

I like to think I'm pretty open-minded, but for cryin' out loud! This movie played out like a bad gay soap opera with the bloodshed and sex (yes, it goes there) tossed in last minute like a plot twist in a *Dora the Explorer* cartoon. What makes it worse is the fact that this movie goes a full two hours! What can you possibly do for two hours with a storyline written on the walls of a bathroom stall!

According to this movie: NOTHING.

This movie was almost as bad as *Troll 2* and worse than *Battlefield Earth*. The fact that this movie was taken seriously and has a small cult following makes it even worse. Generally, any cult movie is good, and followers are a little more in tune with what is good and what is summer blockbuster fodder. The scenes are spliced together with all the grace of an explosive bout of diarrhea, and the only good thing about this movie on the whole was the fact that it ended.

Period.

Gingerdead Man: Those aren't chocolate chips...

Let's face it, Gary Busey is pretty cool.

I saw him one year at the Monster Party. He doesn't shake hands, but he'll fist bump. No worries, he's really cool about it. While I should have been thinking *Predator 2*, I was in the middle of my cerebral torture with this pile of dookie baked to a crisp golden brown. *Chucky* was classic. A doll that is possessed by a serial killer and starts offing people. Still weird, but dolls are scary to begin with.

A killer gingerbread man? Jesus.

Millard Findlemeyer is holding up a local diner and has killed everyone but Sarah Leigh. In case you haven't noticed, everyone in the movie is named after a food brand. (Yeah, I know.) Her fear and her beauty make him leave her alive, but she testifies against him and sends him to the electric chair anyway.

Fast forward two years, and Sarah is now running her family's bakery with her mother. A new corporate place is opening across the street, and the sleazoid CEO is wanting to give Sarah $50K to shut down and go away. She refuses, and he indicates his daughter, Lorna, who is the token b**chy cheerleader in the movie, and says that he can do for Sarah what he's done for her. Sarah shoots him down and storms off to finish the gingerbread man she had started.

After cutting the giant cookie out and putting it into her walk-in oven (never seen one IRL, but hey) she finds Lorna setting a rat free in the bakery. They fight, and Lorna's boyfriend Amos shows up to break them apart. Sarah shoves Lorna into the main power lever for the shop and it short circuits, sending lightening into the oven. Amos and Sarah pull the pan out to find the gingerbread man gone...or is he?

Enter the walking talking homicidal Millard Findlemeyer, now as a killer cookie. The rest of the movie takes place inside the bakery as Gingerdead hunts the characters down. Sarah's mother gets her finger lopped off, Sarah's best friend Julia gets knocked out and decorated like a woman cake, and Lorna's father gets crushed by his own car right before Lorna gets a well-deserved knife to the forehead.

During the madness we find out that Amos and Sarah were childhood sweethearts, and they rekindle their relationship. This plot point simply works to keep Amos alive and does not affect the rest of the movie at all.

In fact, it was forced in with all the grace of an anal probe wielded by Jason Voorhees.

No lube.

Brick returns in a final combat scene and tackles the Gingerdead Man, holding him down while he eats him. Julia and Sarah's mother escape, but Brick becomes possessed by Millard and attacks Sarah. Amos and Sarah shove him into the oven and bake him alive.

The next week they hold a bake sale in front of the bakery. A nurse shows up with a box of gingerbread men left by a mysterious old lady. Credits.

VERDICT: FEED IT TO THE BIRDS!

It was painfully obvious that the bulk of the budget for this movie went to getting Gary Busey to play the bad guy. The brief CGI of the Gingerdead Man coming to life looks like it was copied and pasted onto the print from the internet. Also, I'm still trying to figure out where the gingerdead mix came from.

(Googles and does research)

Ah. Millard's mother got his ashes and mixed them into the gingerbread, then dropped them off at Sarah's bakery.

HOW THE HELL WAS I SUPPOSED TO KNOW THAT!?

This movie bills itself as a dark comedy, but I'm still trying to see what's funny about it. Gary Busey does his best with bad writing, but the only line in the movie worth the high-dollar toilet paper for cleanup is, "Well, I sure ain't the Pillsbury f**kin' Doughboy!"

Robin Sydney (Sarah) has also been diagnosed with Kristen Stewartitis. It's a rare disease that forces your facial muscles into one expression and robs you of any acting ability whatsoever. The icing on the cake? There are two sequels. No, really. Two. I have one. It might never get watched, but I have part 2. Let's see: "The Passion of the Crust."

No, thank you. Gingerdead gives me the squirts.

The House that Screamed: More liked the House that SUCKED.

I don't usually mind indie films, and I have seen a few good ones. This was not one of them.

The House that Screamed took campy porn acting and plotline to a whole new level of sucktacularness that not even *Witchcraft 11* could touch.

The main character, who we'll call Captain Hair Recession due to his EXTREME and obviously fake receding hairline, is a writer who has just lost his family in a house fire cause by his wife (who looks old enough to be his mother) dropping a cigarette on the carpet. His son dies in the fire, though in the iconic (read: hokey) scene where Capt. H.R. is screaming over his dead son, the kid is still kicking and squirming.

Yeah, zombie kid. Go fig.

Capt. H.R. decides to move into a known haunted house and try to write a book about his adventures in the place. What follows is a series of events that would have been more frightening in an episode of *The Smurfs* than in this movie.

The first real haunting takes place while Capt. H.R. is in the bathtub. He hears a knock at the door that will not go away, and the scene cuts to the Grim Reaper knocking on his front door.

Yes, THE GRIM F**KING REAPER!!!

Of course, when he answers the door, no one is there. After another pointless round of this stupidity, he is locked out of the house because it's funny to lock a hairy, half-bald man who can't act out of his house in the middle of the night while he is wearing only a towel and no dignity. He finds his way back in and turns in for the night.

Eventful, right?

By the time we were halfway through day two, I was pleading for there to not be a day three. Not only was I given the finger with day three, I was kicked square in the brown-eye by day four! The acting in this movie was worse than any porn or children's show I have ever watched, and the sound was so bad and overdone that most of the worthless dialogue was drowned in thundering sheet-metal and music played on a cowbell.

No, I am serious. Cowbell.

Insert Christopher Walken reference here.

After his seduction by a morbidly obese zombie hooker (not kidding), he realizes that he is in a world of trouble and does his research only to be visited by a dead Civil War vet (random...) and told that he is essentially screwed.

I will not sugarcoat it, folks. This movie gave me a migraine headache, only cured by turning it off after the credits rolled.

VERDICT: DESTROY!!

Independent films are the bread and butter of the industry, but this movie was the diuretic aftermath. Even though everything about this crappy flick says eighties, it was actually shat onto film in 2000, which somewhat validates the monotone scrolling words at the beginning of this massive waste of mental functionality.

This movie is so bad that any movie critic in his right mind would shoot heroine after watching it just to forget the pain. What were they thinking, anyway? "Hey guys! Mom just gave me a twenty-spot! Let's make a movie!!"

Do not watch this movie, whatever the cost. It will sap you of your dignity and have you thinking that William Shatner's Oscar for Best Actor Ever is long overdue. This movie is the reason doctors prescribe anti-depressants.

Inara, The Jungle Girl: Is Brain Liquification an STD?

Another one for the stew.

I was given this movie by a fan that insists that it is actually the worst movie ever made. I wouldn't go so far as to claim that, unseating *Troll 2* and *Manos: The Hands of Fate* from their porcelain throne, but *Inara: Jungle Girl* certainly holds its own in the category of "Sucktacular."

Of course, it's indie and not even on Netflix, Amazon, or Hulu. I looked, though feel free if you think I missed it somehow. It was actually given to me in a blank cover with a home-printed insert for the cover and a BD-R (Hey, it's on a Blu-ray!) with the cover pic Lightscribed onto the label side of the disc.

The cover actually had email addresses for two of the actresses from the film.

Now THAT is what I call indie!!

The film opens with a dude in military fatigues looking down on another dude in fatigues who has apparently just had his ass kicked. A woman is lying on the ground several feet away, holding a baby in her arms.

Dude standing up begins to give a ridiculously long speech about how things are, how great he is, how our POV guy is going to eat it, and how he raped the girl lying off to the side. He explains that she is the Holy Mother, and that "they" worship her.

In other words, it's a Backstory Word-Vomit.

The guy on the ground shoots the motor mouth, and we then get a musical montage of a redheaded girl eighteen years after the fact. She is mourning the loss of her father and even gives us a couple of scenes of extreme overacting to show us her sorrow.

Like, I don't think they're shooting in slow motion. I think she is ACTUALLY doing it in slow motion.

Well, maybe it IS in slow motion.

Maybe not.

Jeez.

There is a brief scene between her and an old man in her apartment. He tells her that he has been charged with protecting her. She says that she doesn't care about him, her father, or "Liam and his boys." Liam is the son of the motor mouth from the opening.

We get another musical montage of her walking around, drinking, smoking, sulking, more walking around, more drinking, more sulking. Music. Walking. People-watching. Walking.

This movie has been on a good f**king half-hour.

What the hell.

What makes the movie watchable thus far? The lead actress playing who, we are to assume by this point, is Inara, is gorgeous. Unfortunately, beauty does not a good actress make.

Inara, drunk as a skunk, wanders into an alley where she is jumped by "Liam and his Boys." These guys are military and wearing their fatigues while all four of them assault and beat up on a skinny little drunk redhead.

Inara fights back, sobers up a little, and kicks the s**t out of all four of them. What funny is that she isn't surprised at all by her fighting ability. So, what? Am I to assume she's done this before?

She's interrupted by her father's friend and told about a military operation that he wants her to be a part of. She agrees and shows up the next day in her fatigues…

Wait a sec.

I mean I get that she was wearing them during her father's funeral. But hell, I've known military brats who've done the same thing and aren't actual soldiers. But when the hell did she enlist? And are low-rider pants and a midriff official dress code (not that I'm complaining)?

Oh, they're mercenaries. I get it.

(Headdesk)

Liam and his buddies are also part of the platoon, and Liam assaults Inara on the plane while they are flying into the warzone. The plane crashes, killing everyone. Maybe. Possibly. Where the hell is the blood?

Is that dude ACTUALLY dead with his arm perfectly placed under his head? Sleeping? Didn't want to get his hair dirty?

Inara meets the Amazons and quickly joins with them and their cause for no apparent reason whatsoever. I had to have it turned down low because people in the house were sleeping, but I could still hear the sparse amount of dialogue.

And then we are treated to the fourth montage this movie features where Inara befriends the Amazons and learns their ways in a matter of twenty-four hours. She even starts to talk like them because, you know, she's always been an Amazon. We just didn't know that.

Sigh.

Liam and the crowd from the plane survived after all, and they swarm in and gun down the little girl that Inara befriended during her first day with the Amazons. Inara takes command and rallies the Amazons to fight the Mercs.

The Mercs wander down a creek, guns at the ready, and are stormed by Inara and the Amazons. They throw down their guns and draw swords...

Really?

Let's "In Real Life" for a sec. Crazy b**ch with a sword comes running at me, and I am armed with an AK47. Um...kneecap. Foot shot. Probably the last thing a soldier would do is drop his firearm and go toe-to-toe with a crazy chick wielding a sword. And where the hell did the soldiers get swords!? Where were they keeping them!?

The Amazons drive off the soldiers, and Inara hunts down Liam and kills him with the help of her father's old friend...okay, WAY out of left field there. She takes over as the Queen of the Amazons since the former Queen was killed...okay, missed that one too. What the hell is in this coffee?

(Sniffs coffee)

Nope, no liquor. No drugs.

Ooh, the end credits!

SQUIRREL!!

VERDICT: AMAZON POOPING IN THE WOODS.

Outside of holding the world record for the most montages in one movie, this film also tries to resurrect a long-dead genre. Barbarian-chick films died out sometime in the late eighties to early nineties, and *Xena: The Warrior Princess* was really only successful because it redirected the genre to broadcast television with an episodic storyline.

One of the biggest nails in the coffin for this film was the fact that the storyline was almost entirely left to the assumption of the viewer. The dialogue is sparse at best, and even the body language is hammed up for the camera.

I will have to give the crew credit, however. The cinematography is fantastic, and the high-def picture is absolutely on target. A lot of time was put into the costuming and makeup. On the flip, even at the end of the movie after combat scenes and a plane crash, the characters are wearing the cleanest military uniforms and loincloths I've ever seen.

While I understand getting into the action quickly, there is a level of backstory that needs to be revealed as well. *Inara, The Jungle Girl* makes the unfortunate mistake of dumping it all on the viewer at once through montages with all the grace of an open drain on a cistern of s**twater at a waste water treatment plant.

If greater emphasis had been placed on training the actors and actresses in the film, and the writing gone over with a finer-toothed comb, this movie would've been a watchable indie. As it stands, it's not a total a**-biscuit. I'd be more likely to label it a "Fart in the Wind."

Manos-The Hands of Fate: What is the black s**t under your fingernails?

For nearly two years, I have touted *Troll 2* as the worst movie of all time, and believe me, that movie earned it. Before *Troll 2, The Garbage Pail Kids Movie* carried the moniker like a flag at the Special Olympics.

But everyone seems to forget this little gem like that awkward moment when you're at the Clinique counter (waiting on my battered half, in my case) during a crowded day at Belk, and you realize that you trusted the wrong fart a little too much.

Really, that's the best description I can give *Manos: The Hands of Fate*: It is a shart in the pants of the industry. I dare say that this movie is (dun-dun-dun)...

THE WORST MOVIE I HAVE EVER SEEN.

Michael, Margaret, their six-year-old daughter Debbie, and their dog Peppy are all piled in the car near El Paso, Texas looking for a place called the "Valley Lodge." The first thing you'll notice is that it seems as if the actors performed the movie, then went back in later and did voiceovers.

They pass a convertible with a young couple making out furiously (for no apparent reason or significance to the plot whatsoever), and soon have a run-in with the police because Michael is speeding.

Yes, this really is the plot so far.

After skipping a great deal of asinine nonsense written by an insurance salesman (I'll explain in the verdict) we find the family at the doorstep of a mysterious lodge and a gimpy-looking dude in a hat standing at the door.

"My name is Torgo. I watch the place while the Master is away!"

Against Torgo and Margaret's wishes, Michael insists that they stay the night since it is getting dark and they are hopelessly lost. Torgo explains (over and over again) that the Master will not approve of the dog or the child.

While Margaret and Michael gaze at a creepy-looking portrait of the Master and his dog, Torgo goes out back, and we get to meet the Master and his wives. They are all asleep though the women are asleep under the Master's spell.

Torgo claims that one of the women is evil, that the Master has enough wives, and that Margaret belongs to him. He also cops himself a feel. Silly Torgo.

Meanwhile, back at the ranch, Peppy gets loose and disappears into the night. Michael chases him, but Peppy is suddenly killed by something strange in the dark. The Master awakens, and Torgo knocks Michael out and drags him off into the night while Margaret and Debbie sleep.

The women bicker about whether or not to kill Debbie, but all agree that Michael has to die. The Master laughs maniacally (over and over again) and tells them all to be silent, accusing the head wife of being a traitor since she wants Debbie to live.

The police show up and stop the couple from making out. Again.

No, let's take a damn moment here people. This is the third time they've stopped these two horn-birds from playing tongue sabers, and for what? NOTHING. These characters literally have NOTHING to do with the plot. At all. Period. Do not look for symbolism or anything deep because all you will find is a big ol' bag of pointless wrapped up in a bucket of stupid.

The Master punishes Torgo for his actions while they were asleep, making him lay down on the altar while the women gather around. The Master orders them to kill Torgo, and they furiously slap at him and yank at his clothing because you know that s**t's lethal and stuff. Yeah...

Michael wakes up and realizes that Margaret and Debbie have been nabbed by the Master, who is laughing insanely (with the EXACT same laugh over and over again like a f**king broken record). He runs to the back area where they are tied up and frees them after knocking Torgo out.

The family runs to the house but is cornered by the Master, who opens his cape and comes at them menacingly like a creeper at candy store. Cut to black, and open on Thelma and Louise on a road trip when they happen by the lodge. Michael is standing at the door like a gimp.

"My name is Michael. I watch the place while the Master is away!"

Yeah, shocker. I know.

Cut to the back of the place where the Master and his wives are sleeping. We see that Margaret has now joined the wives. Another camera shot shows that...okay, ew. Debbie is now also one of the wives. So not only is the Master a horrible actor with a tarantula growing on his upper lip, he is also a pervert.

Ew, dude. Just ew.

VERDICT: JUST F**KING SHOOT ME.

I was left without words when this movie ended, not about the ending (that was just f**king disgusting, man), but because the acting, the camera work, hell, the EVERYTHING about this movie was just bad.

Okay, the Insurance crack. Harold P. Warren, the writer/director/star (Michael) of the movie was an insurance salesman. The outline for the script was penned on a napkin in a coffee shop, and he raised $19,000 (equivalent to $136,703 in 2014 dollars) to fund this embarrassment.

He rented the camera but had a tight deadline to return it. Therefore, to make the deadline, he shot all night shots since everyone worked during the day. Also, the camera only shot 32 seconds at a time, so the scenes are choppy (and that's being nice) and cut in really bad places.

The experience was hell on everyone involved. John Reynolds (Torgo) ate a shotgun shell a month before the movie premiered, and everyone involved pretty much walked away from Warren after filming was complete.

The acting is atrociously bad, the script being voice-work since there apparently was no way to record sound at all on the set. Jackie Neyman (Debbie) was brought to tears at the premier when she saw her mouth moving on screen and another woman's (yes, not little girl, woman) voice instead of her own.

Since this sinker dropped, there have been a few nods to its horrible quality, and even an 8-bit mobile game was released as well as an episode of *Mystery Science Theater 3000* where the robots sat mostly in silence because they had nothing to say.

It's not that it was the 60's and resources for quality film makers was limited; it's that this movie would've been a mutated dingleberry hanging off of Hollywood's a**hair even if Warren had spent more than $19K on the project. The story, the script, everything was just lousy.

Prime Evil: That awkward smell on my DVD shelf.

After looking at many suggestions and realizing that bashing *Killer Klowns from Outer Space* would likely get me assassinated, I looked to my treasure trove of crap known as *Gorehouse Greats*.

I was not disappointed.

Well, I *was* disappointed. I mean I wasn't in that I found a crappy movie, but I was...never mind.

One movie stood out like a black man at a NASCAR Race: *Prime Evil*. Yeah, I know what you're thinking: gators love marshmallows. Nope, not even close.

The story opens with a bunch of monks in a random Catholic Church in the 1600's putzing around and talking.

Yeah, I know.

One of them feels like the church is a lie and proposes that they turn to Satan instead. He is outcast by a fellow monk, but the Satanist acts quickly and beheads the loudmouthed mannequin.

Yes, the special effects are just that: special.

What follows is not much more than a day-in-the-life movie about this group that has lived for centuries by breeding and killing their offspring or other blood-relatives. The audio is as atrocious as the acting, the music not being much more than seventies horror-twang and bells.

Yet this poop-fest is circa 1988.

Go figure.

The main protagonist, Alexandra, is being tempted by the evil priest to fall in love with him so he can sacrifice her to Satan, who is represented in magnificent grandeur by a slime-soaked retarded puppet that looks like it got frozen in time while cheering after winning the medal for Best Helmet at the Special Olympics. The most this thing does is squirm when a nun stabs it at the end.

The acting, as noted before, is awful. It's not as bad as *Troll 2*, but it's campy B-movie acting gone wrong. I'm still trying to cope with the fact that a grown man called another grown man "fart breath."

Of course, being a B-movie, there are gratuitous boobies and gore, but the gore is about as gruesome as $0.99 fake blood can get.

Add in the random characters that do not add to the plot whatsoever and you get possibly the most boring Good vs. Evil Satanic Cult movie since *Blue's Clues vs. Barney and Friends*. The most annoying character was probably the hit man the cult hired to collect ladies and kill for them, but he is trying too hard to be Jason Voorhees and looks more like that creepy dude that NEVER misses a junior girls' soccer game even though he is single and lives at home with his mommy.

VERDICT: DELETE.

This movie could have been at least mildly entertaining, but with bad writing, bad camera work, bad acting and bad audio, it ends up being about as appealing as a Texas Pete enema.

This movie was shat to film in 1988, but some a**hole decided to bring it back from the pits of Hell for this collection because some nimrod somewhere thought it was a cult classic.

I would rather have my eyelids peeled back like Malcolm McDowell in *A Clockwork Orange* and be made to watch reruns of *Teletubbies* than watch this movie again. Get the one about gaters, instead.

And don't forget the marshmallows.

Satan's Slave: Lazy as HELL.

Once again into the *Gorehouse Greats* $5 12-pack that my in-laws gave me a while back. I keep calling it a Cornucopia of Crap, and I have yet to be disproven. The latest one that stood out for me was *Satan's Slave*. I figured, "Why not? What's a few brain cells?"

The movie opens with Stephen Yorke. He is handsome and rich, and has who appears to be Adrienne King (read: that chick from the original Friday the 13th) in his house ready to give him a serving of all natural British nookie. Stephen, for no reason, goes into an aggressive fury and tries to rape her.

Oh, yeah. It's not Adrienne King. Sorry, kids.

She gets away, and he kills her. The entire purpose of the ten-minute long scene? He's loopy.

Onwards and upwards to the city where Catherine Yorke decides to join her parents on a trip to her reclusive uncle's house in the country. Suddenly, as soon as they hit the driveway, Daddy loses control of the car and they barely dent the front end on a tree.

But, apparently, it was enough of an impact to kill Mom and knock everyone else out.

Catherine comes to and is pulled from the car just before it explodes like a tie fighter in *Star Wars*. No, seriously. A fender-bender and the car blows like a bad case of the squirts.

Come to find out, Stephen is Catherine's cousin, and her uncle is played by Michael Gough. Catherine stays on with her relatives while funeral arrangements are made, and she develops a relationship with her cousin. She eventually ends up sleeping with him.

Guess no one loves you like family.

Uncle Yorke and Francis, the lady of the house, jump on Stephen for moving too slow. Quite obviously they are all planning something. Ooh, shock.

By the way, we are now a full hour into the hour and a half movie, and this is all that has happened.

Meanwhile, back in the city, Catherine's boyfriend jumps off the roof of their high rise after hearing things in the elevator.

That quick.

Francis soon feels for Catherine and fills her in on what is going on. Uncle and Stephen are Satanists, and they plan on using her to revive their old priestess. Francis is later killed by Stephen, and Catherine is on the run only to discover that her father is one of them, having survived the explosion. It was all a plot.

The end.

Shoot me.

VERDICT: Another one for the toilet.

This movie was more monotonous than golf and slower than Christmas. If it wasn't the bad acting or the off-subject remarks made by the characters, it was the ability for me to guess what was going on before ANY of the characters in the movie had any idea at all.

It's one thing if I know what the villain is up to and the main characters don't, but when I know the heinous plan before the bad guy even does, I chalk that up to pathetic. It ends on a dull note with cultists surrounding Catherine and her screaming. Again, pretty much random and out of nowhere.

Kind of like—SQUIRREL!!!

Sgt. Kabukiman, NYPD: Blatant silliness, a fool as a painted fool, gratuitous boobies

Believe it or not, there is a studio dedicated to crap movies.

Let me back up a bit. Years ago a little studio called Troma opened and began producing low-budget independent films. They later had a smash hit call *The Toxic Avenger,* which gave them a mascot for the company and some attention.

Then the collective ADD of the public kicked in.

Now Troma films are considered cult movies, and they are always done on the cheap. Ever see the famous car explosion scenes in a Troma movie? Yup. Same scene borrowed for cost efficiency. And it came from none other than *Sgt. Kabukiman N.Y.P.D.*

Obviously, I felt like I was walking into another session on the film industry's toilet with this being the weird stain left by the last guy. Yet, my Sucky-Sense wasn't going haywire.

That's right: Sucky-Sense. Suck it, Spider-Man.

Harry Griswold is a bumbling New York City Detective who has, with no doubt, the WORST luck of any human being on the planet. Unbeknownst to Harry, the Kabuki actor he is about to see in a performance is backstage partaking in a ritual to bring about the spirit of Kabukiman to combat the encroaching evil.

During the show the head benefactor, billionaire Reginald Stewart, gets up and leaves. Just as he exits, a group of thugs begin to shoot up the theater. The old Kabuki actor is gunned down, taking Harry to the floor with him. He transfers the spirit of Kabukiman to Harry and dies.

Harry begins to undergo strange changes, such as spontaneously having his pants replaced by a kimono and his face seeming to grow makeup. The old man's granddaughter, Lotus, aggressively forces her help on Harry so that he may harness his Kabukiman powers before the evil arrives.

Oh, I'm not done.

OF COURSE, Stewart is the bad guy. He and his flunkies are trying to enact an ancient ritual to give him ultimate power, and only Kabukiman can stop him.

After a few major blunders, Harry agrees to Lotus's help and fights to rid the streets of New York of crime and corruption. When Lotus is kidnapped by Stewart, Kabukiman uses her monkey to help find her and defeat Reginald Stewart.

The final battle takes place in a shipyard. Stewart is able to perform enough of the ritual to be transformed into an inhuman beast that is Kabukiman's match. But, before the final piece of the ritual can take place, Kabukiman is able to distract Stewart from his goal. Stewart is destroyed, and Harry is reinstated to the police department.

No, really.

The movie is that brief, aside from a lot of shenanigans and blunders on Harry's part. In one scene he tries to "conjure" Kabukiman on the fly and is turned into a clown.

The goons are complete idiots, often calling each other "weenie" and trying to carry out their schemes in the most ridiculous ways possible. One in particular wears a long blonde wig and carries himself as a transgender.

VERDICT: Believe it or not, it's worth a look.

Okay, bear with me. The movie is s**t, don't get me wrong. But, it's a Troma film. This makes it a different animal than your basic s**t movie. It's SUPPOSED to be crappy. The dialogue is cheap and puts forth the basic stereotype of each character. Harry is the lead and the everyman, so he's laidback but clumsy. Stewart is the scheming billionaire villain, so he wrings his hands and acts all creepy and slimy. Lotus is the mysterious Japanese girl, so she acts all…mysterious.

Yeah, ran out of adjectives.

This movie is spoof on super-hero movies, so there are nods to a good many of them (Kabukiman flies like Superman, and the scene changes are reminiscent of the old Batman series). It makes no bones and has no confusion about what it is: a live-action cartoon.

I was surprised at the gratuitous boobie-shots in the flick, as it carries a PG-13 rating. It also has a lot of gore, as is expected of any Troma film.

If you like cheap humor and self-representation, check into it. It's silly, stupid, and devoid of any purpose in the industry other than to make drunks and meatheads laugh. If you're looking for an awe-inspiring epic that makes your heart race and your sense of justice swell in your chest…yeah, you picked the wrong movie.

Troll 2: Tom Selleck's chest hair was not this bad.

I never thought it possible that a movie could be worse than *Battlefield Earth*, but then Jared, one of my followers and fans, suggested *Troll 2*.

Thanks, Jarred. You might as well have recommended I eat a yogurt-covered turd glazed with liver sauce.

I'd say the movie is a joke, but unfortunately, it's not even funny enough to be considered such a high rating. In fact, toilet film has better appeal than this steamer.

Troll 2 opens with some dude dressed like a Swedish Butt Pirate-Ninja prancing through the woods (no, he really *was* prancing) for his life from a group of goblins trying to eat him.

Yup. That's right.

The movie is called *Troll 2*, but there is not one single troll in the entire movie! It's about goblins! The original title was *Goblin*, but they changed the name to try and capitalize in the original *Troll* following.

And get used to the prancing because no one in this move flat out runs. Every single character in this movie prances for their lives when being chased.

It ends up being a story that Grandpa Seth is reading to Little Joshua. Turns out Seth is dead and he's Joshua's imaginary friend.

The Waits family is supposed to go to Nilbog for vacation on a home swap that they have arranged with a family who lives there.

Right away I have to wonder how stupid these people really are. Nilbog? Goblin?

Hmmm (scratches head).

Moving along because the movie draws out every friggin' little story point to utter death…the family ends up in Nilbog to discover that the place is a dump. Mr. Waits explains that "farmers don't usually come out this time of night."

It's the middle of the day. Really. The line is delivered while the sun is at high freaking noon.

There is a feast laid out on the table for the family, but Grandpa Seth warns Josh that it's tainted. So Josh decides to pee on it.

Really. That simple.

I can go on and on with each scene pointing out the absurdity, but I won't. Let's talk about the atrocious acting combined with abhorrent writing.

Two Italians who speak no English wrote the script, so it's all a sort of "pidgin" English. Combined with the cartoonish way that some lines are actually delivered directly to the camera, this makes the movie laughable.

The goblins are dudes wearing burlap sacks and rocking rubber masks that look like they came from the rotten bowels of Dollar Tree. They keep trying to serve up green food because they want to turn the humans into plants for consumption.

Yup! Not just ANY goblins! VEGETARIAN GOBLINS!! WHAT THE HELL!? They're f**king vegans! How many stories have we heard about goblins eating people!? *Nothing* was said about them eating people after turning them into artichokes!

As much as I wanted to look for good points, this movie just kept getting worse and worse. And it didn't help that it tried to take itself so seriously.

I have to wonder what the hell they were thinking on the music. Each scene of action or terror is accompanied by disco dance music. No, really. I can't make this crap up. I could go on and on, but the more I go on, the longer I have to live with the pain of this move scorched into my retinas.

VERDICT: Oh my Gooooooooooooooooood!

This movie makes licking the walls of a public porta-john look like a phenomenal idea. The director/writer still flaunts this movie as a masterpiece, not willing to accept that he actually manufactured something about as entertaining as being castrated by a rabid wiener-eating badger.

It's one of those movies that should have been no more than an hour but drags on for twice as long. It was made longer by that fact that I had to pause it and walk away about every three minutes just to collect myself and get rid of the headache.

Being in this movie actually made one of the actors a permanent shut-in. No one has heard from her since!

I thought that maybe being an eighties flick would lead to some forgiveness, but no. It was 1990, my friends.

This movie was not shat onto film; it was just shat.

Zombie Ass-Toilet of the Dead: From the diuretic bowels of Hell...

What the absolute f**k did I just watch?

It takes a lot to make me uncomfortable, and this movie achieved it. I mean, I get it. It's live-action anime. It's supposed to be silly, and it's gross as hell since it's also a Japanese Gore Flick. I mean look at *Tokyo Gore Police*, for example.

That movie was also retarded.

What kills me is that these movies are supposed to be funny. I mean, I guess since I'm not Japanese and not immersed in the pop culture over there that maybe I just don't GET the humor. I'm open to that idea entirely. But I also like the occasional s**t joke. Who doesn't?

The storyline is thin, that being a compliment, so I'll do my best.

Megumi and her friends are traveling away on a weekend excursion to find a parasite for Maki to eat so that she can stay thin and try to boost her nonexistent modeling career. Aya, her boyfriend Take, and their goofy nerd pal Naoi, are along for the ride.

As it turns out, Megumi's sister was tormented in school for farting and ended up killing herself over it. Meg is still having issues with it. The group ends up catching a fish in the stream out in the woods. Naoi cuts it open and finds a worm about a foot long inside. Maki promptly grabs it and swallows it.

Bear with me. It only goes downhill from here.

Maki runs off to a nearby outhouse and tries to take a dump when a zombie emerges from the s**t pool underneath and grabs her naked a**. She runs out to the others and is chased by a horde of zombies covered in poop.

They are attacked by a zombie who bites off Take's finger. They run as more approach, and Maki suddenly falls ill and begins to fart massive yellow clouds of gas. She is overtaken by the zombies, and the group flees to a small shack they find in the woods where they are saved by a doctor. He shoots a zombie, and we discover that they do not bleed. There are no organs.

They are literally full of s**t.

Bad Movie Beware!

Doc Tanaka lives alone with his daughter and offers shelter to the group from the zombie horde. He feeds them a pasta dinner served up by his daughter, Ko. Tanaka explains that the zombies are being controlled by a parasite and that they can transmit it through bites. Take succumbs to his injury, farting explosively and nonstop as his head begins to bulge.

As it turns out, the parasites react violently to drugs, and Take's head explodes from the pressure. Later on the others begin to feel cramps, and Megumi happens upon Ko and Tanaka in a closed room while on her way to the toilet. Tanaka feeds a six-foot long parasite to Ko, then gives her an anti-parasite drug that makes her poop out the old dead one.

They see her, and Tanaka confesses that he is farming the zombies to keep Ko alive. The pasta was filled with parasite eggs, though Megumi had refrained from eating. She escapes with Aya and Naoi but realizes that she needs to serum and leaves them to fend off a horde of zombies.

Before the fight goes much further, the zombies all bend over double and parasite heads pop out of their brown-eyes. As if this isn't enough, they attack butt-first.

What in the name of all that is holy...

Ko and Megumi show down, and Megumi knocks her out. Naoi sacrifices himself to save Megumi. He succumbs to the parasite and takes Tanaka with him. Aya meets up with Maki, who is bent over double with a worm sticking out of her tucous. Maki happens to be carrying the queen and attacks Aya with multiple tentacles.

Megumi arrives in time, and Aya begs to be killed before she transforms. Megumi finds Tanaka's gun and shoots Aya in the face and Maki several times in the face. Aya dies, but Maki is far from dead and transforms into a horrific monster...filled with s**t.

They take the battle to the air, the monster flying with wings while Megumi uses a gigantic never-ending fart to propel herself around. Megumi ultimately wins and stumbles back to the car to find a zombiefied Tanaka waiting on her. She ends the film with a jump kick to his head.

Oh, Lord Jesus, it's the END!! THANK GOD!!

VERDICT: SOMEONE FORGOT TO FLUSH.

I make a lot of s**t jokes, but I never thought I'd watch an entire movie that is intended to be one large s**t joke. It failed miserably.

It's not a s**t joke; it's just s**t.

The acting, believe it or not, is superb. The Japanese take film and performing arts of every kind VERY seriously. Even people who do voice work for anime are held in very high esteem.

The movie itself on the other hand...let's face facts: I knew what I was getting in to. *Zombie Ass* is not the kind of title one would see at the Oscars. It's a live-action anime, so it's going to be over the top. But, it's still a bad one. The story is weak with really no background on the characters. Megumi, as it turns out, has always had a parasite that she keeps under control. We find this out DURING THE FINAL BATTLE.

The effects are also...well, s**tty. They went a bit on the cheap for a lot of it, and some of the zombies actually had personality and spoke.

Bottom line: this movie is a boil on the a**of the industry, with none other than *Troll 2* still being the only movie that tops the pure mountain of s**t.

I can't really come up with any s**t jokes, which kills me since I just watched an entire movie about farting and zombies that bleed s**t. It's actually been a challenge for me to write this review.

It's difficult to balance a laptop in your lap while wiping.

There You Have It!

That's not all of them, but I've managed to stuff most of my reviews into this book.

As you can see, I've watched some fun movies, but I've mostly watched the scum at the bottom of Hollywood's toilet. The indie film industry also got to incur my wrath, and some of those fell prey to my site.

And my poor intelligence fell prey to the stupidity of a good many of these movies.

I've been through good and not-so-good times with Fail-Flix. I've gained and lost "likes" on the Facebook page, and I've gone through times when I can crank the reviews out and times when life has just gotten in the way.

I don't plan on stopping any time soon, though. The site is going strong, and I plan to do another book when I have more reviews to fill it up. Until then, pop the popcorn, grab a beer, and be on the lookout for more cinematic poo-poo!

Thanks for reading!

Acknowledgments

Oh yeah, I gotta do one of these too, don't I?

First, I want to thank my wife, Melissa, who heads up Clicking Keys. She's the one responsible for the birth of Fail-Flix, and she's been supportive of the whole ordeal ever since. She's been editing every review since last year and has edited every review for this book. Without her help, I'd still be posting everything on Facebook and typing up a hot mess, to boot.

I want to thank Faith Hunter, John Hartness, D.B. Jackson, A.J. Hartley, Misty Massey, and all of my other writer friends who have inspired me to keep writing, and have pushed me to keep at it. Particularly Faith, who once told me to "Stop trying to be so damned poetic!"

I want to thank Christopher Ross, who provided more than a few movies for the site last year. The man can certainly pick some crap!

Most of all, I want to thank all of my fans who have stuck with me through thick and thin, good times and hard times, and have enjoyed my reviews. You guys are the main reason why Fail-Flix is alive and moving forward, and it wouldn't be possible or worth it without your support!

Thanks!!

About the Author

When he isn't working or chasing his kid around, Jason Gilbert is playing video games, listening to music, reading, writing, or watching crappy movies for Fail-Flix. He enjoys movies and television shows in general, and prefers horror and all things weird and disturbing. In short, he stays pretty active, and goes until he passes out (they make meds for that, but he doesn't take them). He likes a dark beer in the evenings and listens to too much heavy metal music. Jason lives in South Carolina with his wife, his daughter, and the family cat.

Made in the USA
Charleston, SC
30 April 2015